Tries and Conversi

South African Rugby League players

Peter Lush and Hendrik Snyders

London League Publications Ltd

Tries and Conversions
South African Rugby League players
© Peter Lush and Hendrik Snyders. Foreword © David Barends

The moral right of Peter Lush and Hendrik Snyders to be identified as the authors has been asserted.

Cover design © Stephen McCarthy.

Front cover: Left: Green Vigo playing for Wigan (Courtesy *Rugby League Journal*); right: Tom van Vollenhoven on the attack for St Helens (Courtesy Alex Service)
Back cover: Top: Wigan's Trevor Lake tackling Tom van Vollenhoven in the 1966 Challenge Cup Final at Wembley (Courtesy Alex Service); bottom: Enslin Dlambulo offloading the ball for Bradford Northern against Wakefield Trinity in 1963 (Courtesy Robert Gate).

A CIP catalogue record for this book is available from the British Library.

First published in Great Britain in April 2015 by London League Publications Ltd, PO Box 65784, London NW2 9NS

ISBN: 978-1909885-07-3

Cover design by Stephen McCarthy Graphic Design, 46, Clarence Road, London N15 5BB

Editing and layout by Peter Lush

Printed and bound in Great Britain by Charlesworth Press, Wakefield

This book is dedicated to the memory of Dawie Ackerman, the first captain of a South African Rugby League team, and Winty ('Short Man') Pandle, a member of the first unified Black South African national Rugby Union team selected in 1953 for an overseas tour that never took place.

Foreword

I am very honoured to have been asked to write the Foreword to *Tries and Conversions* – the South African Rugby League Players book. This is a collection of sporting biographies of many South African, Zimbabwean and Namibian players who, because of circumstances beyond their control, chose to further their careers by leaving their homeland. Most of these players came to the North of England. Others, in the early 1960s, played rugby league in South Africa.

The players who came to England were pioneers on a

pathway that I followed in 1970. I hold those players in high esteem, because many of them chose to follow that path for the best of reasons. I followed their example and played in West and North Yorkshire.

I gradually became aware of the difficulties that they could have faced and the determination they showed. They made me proud to be a South African. They became a source of inspiration for me and in some cases professional sporting roles models, as I followed my professional career with Wakefield Trinity, York, Bradford Northern, Featherstone Rovers and Batley.

I believe their inspiration led me to develop my own philosophy of sport and life: "You should give more then you take to your family and your team; respect people for who they are, and being fair to all, should translate this into true sportsmanship on the field."

David Barends
February 2015
Hemsworth, West Yorkshire
Elim, District Bredasdorp, Cape Province

David Barends had a distinguished rugby league career and is the only South African to play for Great Britain. This is covered fully in chapter 17.

The photo shows David wearing his 'honorary Springbok' tie and blazer.
(Photo: Peter Lush)

Introduction

Today, South Africa has slipped alarmingly down the world rankings in rugby league. The sport in South Africa has a low profile, and there are only a handful of South African players in professional rugby league.

However, since James Megson and William Mart signed for Leeds and Hull Kingston Rovers respectively in 1910, South African players have, at times, made a rich contribution to the sport's history. Wigan in the 1920s had a major South African presence. In the late 1950s and early to mid-1960s, South Africans were prominent in both British and Australian rugby league. Again in the 1990s, a layer of South African players played in Britain and Australia.

In South Africa, rugby union and association football are the major winter sports. Traditionally, the main sport for the African population has been association football, although this also had support from the white British population. For the Afrikaner and Coloured populations, rugby union is their major winter sport, although it is played by the African population as well.

Rugby league, from its earliest days as the Northern Union, has a long history of players crossing both international and sporting boundaries to participate in the sport. International stars, often recruited from rugby union, could be a major draw for spectators at a time when association football in the United Kingdom rarely included overseas players, and the attraction of new international recruits could be an important source of additional income at the turnstiles for their clubs.

Today, national boundaries play little if any role in the composition of major club sports teams. In association football, players of British origin make up one third of the English Premier League's teams. In cricket, rugby union and rugby league, non-British players make a significant contribution, although the rugby codes find it slightly more difficult to import players with many of their targets being outside the European Union. In Australia, the NRL includes players from New Zealand, Papua New Guinea and the other South-Sea islands where rugby has a base. Some abandon their heritage to try to play in State of Origin, the annual prestigious New South Wales versus Queensland series, which only includes players qualified to play for Australia; while others recall it when they want to play for their homeland again towards the end of their careers.

For much of the period until the early 1980s, transfer bans between England and Australia and New Zealand were in place, to stop international moves destabilising domestic competitions. However, until union went 'open' in 1995, rugby union signings were also important for rugby league clubs as new 'stars'. If these players brought with them the kudos of being international recruits as well, so much the better.

Apart from players moving within rugby league between England, Australia and New Zealand, the major sporting migration into rugby league was from rugby union in South Wales. Over the generations, hundreds of players 'went north'. These included many prominent Welsh rugby union internationals, but also players at lower levels of the sport.

These players faced the challenge of adapting to a new sport, and were at times targeted by the opposition because of resentment of the signing-on fees they received, as well because of any threat they could pose on the pitch. But they spoke the same language, were moving a three or four hour journey from 'home', and often the villages and towns they moved to in the north of England were not that different from those at home in south Wales. However, some players did find it difficult to settle, as Jim Mills recalled in his biography, *Big Jim*, when he at times felt lonely and isolated having signed for Halifax at the age of 20.

Welsh rugby union historian Gareth Williams argues that the main reason for players to 'go north' was economic, especially between the wars, to escape the poverty and unemployment in south Wales. Certainly, when the post-war boom stabilised the Welsh economy in the 1950s and 1960s, the movement of rugby union players to rugby league slowed to such an extent that the Wales rugby league team was disbanded for 15 years, only reforming in the late 1960s and then playing its 'home' games in the north of England. This does reflect the sport's overall weakness in South Wales, where for a long time it did not exist in any organised way.

Some rugby union internationals moved from Australia and New Zealand to play rugby league in England. But even these moves were often stopped by the transfer bans. The other migration of rugby players was South Africans, which has largely been forgotten by rugby league. When the sport was relaunched in South Africa in 1988, and the national team played its first matches for almost 30 years in 1992, there was some interest in the sport's history. The *Rothman's Rugby League Yearbook* had a feature on it, including profiles of some of the players who had come to Great Britain in earlier times.

And, of course, individual club histories have featured their particular heroes. However, this book aims to look at their collective experience. The fundamental question, why did they come, is the most difficult to answer.

Until 1994, when the first democratic elections for all South Africans were held, South Africa was a society deeply divided both legally and socially on racial lines, with rigid divisions between the white population, itself divided into the Afrikaner and English groups, the Coloured (mixed-race) population and the majority African population. Before the Second World War, there was a system of discrimination, with the African majority having very few, if any civil and human rights. The black majority lived in poverty, and were used as a source of cheap labour for the white minority owned industries, in particular mining.

The Afrikaner dominated National Party's victory in the 1948 General Election saw this intensified into what became known as Apartheid – separate development. From 1950, laws were introduced banning political opponents, and dividing every aspect of life on racial lines. Living areas were strictly defined by race, and inter-racial marriage was banned. Sport was divided on racial lines.

In 1960, a demonstration at Sharpeville against the Pass Laws (which required all Africans to carry a 'Pass' to allow them to be in a particular area) was attacked, and 69 demonstrators were killed. However, after March 1960, repression intensified, and in May 1961, South Africa left the Commonwealth, which was a further step in politically marginalising the white British population, although they still had a very high standard of living, and the considerable British immigration to South Africa continued. In 1961, Umkhonto we Sizwe (MK), the armed wing of the ANC, started their sabotage campaign of attacking government and industrial targets, which heightened the tension in the country.

The ANC (African National Congress) and the PAC (Pan African Congress), two of the main organisations opposed to the government, were banned. In 1962, Nelson Mandela was arrested, and in 1964, at the 'Rivonia' trial, along with other ANC leaders, he was sentenced to life in prison for their campaign of sabotage and opposition to the government.

Sport has always been an important part of South African society. As international opposition to Apartheid developed in the 1960s, South Africa was gradually excluded from most international sports bodies. Rugby union was one of the final sports to break off official links with the Apartheid regime. Opposition to the 1969–70 South African rugby union tour to Great Britain, which included demonstrations at matches and pitch invasions during the games, saw the cancellation of the 1970 cricket tour to England and Wales.

In the early 1960s, the Rugby Football League (RFL) supported the attempts to establish rugby league in South Africa, despite concerns by some of the sport's followers about working within the country's political system. When rugby league was launched again in 1988, the RFL would not offer any support because of the international sports boycott. In 1990, Nelson Mandela was freed, and moves started towards dismantling Apartheid. This resulted in the election of an ANC-led government in 1994, and Nelson Mandela became the country's first black President. As other sports started to play with South Africa, so rugby league supported its fledgling organisation in the country.

An understanding of South African society is important to appreciate the difficulties players faced when coming to play in England. Those who came to England in the 1920s probably switched codes mainly for economic reasons. Most seem to have been of working class backgrounds, and the signing-on and match fees would have been very tempting for them. Working class white South Africans, particularly from an Afrikaner background, while better off than the Coloured or African communities, often were not particularly prosperous at this time. A rugby league agent in the 1920s explained that a player could receive his signing on fee, play in England for a few years and then go home and start a business.

Around 40 players, some of them Springboks[1], came between 1957 and 1963. Their main motivation seems to have been economic. Rugby union in South Africa was strictly amateur, and as the officials became aware of the loss of players, those who came to England, and at least 160 who switched to play rugby league at home, issues such as tour expenses and loss of earnings while on tour were raised. Rob Louw and Ray Mordt, who joined Wigan in the 1980s, said that they had earned nothing from rugby union despite playing for the Springboks regularly, and wanted to be rewarded financially for playing rugby.

There is limited information about what jobs the players did. Even those in manual trades would probably have had skilled jobs or supervisory roles, which were reserved for whites. Of the players who toured Australia and New Zealand in 1963, which included four who had been playing in England or Australia, 14 had white collar jobs, seven had blue collar jobs and one was a farmer. However, of the white collar workers, six were clerks, and a couple were sales reps.

---

[1] The Springbok is the long-established symbol of rugby union in South Africa, and players who have played for the national team are known as Springboks. A springbok is an antelope-gazelle based in South Western Africa; the word 'spring' in Afrikaans means 'jump' and the 'bok' means a male antelope or goat.

However, the structure of South African rugby union meant that the Springboks took preference over everything else, so in some seasons the Currie Cup, the main provincial competition, was not played. For players who wanted to progress, there could be a lack of opportunity to do so. Rugby league offered an alternative, along with financial rewards.

What is never mentioned is politics. Interviewed in Australia after democracy for the whole population had been won in South Africa, South African Wigan and North Sydney star Fred Griffiths, who signed for Wigan in 1957, reflected that apartheid was part of life, and he had not been aware of any alternatives. This was not uncommon. The Labour MP Peter Hain, who was brought up in South Africa until his family were forced to leave in 1966, has recently written a biography of his parents, who were active in the South African Liberal Party, which opposed apartheid, in the 1950s and 1960s. In the early 1950s, before they became politically active, he says that "Like the vast majority of white South Africans, Ad and Wal continued to enjoy a life of comfort and pleasure. Whites benefited from the good fortune apartheid conferred upon them, yet were curiously insulated from its unjust and oppressive conditions." [2]

The year Fred Griffiths left South Africa, there was the 'Treason Trial', in which over 100 ANC leaders were on trial, and other protests against apartheid. But there is no record of a white player mentioning political instability, or the ongoing violent repression of the majority community, as a reason for leaving South Africa.

In the 1950s and early 1960s, the Afro-Caribbean population was growing and becoming more established in England. The white South Africans often found themselves playing with and against black players. One even found himself with a black coach, and it is believed that this was part of the reason he failed to make it in the sport. But coming to the north of England from South Africa must have presented so many challenges in lifestyle, climate, language and status that this was just one more issue of many they faced.

For the few African and Coloured players who came to England there was a much greater sense of opportunity. They came to a country where racism was an issue, but nothing like the organised, structured, repressive regime they faced in South Africa. Proportionately, although the numbers are very small, far more settled in England, or in one case moved to Australia, then the white players. One, who was an open supporter of the ANC, which was then a 'banned' organisation in South Africa, found that his South African passport would not be renewed, and was forced to settle in England.

There was concern expressed in 1957 in the rugby league press about the British Lions playing France in South Africa, and what would happen to Billy Boston, the black British winger if he went to South Africa. In the end Boston was injured and the question of his entry to South Africa was not tested. Similar concerns were raised in 1962 when the Lions visited again; this time Boston was again injured. Rugby league had a good record of including players from different racial backgrounds, and black players had played for England and Great Britain years before they played for the England association football team, or the rugby union team since before the First World War.

As this book shows, some South African players made a great contribution to rugby league clubs in England and Australia. Others failed to make an impact, which finished their

---

[2] *Ad & Wal* by Peter Hain, 2014, p.66

rugby careers as there was no way back to rugby union. For some, their time in England ended in tragedy.

Also of great interest are the players who switched to rugby league in South Africa. Again, their motives are unclear. There was a mix of experienced and inexperienced players. Certain rugby union clubs were hard hit by 'defections', and at times team-mates seem to have stuck together in changing codes. Again, a combination of being rewarded financially for their efforts and wanting a new challenge on the pitch seem to have been prevalent.

Records and information about South African rugby league players are often scarce. Considerable research has gone into this book, but there are almost certainly players that we missed. Also, some players are covered more than others. However, we hope that readers enjoy the book anyway and let us know about anyone who has slipped through the net. The full story of rugby league in South Africa remains to be told in a future work, this is just the start.

Peter Lush and Hendrik Snyders
March 2015

Thanks

Thank you to the following people and organisations who wrote pieces for this book, shared research, agreed to be interviewed, contributed photos or supported and helped us in many other ways: Alex Service, Gary Slater, Robert Gate, Andrew Hardcastle, Phil Fearnley, The Oldham Rugby League Heritage Trust, Graham Morris, John Pitchford, Bill Dalton, Graham Williams, David Thorpe, Mike Latham, Harry Edgar & *Rugby League Journal*, David Williams (rlphotos.com), David Hinchliffe, Leon Kaplan, Dave Makin, Jan 'Das' Prinsloo, Johnny Buys, the South African Rugby Union Springbok Experience Rugby Museum, librarians at the British Newspaper Library and The Huddersfield local history library, Professor Tony Collins and the RFL Archives, Dave Farrar and many others. Thanks to everyone who was interviewed for the book and David Barends for contributing the Foreword. Thanks to Steve McCarthy for designing the cover and Charlesworth Press for printing the book.

Of course, despite all this help, if any omissions or errors occurred, they are the responsibility of the authors.

About this book

We have interpreted 'South African' fairly widely to include players from Rhodesia / Zimbabwe and South West Africa / Namibia. We have used the names of countries, provinces and cities that were in use at the time the events took place.

Writing a book covering this period inevitably means using language of racial classification from the Apartheid era in South Africa. This does not imply acceptance of these terms by the authors or other contributors to this book. For readers not familiar with the definitions under Apartheid: the majority community are described as black or African; in the past the terms 'Bantu' and 'Native' were also used. Within the African population, there are various tribal groups, including the Xhosa, Zulu, Sotho, Tswana, Pedi, venda, Ndebele, Tsongs, Pondo and Swazi. The 'Coloured' community were generally of mixed race, and had a strong presence in the Cape regions. Afrikaans is their first language. The Indian community was seen as separate, and had a strong presence in Durban and what is now Kwa-Zulu Natal. The terms 'Non-European', or 'non-white' were used on occasions as catch-all terms. The whites are split into the Afrikaner population, who speak Afrikaans as their first language, were the dominant political force under Apartheid, and have origins in emigration from Holland. The English white population have their origins in British colonial rule, and speak English as their first language. There is also a small Jewish community. South Africa today has 11 official languages, although English is widely spoken. The population today is over 50 million.

This book was very much a joint effort, which was originally conceived as a history of the sport in South Africa, including the South African players, after Peter and Hendrik met at South Africa's first Sports History Conference, held at Stellenbosch University in 2008. However, the book as originally planned would have ended up with around 250,000 words, so they decided to split the project into two. The history of the sport will follow in a couple of years, we hope. Most of the rugby union information was researched by Hendrik, and most, but not all of the rugby league information by Peter. We used material that had been previously researched for our papers on rugby league at the Conference, and for articles in *Our Game* and *Rugby League Review Number 2*.

About the authors

Peter Lush grew up in London, where he still lives. He has been watching rugby league since he went to a game at Fulham in October 1980 with Dave Farrar. In 1995, with Michael O'Hare, they wrote *Touch and Go – A history of professional rugby league in London*, and Peter and Dave set up London League Publications Ltd. The company has now published over 80 books, mainly on rugby league. Peter often works on book development and design, but other books he has written or edited include *I wouldn't start from here*, *Tries in the Valleys*, *From Fulham to Wembley*, *The Rugby League Grounds Guide*, *Rugby League Review 2007*, *Rugby League Review Number 2*, (all with Dave Farrar), *Trevor Foster* (with Simon Foster and Robert Gate) *Peter Fox – The Players' Coach* (with Graham Williams), *Hendon Football Club* (with David Ballheimer), *Big Jim* (with Maurice Bamford) *Rugby Football: A United Game* (an historical novel) and two cricket grounds guides. He was joint editor of the rugby league magazine *Our Game*, and has written for various magazines, journals and newspapers on the sport. From 1982 to 1985 he studied for an MA in Industrial and Social History at Middlesex Polytechnic (now University). Much of his work was on the history of the South African trade union movement, supervised by Dr Norman Levy. He subsequently worked with campaigns to support trade unions in South Africa. He first visited the country in 1992, and then again in 1995, when he visited social housing projects and saw Nelson Mandela launch the Reconstruction and Development Programme in Cape Town. He attended the country's first Sports History Conference in 2008, at the University of Stellenbosch. He presented a paper on *Rugby League and South Africa*.

In real life he is the director of Training Link, a charity providing basic skills training to help people find work, in central London. He is also a magistrate in East London, and sits as a member of Employment Tribunals.

He would like to dedicate his work on this book to Rosemary, with much love.

Hendrik Snyders works as Museum & Heritage Manager at the South African Rugby Union (SARU). In this capacity he heads the Springbok Experience Rugby Museum at The Victoria & Alfred Waterfront in Cape Town. He has been involved in rugby for at least 35 years both as player and administrator in both the pre- and post- rugby unification period. Prior to assuming his current position, he worked as the full-time Team Manager of the Boland Cavaliers provincial rugby team that participates in the Vodacom Cup and Currie Cup Competitions of SARU. He also had a short stint as the founding President of the erstwhile West Coast Rugby League Province and West Coast Raiders team of the South African Rugby League (SARL) under former President, Dave Van Reenen.

He studied history, education, science & technology studies, business administration and applied parliamentary research at the universities of the Western Cape, South Africa, Stellenbosch and Cape Peninsula University of Technology respectively. He has published in peer-reviewed academic journals on both rugby codes, memory, rodeo and Australian Football. Current research includes the history of Sevens Rugby in South Africa, Mandela and Rugby and SA – USA Rugby Relations. He would like to dedicate his work on this book to Eth in appreciation for her patience, love and support during challenging times.

How union and league were organised

South African rugby union is organised into provincial unions, which run competitions for clubs which are affiliated to them. At provincial level, the Currie Cup was the main competition. Prior to 1990, rugby was divided on racial lines, with separate organisations and competitions for white, coloured and black players, as explained below.

Ever since the formal establishment of rugby football in South Africa and the formation of two separate ethnic controlling bodies to administer the game in the late nineteenth century, race, politics and rugby became inseparable. While the South African Rugby Football Board (SARFB, established in 1889) administered White or 'European' rugby, the South African Coloured Rugby Football Board (SACRFB – established in 1897) took responsibility for all Non-European or 'Black rugby'. Each also administered their own segregated provincial competitions, the Currie Cup and Rhodes Cup respectively.

In 1935 a group of ethnic African clubs broke away from the SACRFB and at a meeting in the Peacock Hall in East London established the South African Bantu Rugby Football Board under the leadership of James Mwela Dippa. The new body likewise established its own provincial completion, the Native Recruiting Corporation (NRC) Cup, with a trophy donated by the Chamber of Mines. Whether this divide in the ranks of Black rugby was as a result of inter-racial tensions, or simply as an independent attempt to organise sport among Africans as a means to provide "a healthy outlet for his superfluous energy" as was stated in its official correspondence, is not clear. It did, however, complicate the attempts of Black rugby's founding fathers to use rugby and sport as tools towards integration and assimilation.

By 1959, following a new racial awareness among the indigenous population in the spirit of "Uhuru" (freedom) that swept the African continent, the SABRFB dropped the racial tag 'Bantu' which they regarded as derogatory and insulting, from their name and reconstituted itself as the South African African Rugby Football Board (SAARFB). It also replaced the NRC Cup with the Zonk Cup to disassociate itself from the Chamber of Mines, the former trophy sponsor and user of cheap African migrant labour.

In the same year, a group of Western Cape rugby administrators, citing serious strategic concerns with regards to the management of the Kimberley-based mother body, broke away from the SACRFB to form their own organisation called the South African Rugby Football Federation (SARFF). As a result, South African rugby at the beginning of the 1960s was administered by four different controlling bodies distinguished by both race and ideology.

As a result of increased domestic resistance to apartheid which resulted in events such as the Sharpeville shootings, South Africa was set on a different political path. These events impacted on all levels of society including the sporting fraternity.

On 28 May 1966 the SACRFB like its African counterparts earlier, decided to drop the racial reference in its name reconstituted itself as the South African Rugby Union (SARU). It finally wound up its affairs on 31 July 1967 with the shelving of the Rhodes Trophy which was now seen as inappropriate, given the role of its donor Cecil John Rhodes in South Africa's history. In its stead a new trophy, the South Africa Cup, was inaugurated with effect from 1971.

With the growth in international opposition to apartheid since the start of the 1970s, opportunities for the Springboks to play against their traditional opponents also decreased. As a counter strategy, the SARFB engaged in talks with its Black counterparts to try to bring about rugby unity. These talks, which started in the 1960s, failed because of SARU's unwavering commitment to the principle of "No normal sport in an abnormal society".

By 1978, following the implementation of the National Party Government's multi-racial sports policy which allowed limited competition between Whites and Non-whites, the SARFF, SARFB and the SAARFB, which after dropping the racial reference "African" from its name reconstituted itself as the South African Rugby Association (SARA), decided to merge to form the South African Rugby Board (SARB). The South African Rugby Union (SARU), however, refused to participate and instead increased the pressure in their fight for the establishment of a non-racial society. This effectively reduced the number of national rugby controlling bodies in South Africa to two ideologically distinctive organisations.

Along with change in the political arena in the late 1980s, the process of rugby unity also got a new impetus. Following talks between the still-banned African National Congress (ANC), the SARB and SARU in Harare in October 1988, a decision was taken to finally move towards the establishment of a unified rugby body as part of the process to normalize politics. Finally on 20 March 1992, the two rugby opponents met in Kimberley to establish the non-racial South African Rugby Football Union (SARFU), now known as the South African Rugby Union.

British rugby league: In 1901–02 when Alf Larard joined Huddersfield on his return from South Africa, the Northern Union (British rugby league) had a structure with the Northern Rugby League as a 14 team senior competition, with the Yorkshire and Lancashire Senior Leagues beneath it. From 1902–03 to 1904–05 the sport had two divisions. In 1906–07 these amalgamated into the Northern Rugby League. In 1907, the sport used a top-four play-off to decide the Championship. The Northern Union changed its name to the Rugby Football League in 1922. This system lasted until 1962–63, when for two seasons two divisions were used again. From 1964–65 to 1972–73 one division was used again. In 1973–74, two divisions were introduced and in various forms, including the current three divisions, this is how the sport's league format has functioned ever since. Recently, a franchise system was used to decide membership of Super League, but this was abandoned in 2014, and the bottom two clubs were relegated to the Championship.

In 1896–97, the sport introduced the Challenge Cup, a knock-out competition. In 1929, the final was played at Wembley for the first time, and playing in a Wembley Challenge Cup Final has always been one of the main achievements of a player's career.

In 1905–06 the Yorkshire and Lancashire Cups were introduced. These competitions were usually played in the first half of the season, and were taken very seriously, often producing hard fought 'derby' matches. The County Cups were abandoned in 1992. Various other cup competitions have been run over the years.

Generally, British rugby league has been based in the north of England, in Yorkshire, Lancashire and Cumbria. There was a short-lived growth of professional clubs in South Wales before the First World War, and some short-lived geographical expansion attempts in the 1920s, 1930s and early 1950s. It was not until Fulham RLFC was launched in 1980 that the sport started to spread its geographical base in a more sustained way. Until 1996, and the establishment of Super League, the vast majority of rugby league players were part-time professionals. In the decade leading up to the launch of Super League, some of the top clubs had players who were full-time.

Contents

Appendices

Left: Ernie and Ossie Deysel, two brothers who joined Leeds from Rhodesia in 1958. Although many supporters remember them, they made little impact and only stayed for a few months at the club.
(Photo: Courtesy Dave Makin).

Below: Chris Landsberg playing for Leigh. He only played for just over one season before returning to South Africa. His brother Percy played for St Helens.
(Photo: Courtesy Michael Latham).

1. Tom van Vollenhoven

There are currently (January 2015) 23 players in the British Rugby League Hall of Fame. Only three players are not British – Brian Bevan and Albert Rosenfeld are Australian. Tom van Vollenhoven is the only South African.

The signing by St Helens of Tom van Vollenhoven was enormously significant for rugby league. Deprived of international stars to play at club level by the transfer ban between Britain and Australia and New Zealand, the South Africans who followed in van Vollenhoven's footsteps had a huge impact on English rugby league in the late 1950s and 1960s. Not all were successful, but their stories form the major part of this book.

St Helens rugby league historian Alex Service recalls the rugby league career of Tom van Vollenhoven, while Hendrik Snyders looks at his time in rugby union.

The date was Friday 12 February 2012. It was a truly memorable evening for the players, officials and supporters of St Helens RFC, who were about to see their long-time goal of a new stadium to replace their historic but aging stadium at Knowsley Road come to fruition with the first Super League fixture at Langtree Park. Before the kick off, a guard of honour of Saints' past players fanned out from the players' entrance onto the pitch. They were waiting for the greatest winger in the club's history – Tom van Vollenhoven – to deliver the match ball. There was a thunderous roar as a slightly stooped figure in a blue blazer made his way out to the middle. At the end of the line, somewhat appropriately, was Glyn Moses, the amiable Welsh full-back who had been in the team when Tom had made his debut all those years before, against Leeds at Knowsley Road on 15 October 1957. Glyn held out his arms in anticipation of a pass, much to the delight of his colleagues, but Tom held firm. He had a job to do, after all and would not be distracted. Here was the man who had put the ball down for a record number of tries: 392 of them in 409 appearances for St Helens, in his 10 years as a Saint. The crowd's applause signalled another perfect touchdown, this time on the centre spot and Tom returned to the South Stand to watch the Saints defeat Salford City Reds 34–0 at the start of another much-anticipated era in the club's history.

Before Tom van Vollenhoven, the fans' first idol was Alf Ellaby, one of the greatest players in the pre-Second World War era. Nicknamed the 'Hat-trick King' for obvious reasons, Ellaby became the first Saints' player to top the rugby league try-scoring charts, which he did on three occasions and he also established a club record of 50 tries for a season. When he was transferred to Wigan in the early 1930s, quite a number of fans switched to Central Park to watch him. It seemed as though his deeds would be enshrined in the record books at Knowsley Road for ever. He was a huge star and everyone who followed him on the right wing was always going to be compared to the great man. The Saints had some fantastic wingers in the immediate post war years, such as Stan McCormick, a £4,000 world record buy from Belle Vue, Steve Llewellyn, from Abertillery RUFC, who specialised in sensational 'swallow dive' finishes over the line and local product Frank Carlton in the mid-

1950s, who was a real flyer too. They were international class, but not in Ellaby's class, according to the older supporters.

Coach Jim Sullivan had steered the club into the rugby league's elite, with a league Championship in 1953 and Challenge Cup victory in 1956, but by the autumn of 1957, supporters' continual criticism of the team's 'creeping barrage' style of play, as one correspondent put it, galvanised the Saints' board into looking for a new star. They targeted Karel Thomas van Vollenhoven, a supremely-gifted all-round athlete, who could run 100 yards in 9.8 seconds; Tom was selected for the South African rugby union team for the visit of the 1955 British Lions. In the second test at Newlands, Cape Town, he roared in for a fantastic hat-trick as the visitors were beaten 25–9. He thus became the first South African player to score three tries in a test match in his own country.

Little wonder that he began to attract interest from leading rugby league clubs like the Saints. His signing, a top-secret affair from under the noses of the South African rugby union authorities – and under intense competition from Wigan – is a story in itself and cost the club £7,230. It was the biggest fee paid for a rugby union player or for a transfer between professional clubs at the time, but was money well spent! Indeed, he was to 'electrify the crowds' with his pace and finishing ability, just as Alf Ellaby had done all those years before. Tom had blond-cropped hair and at five feet 10 inches tall and 12 stones, he was not as physically dominant-looking as Ellaby had been, but he possessed fantastic strength for his size. "I remember sitting on the bench at Hull when Vol had one of his first runs down the touchline," recalled Steve Llewellyn. "As defenders came across to bury him, he warded them off with his hip. Sully said: 'Did you see that – incredible!' He could ride tackles superbly and had phenomenal all-round ability."

Here was the new kid on the block scoring freely in his new code. Given that he was in a side containing many great players, such as Austin Rhodes, Alex Murphy and Vince Karalius, there was a distinct possibility that Tom van Vollenhoven would soon be rewriting the record books for himself. Since making his debut – with a try – against Leeds at Knowsley Road, on 26 October 1957, in front of 23,000 fans, van Vollenhoven raced over for 45 tries in 34 appearances. In February 1958, Alf Ellaby, the 'Hat Trick King' met the 'Young Pretender' before a match against Oldham at Knowsley Road and was clearly impressed by what he had seen: "[van] Vollenhoven is amazingly fast and from the way he moves has grit and natural ability," he wrote later. "Speed by itself is not the main essential to be a wingman except, possibly with the clear run in. Your best wingmen may be yards slower, but with sudden acceleration, deceiving footwork and change of pace the really clever footballer can beat the pure sprinter."

Alf Ellaby wasn't the only one to be impressed. Peter Harvey was in his late teens when he first watched Tom from the Knowsley Road terraces: "The first three years was a brilliant time to watch him. He was literally magic. I used to go behind the posts to watch him, rather than the Popular Side. It was best to watch the great man running in a straight line to appreciate his magic, because Vol could run in a straight line and beat people with his change of pace. He would take a line five yards off the touchline which gave him enough

2

room on the outside if he wanted it. Then he would hold his line and actually stop people as they ran at him and then accelerate away. I could never quite work out how he did it. Even when we played together at Saints I would be asking myself 'How did he do that?' It was just artistry and with Vol you were looking at an artist. Like all true art you can't analyse it. You do not know why true art is good, you look at it and say that something is much better than the other. In Tom's case, it was the ease with which he did everything and the ability to change pace when everyone else was running flat out. He used to do it in training. He would just accelerate away like Seb Coe used to do in his pomp. You could see him change gear because his head would go to one side. That was Vol stepping up from threequarter pace to overdrive. When you thought he was running flat out – and as people went to tackle him – he would accelerate away."

Tom van Vollenhoven did go on to usurp the great Alf in the record books for the Saints. The Flying Springbok equalled Alf's feat of scoring six tries in a match; beat his seasonal record, with 62 in 1958–59 and overhauled Alf's career total, with 392 tries from 409 appearances. In fact, Alf's Saints' total was also beaten by another local lad, Les Jones, with 282 tries from 1967 to 1983, pushing him into third place on the all-time list. It should also be noted that following his stint with Wigan, Alf rejoined the Saints for a couple of seasons before the war, but was not exactly as prolific as he had been before, with nine tries in 28 appearances.

Tom van Vollenhoven helped to take the St Helens club to the next 'stage' of success, with Lancashire Cup, League Championship and Challenge Cup victories within the first four years – hitherto unparalleled achievements. In his early days Tom had Duggie Greenall at number three as both 'minder' and provider producing sensational results when he first came. The Flying Springbok topped the charts in three successive seasons – 1958–59, 1959–60 and 1960–61. Tom scored a massive 62 tries in the 1958–59 campaign, overtaking Alf Ellaby's existing individual record of 50 tries set in 1926–27. Despite being plagued by hamstring trouble, he also scored a magnificent hat-trick, as Saints beat Hunslet 44–22 in the 1959 Championship Final at Odsal. "We were losing 12–4 early on," remembers full-back Austin Rhodes, "but then Vol scored this fantastic length-of-the-field try, the best I have ever seen, and we went on to win the match."

Remember as well the sheer poetry in motion of his marvellous Wembley try against Wigan in the 1961 Challenge Cup final and the fabulous inter-passing with his centre, Ken Large. Talking of centres, Tom – like Ellaby – ended up with a goodly number after the initial pairings with Duggie Greenall and Large brought most success. It is interesting to note that St Helens came very close to signing Wigan's Eric Ashton at the turn of the 1950s. Looking at Eric's remarkable achievements with Billy Boston outside him, we can only imagine how good a partnership that could also have become for the team. Eric and the Van would have been a truly frightening prospect for opponents, in fact.

Ten years at top level did have a marked effect on Tom. Austin Rhodes maintains, for example, that he never quite reached the dizzy heights of his first three seasons and that the ramifications of his 1959 hamstring injury tempered his sizzling pace somewhat. It was an era, of course, when one of the main objectives was to nullify the opposition's star players and get them off the field, if possible. Tom suffered from knee trouble in the mid–1960s too. He played at Wembley against Wigan in the 1966 Challenge Cup Final, but missed the Championship Final the following week at Swinton, when Tony Barrow deputised. He was still a good 'un, however, and scored a hat-trick in his last 'derby' game against Wigan, at Knowsley Road in 1968. This was in his testimonial season and his Committee sold a unique seven inch single, *the Vollenhoven Calypso,* that it inevitably 'topped the charts' locally. Like many, I still have my copy and it remains highly-prized!

The St Helens club had capitalised on the 'Vollenhoven effect' by building a new main stand, with demand for season tickets at an all-time high. They were great times to watch the team and Tom's presence meant that other South African players were tempted to come over and try their hand in the professional code. One of the most effective was Jan Prinsloo, who played 89 times for the Saints, scoring 70 tries. He had pace, certainly, but also used his strength to great effect, a bit like Castleford's Justin Carney, in the Super League era. There was one memorable headline after one game: "Jan and Van Pan 'em" which many older supporters remember to this day. In 1962, Saints also signed another winger – Len Killeen, who went on to become a fantastic points-scorer and match-winner supreme, one of the stars of the club's four trophy season in 1966 and a Lance Todd trophy winner to boot.

Although resident back in South Africa, Tom has returned to St Helens on a number of occasions, including the 1990 Ground Centenary celebrations and the Saints' Greatest 17 inaugurations, as part of the farewell to Knowsley Road. The two wingers chosen were, naturally, van Vollenhoven and Ellaby. Ironically, Alf was given the left wing slot! Tom and his wife Leonie are always welcome in St Helens. His name is familiar to everyone in the town, whether they are current or past supporters, or even those with no sporting interest whatsoever, such are his enduring achievements as a Saint. He remains my favourite all-time rugby league player, with Alex Murphy a close second. And yes, there are people who never went to watch a game again after Tom retired. After all, they had seen the best. Who could ever measure up?

Paul Wellens, another member of Saints' Greatest 17 and a superb full-back during his stellar career mentioned one of the problems of players [wingers] trying to 'win over' the fans with Tom van Vollenhoven still in the memory. When Darren Albert came to St Helens from Newcastle Knights in the early 2000s, he had natural pace and seemed to glide across the turf at Knowsley Road to score some excellent tries. According to Paul, at times, no matter what Darren did, it was always a case of 'that was good, but he's no Vollenhoven'! No slight on Darren, of course, merely a measure of how Tom's achievements have firmly ingrained themselves in our consciousness. Now, what about that Tommy Makinson?

From a national perspective, other than for the establishment of the South African Bantu Rugby Football Board (later the SA African Rugby Board) following a breakaway from the South African Coloured Rugby Board, the 1935 rugby season in South Africa was unremarkable. On the white rugby front, the South African Rugby Football Board season was not a Currie Cup year and there were no international tours. Whether it was by coincidence or as a result of the deliberate alignment of those planets that determined the fate of men on 29 April, everything was set for the birth of Karel Tom van Vollenhoven, in the little Eastern Free State town of Bethlehem.

Born to working-class parents in a deep rural area, the young van Vollenhoven went to primary school close to his home. He then entered Voortrekker High School in 1949, the year of a New Zealand tour to South Africa. Coming from a rugby-playing family and blessed with natural speed and agility, he soon made his mark and was duly selected to represent the Orange Free State under–19 provincial side in three matches. This started him on a path that few could have foreseen given the fact that he at one stage struggled with poor health.

For economic reasons, at the age of 17, he left school to join the South African Police in 1952. Based in Pretoria, he joined the local club and entered the uncompromising world of the Carlton Cup and Senior League competitions in the Northern Transvaal Rugby Union. His club, Pretoria Police RFC, was one of the leading lights in the province and had established itself as the 'backbone' of the capital-based union and as a prolific producer of provincial and national players. They were habitual winners of the premier league. In this setting, he soon won selection for the Northern Transvaal under–19s. The season, however, was mediocre with no major championship wins.

Within 12 months, van Vollenhoven was in the Police first XV and enjoyed an early taste of championship glory when his club won the 1953 Senior League title. However, the provincial side still struggled to make an impression. On the back of his club's success, van Vollenhoven, at the age of 19, made his first class provincial debut for Northerns. He was not, however, considered for the match against the touring Australian Wallabies and missed the glory of being part of the first Northern Transvaal team to beat an overseas touring team. Future league player Chris Geyer contributed a try to their 27–11 win. Van Vollenhoven did play in some of the provincial friendlies.

Van Vollenhoven kept his place in the provincial side for the next season, which included the Currie Cup. After a strong display in the elimination rounds, the team secured a place in the final against Western Province at Newlands. Van Vollenhoven distinguished himself by creating scoring opportunities for his team mates and contributed to Northerns remaining competitive throughout the game. Controversial refereeing, however, denied them championship glory as they lost 11–8.

With his consistent form and growing reputation, it was no surprise when Tom finally won Springbok honours during the 1955 British Lions tour. He made his Springbok debut on 6 August at Ellis Park in the first test. The Springboks narrowly lost 23–22 following a failed conversion by Jack Van der Schyff. The debutant, however, did not score. Van Vollenhoven's crowning moment in the national jersey followed a week later when he scored three sensational tries, each a hallmark of his overall ability. They demanded skill, speed, vision and agility to help to beat their opponents at Newlands. This performance made him a national hero since he emulated other former Springbok legends such as 'Boetie' McHardy and Jan Stegmann in scoring three tries at the famous 'home' of rugby. Also, he was the first to do so in a home test. Others who excelled in this game were Wilf Rosenberg, Tommy Gentles and Dawie Ackerman, all of whom later played rugby league.

A few days later, playing for Northern Transvaal against the tourists, he scored a sensational try after fielding a poor Lions touch-kick. He used his amazing speed and side-step to outsprint the opposition. This feat was repeated in the last test of the four match series in Port Elizabeth. Van Vollenhoven ended his debut series with five splendid tries and four tests at his credit. To crown a very satisfying season, he contributed a magnificent long-distance try for Northern Transvaal against the Junior Springboks in their 29–14 victory. He picked up the ball in his own 22 and out-stepped and outran his opponents over the length of the field. Equally pleasing was his team being crowned the Northern Transvaal Senior League and Carlton Cup champions.

In the period 1954 to 1955, van Vollenhoven played 15 representative games for Northern Transvaal in Currie Cup in centre and wing positions. In what proved to be his last South African season, van Vollenhoven, at the age of 20, was included in the Springbok team scheduled to tour Australia and New Zealand in 1956. Playing under difficult conditions, the national team – after winning the series against Australia – was soundly defeated by New Zealand in an injury-riddled tour. Van Vollenhoven played in 19 of the tour matches and three out of six tests. He scored regularly against a variety of opponents including a hat-trick of tries against Wanganui – King Country and four against the combined XV of Nelson-Marlborough-Golden Bay-Motueka for an overall total of 19 tries. His local club also repeated their feat of the previous season by winning the Carlton Cup to bring the curtain down on a short, but eventful, local rugby union career.

At the end of the 1956 season, van Vollenhoven, for economic reasons, resigned from the Police Force in exchange for a career in the copper mines of Northern Rhodesia (now Zambia). Based in the Chingola region, he joined the NChanga RFC at the start of the new season and played in a local league. Van Vollenhoven continued to show good form and soon established himself as a major crowd attraction far from his natural stomping ground. At the start of the representative season, he won selection for the Rhodesian national side.

Van Vollenhoven made his debut for Rhodesia in a friendly against an Oxford-Cambridge 'Blues' XV in a season-opener. Far from being a run-of-the-mill touring team, the visitors had six internationals: Mulligan (Ireland), Allan (Scotland), McClung (Scotland), Davies (Wales) and Currie and Robbins (England). With this experience, the tourists placed a stranglehold on the local forwards and deprived the Rhodesian backline of quality possession. This left van Vollenhoven with very little ball to work with, and made for an unsatisfactory debut. Their defeat, 51–14 was a good wake-up call for the team in the process of preparing for the 1957 Currie Cup. During the season, Rhodesia played eight matches; won five and drew three. Van Vollenhoven, at the back of a focused Rhodesian team, scored a try against Eastern Transvaal, described by Jonty Winch as the 'one bright moment' of the match, Griqualand West in Kimberley – 'an exhilarating try beating several defenders by sheer speed' – and North-Eastern Districts at Aliwal-North. Their momentum was stopped by defeat against Transvaal which brought to its end one of Rhodesia's best-ever seasons and van Vollenhoven's provincial rugby union career. Prior to signing for St Helens, he helped Northern Rhodesia defeat Southern Rhodesia in the Clark Cup. With his Rhodesian adventure behind him and a much enhanced reputation, he left Africa for the cold of the rugby league fields of northern England. A glorious career awaited him in St Helens.

Top left: Tom van Vollenhoven on his way to scoring on his St Helens debut against Leeds in 1957.
Top right: Tom van Vollenhoven scoring against Leigh in the 1963 Lancashire Cup Final.
Bottom: South African Saints in the late 1950s: Jan Prinsloo, coach Alan Prescott, Percy Landsberg, club secretary Basil Lowe and Tom van Vollenhoven. (All photos courtesy Alex Service)

Len Killeen and Tom van Vollenhoven training for the 1966 Challenge Cup Final.
(Photo courtesy Alex Service)

Tom van Vollenhoven and Jan Prinsloo team up with Duggie Greenall in a bout of handling
practice at Knowsley Road in 1959. (Photo: Courtesy Robert Gate)

2. Hugh Frederick Murray

The first South African who was born in the country to establish himself as a first team player in English rugby league was Hugh Frederick Murray. He was born in Kimberley, the capital of the Northern Cape, on 29 December 1901. Kimberley is famous for diamond mining and the siege of October 1899 to February 1900. At the time of Murray's birth, it was one of the largest cities in South Africa because of an influx of people to work on the mines.

He came to England in October 1920, and joined the Wakefield rugby union club. It is not known why he came to England or to Wakefield. According to *Burglar Bill*, a Wakefield RU memorabilia and memories newsletter (August 2012 edition), he "quickly slotted into a Wakefield team that was at the start of a 'glory period' which would see them reach five consecutive Yorkshire Cup [finals], winning two." Murray played for his new club in the 1921 final. Wakefield lost 13–3. The *Wakefield Express* (quoted in *Burglar Bill*) said that Murray "has a very fine turn of speed". He scored 12 tries in 10 first team games at Wakefield.

Rugby union in Yorkshire at this time was starting to recover from the decimation of clubs moving to the Northern Union which had seen them with 14 clubs in 1902, compared with 150 10 years earlier. However, quality players in rugby union in the county must have been easy targets for the rugby league scouts, with none of the problems of being recognised or challenged on their trips to South Wales. In 1921, Murray switched codes and joined Batley. On 17 September, in a 3–0 win at York, he made his first team debut on the right wing and became the first South African born player to play in a first team rugby league game in England. He played 22 first team games that season. His first nine, until 3 December, were on the right wing; after that he switched to the left. He scored five tries, but faced competition for a place from two other union converts – Bryn Williams from Llanelli on the right and George Kilbey from Northampton on the left. In March 1922, the *Hull Daily Mail* said that he was "a young robust player of a different stamp, who depends chiefly on determination and courage." The report also said that he had "given some satisfaction" to his new club.

Traditionally, Batley have often been one of the game's smaller, less successful clubs. They won the Challenge Cup three times in the competition's first five seasons: 1897, 1898 and 1901, and were runners-up in 1910. The club was hit hard by the First World War, but managed to rebuild largely through recruits from rugby union. This led to one of the most successful periods in the club's history, and Murray played his part in it. Brian Cartwright's club history, *A "Ton" full of Memories*, published in 1986, says that he was called Herbert, and apparently his nickname at the club was 'Bob'.

In 1922–23, Batley reached the Yorkshire Cup Final. Murray played 29 matches in the first team that season, mainly on the left wing with Williams playing at centre. He scored 14 tries, and was second highest try scorer, behind Williams. In the Yorkshire Cup semi-final, Batley travelled to Headingley to face Leeds, and won 28–0, one of the most remarkable wins over their Yorkshire rivals in their history. They returned to Headingley for the final, but lost 5–0 to York. Murray played in both matches.

Batley 1923–24: Hugh Murray is in the middle row, one from the right. (Photo: Courtesy Robert Gate)

The following season saw even more success. Murray played 27 first team matches, despite missing three through suspension for 'charging' early on in the season. He was joint top try scorer with George Davidge, both touching down 17 times. In the Yorkshire Cup, Batley reached the semi-final and lost 10–9 to Huddersfield. But in the Championship, they finished runners-up, with a 70.83 per cent success rate, behind Wigan who were on 81.57.

In the Championship semi-final, Murray contributed two tries to a 38–0 victory over third-placed Oldham. The Lancashire club were missing four players who were en route to Australia and New Zealand with the British Lions, as was Batley's skipper Frank Gallagher.

A week later, Batley faced Wigan at Broughton Rangers' The Cliff ground. Again, Wigan had players missing, but still expected to win. Their South African stars, Gert van Rooyen and Attie van Heerden were both in the Wigan team. However, Murray scored twice for Batley, who won 13–7 to take the Championship back to Yorkshire. Graham Morris comments that Batley thoroughly deserved "their moment of glory". Batley had also won the Yorkshire League, with 40 points from 26 matches, four ahead of runners-up Huddersfield.

The Championship Final seems to have been almost the end of Murray's rugby career. He had been found guilty of assault in court and was fined and asked to pay costs. At the start of the 1924–25 season, he played the first three matches for Batley, but did not play for the rest of the season. The piece on him in *Burglar Bill* says that he had played for another club without Batley's permission. Batley asked for his reinstatement, which the RFL refused. Apparently he had asked to go on the transfer list after the court case.

Off the field, in 1922 he had married Ella Schofield at Dewsbury Registry Office. Their daughter was born a week later. In 1928, she filed for divorce – something more complex and unusual than today – and it seems that Murray had returned to South Africa. He did not marry again, and by 1947 was living in Brakpan in the Transvaal. He died in Johannesburg on 5 January 1957.

3. 1895 to 1914: Early days

As the Northern Union code developed, it was clear to the game's organisers that it had to develop beyond its roots in the north of England. Some of this development took place within the British Isles. The game put down tenuous roots in South Wales for a few years from 1908 onwards, but these clubs, faced with trying to draw fans from both rugby union and association football, did not last until the start of the First World War. A Northern Union club in Coventry was another short-lived development, and one-off matches were played in other areas to try to promote the game.

The most important developments were the establishment of the sport in Australia and New Zealand. The importance of international competition and tours was clear to the game's early officials, and international matches were well established by 1914.

The history of the development of rugby league is full of missed opportunities. One came in 1910, when the sport's leaders in Britain turned down a request to tour from a 'Coloured' team in South Africa. Had this tour taken place, and rugby league established a link with the Coloured and / or African people in South Africa, the history of the sport could have been very different.

As it was, the main links between rugby league and South Africa before the First World War were through individual players. In 1895, Ben Andrew left Oldham to emigrate to South Africa, and played for his new country in the second test against the 1896 British Lions. He never played for Oldham in the Northern Union, but one of his team mates in 1896 was Arthur (Alf) Larard, who on his return to England did play in the new code for Huddersfield.

Arthur (Alf) Larard

Alf Larard played rugby league for four seasons at the end of his career. He played at centre, occasionally at half-back or on the wing for a struggling Huddersfield side, who only really found success during his time at the club when they were in the Second Division in 1904–05. However, he has a unique place in the history of South African rugby union, because he scored the try when the South African team first beat the British Lions in 1896.

Larard was born in Hull on 30 December 1870, and arrived in South Africa in 1888, aged 17. In the 1890s he played for the Diggers club in Johannesburg, the centre of the gold mining industry. He also established himself as a member of the Transvaal provincial team.

During the 1896 tour of the British Lions to South Africa, Larard was selected to play against the tourists when they started the Transvaal leg of the tour. He was selected on five occasions for both representative teams of his union and his adopted country. In the first match on Wednesday 12 August 1896, he represented the Johannesburg Country XV before 5,000 spectators. Despite fielding a virtual full Diggers team (10 out of 15), the Johannesburg side still lost 7–0. Three days later, on Saturday, 15 August 1896, Larard played for the Transvaal provincial side against the tourists in Johannesburg. Despite this team being much more representative of all the union's clubs, the home side still lost 16–3 before a crowd of 7,000. Four days later, on Wednesday 19 August 1896, Larard and his

Transvaal team mates met the tourists for a second encounter in Johannesburg before 4,000 spectators. For the second time they were defeated, this time 15–5.

South Africa lost the first test to the Lions 8–0. Team changes saw Larard selected for the South African team at half-back to play the Lions in the second test on 22 August. He was the 47th player to be chosen for the South Africans. The match was at the Wanderers club in Johannesburg, and a 5,000 crowd saw the South Africans lose 17–8. He was dropped for the third test, which the Lions won 9–3, but recalled for the final match of the series, on 5 September at Newlands in Cape Town. A 3,500 crowd saw South Africa win 5–0, and Larard scored the try.

In the *Annals of South African Rugby*, the prelude to this historic try is described as follows: "South Africa then started one of the finest movements of the day when Larard, Aston, Anderson and Hepburn, in a pretty inter-passing movement, carried play into the British '25'. Here Bulger kicked out and Byrne obtained from the throw-in. He was tackled, and Anderson took the ball out of his hands to run right through. When tackled by Meares he led out to Larard who ran over under the goal posts. 'England raised objections but the try was allowed' and Hepburn converted to make the half-time score 5–0"

A.C. Parker wrote that the day "will forever be a date to be underlined in green and gold in the history of South African rugby... South Africa recorded their first international victory by five points to nil after a titanic struggle." [1] He described the try as follows: "Larard initiated a brilliant thrust, sustained in turn by Aston, Anderson and Hepburn, that was only checked in the British '25' when Bulger managed to find touch. The chance of a score seemed lost when the British gained possession from the throw-in, but as the ball reached Byrne he was hit hard, low and true by Aston. The next moment Anderson had snatched the ball from Byrne's hands and run clear. Meares, the full-back, still barred the way but Anderson committed him to the tackle and Larard, with the anticipation of the natural footballer, was up to take an inside pass and cross between the posts." [2]

Larard was well regarded in South Africa. Parker says that he was "given a rating later by A.F. Markotter as the greatest of all South African scrum-halves." [3] Paul Dobson says that Larard was given a gold medal to commemorate his feat, but also comments that "Larard had a dubious side. They say that he had actually played rugby league before coming to South Africa and it is doubtful if the Rules on Amateurism, formulated in 1895, allowed him to play." [4] Given that he left England in 1888, seven years before the formation of the Northern Union in 1895, that would have been an achievement. However, accepting the gold medal could have breached his 'amateur' status. There is no record of any action being taken against him by the SARFB.

Larard served with the Imperial Light Horse regiment in the Boer War, and returned to England in 1901. He joined the Huddersfield Cricket and Athletic club, which played in the Northern Union. He made his debut against Salford on 28 September. The report in the *Huddersfield Daily Examiner* said that he was "weak" and "has a great deal to learn." The paper also quoted 'Impressionist' in *Umpire* who said: "...this was the first match in which he has played since he came from South Africa where he made for himself a good name, not only as a football player, but as a cricketer. He is an old Rugbyite and this was his first appearance under NU auspices. It has cost him something to sever himself from the old regime and take up service under the newer organisation and he has been frank enough to ask the members of the committee to tell him where he could improve matters. Larard played half-back up to half-time but then he and Bullivan, who had been playing threequarter, exchanged places, ... Larad's chief difficulty seemed to be gathering the ball from the scrimmage and some of his passes were not well judged., but otherwise he did not play a bad game for a start. Under the new conditions, I fully expect that he will soon get accustomed to them and will prove a good half-back as he is a powerfully built player..."

He soon adjusted to play in the Northern Union and played twice for Yorkshire, against Cumberland and Cheshire. However, he found playing in the English winter a change from South Africa. The report of Huddersfield's match at Swinton on 30 December said: "It appears that this climate is almost too much for him as he has spent so much time in a tropical country, and on Saturday he complained sadly of the cold, which prevented him playing as well as he otherwise would have done." By the end of the season, the reports said that he worked hard, sometimes made mistakes, but against Leeds at Fartown at the end of March made two tries.

Larard was also an accomplished cricketer, and missed an early match for Huddersfield in the 1902–03 season because he was "engaged on the cricket enclosure." After Huddersfield's 4–2 win over Batley at the end of September, the *Examiner* said that Larard "was the best of the quartet. He ran strongly and well, handled the ball whether in fielding it or in taking and giving passes and I never saw him kick so well before. He made better use of touch than any man on the field. His defence was equal to his attack, and several times he brought his man down in grand style. One of his comrades in the summer ... waxed very enthusiastic and was heard to describe Larard as a 'little hero', a description that was very well merited."

In January 1903 there was correspondence in the *Examiner* about the best selection for Huddersfield. The rugby writer replied to one correspondent: "It will be noted that he leaves Larard altogether out of the side. This I think is a big mistake, for he and Deere have shown the most consistent form of any of the threequarters and I should certainly not leave him out, especially now we are coming to the time of year when we can reasonably hope for dry grounds. All that have followed the team regularly know that Larard on a wet ground is quite a different player from Larard on a dry ground. Personally I should like to see him tried on the wing again, and if not there I should put him at half along with Holroyd and see how they might do together, if that does not work put him in Winpenny's place, with F. Dewhirst and Holroyd behind the scrum." [5]

Larard continued to play regularly for Huddersfield, mainly at centre but occasionally on the wing. Huddersfield were struggling in the league, mainly due to a weak pack, which was a crucial area at a time when the game was still played under rugby union rules. The report on a 2–0 defeat at Oldham in September 1903 said that "Larard ...played a really fine game throughout... He not only ran and passed with judgement, but tackled well, some of his efforts in that line being worthy of highest praise." However, a poor season saw Huddersfield relegated to the newly formed Second Division for 1904–05, Larard's last season in the Northern Union.

Playing teams that were relatively weak, including Normanton, Millom, Pontefract, Castleford [6] and Lancaster, Huddersfield started the season very well. Larard was appointed captain. After a 19–0 opening day victory over Normanton, the *Examiner* commented: "It was a handsome commencement of the season, which, I hope, will often be repeated. I don't see why it should not be, now that the team is in the hands of a captain like Larard, who, on Saturday, set his men a rare example in the matter of hard, unflagging effort to score; and, although he did not himself succeed in crossing the line, he many times made the play open, and gave his companions at the threequarter line opportunities of scoring, with the result that tries were obtained, and Larard, therefore, is entitled to some share in the total of results which the tries indicate. Larard will be able to show his men what he wants doing, and now that the team is on a new footing there is a prospect of matches being won, and won in the best style, for every man will be serious to fall in with the captain's desires, and the captain is, I know, very anxious to lead his men back to the First Division. Throughout the game on Saturday, Larard made only one mistake, when he failed to pick up the ball when it was rolling towards his own goal, with Readyhough there to stop it, which the full-back did in time. If Larard will always play as he did on Saturday there will be no fear as to the general result."

However, after a 7–2 win at Brighouse on 7 November, the *Examiner* said that "...they gave the poorest display of the season. I allow that the injury to Larard was largely responsible for the dislocation of the threequarter line – would it not have been better if he had retired – but that is no excuse for the miserable display given by the forwards..."

Larard never really recovered from the knee injury he suffered in that game. In the spring, Huddersfield had a good run in the Challenge Cup, beating Victoria Rovers and York before drawing 3–3 with mighty neighbours Wakefield Trinity. The match report said: "Larard and Deere were the weakest spots in our attack. The former seems for the time being to have lost the dash and go that was so irresistible before he was damaged, and his taking of passes was three times at fault."

Larard played in the replay the following Wednesday at Belle Vue. Huddersfield lost 7–0 before a 10,000 crowd. The match report said that "Larard had evidently played enough." For the next match, against Pontefract, it was announced that he had "stood down", and then against Dewsbury the following week it was reported that: "Huddersfield were handicapped by the absence of A. Larard, captain, who has retired from the position."

In four seasons he made two appearances for Yorkshire, 99 for Huddersfield, and scored 14 tries for the Fartown side. He died on 17 August 1936 of a heart attack while on holiday in Cornwall, where he was buried. He was working as a travelling salesman. His obituary in the *Examiner* said that "He was good at most sports, and when he retired from rugby he played for some time with the Huddersfield United Hockey club. In addition to being proficient at billiards, he was an outstanding match player at the Woodsome Hall Golf Club."

Alf Larard's career in the NU was when he was reaching the veteran stage as a rugby player, and was often in a struggling Huddersfield side. Had he not gone to South Africa, and had played his whole career in rugby in the north of England, he undoubtedly could have been one of the stars of the early Northern Union, because he would have been 24 years old when the split occurred in 1895.

Two other players did travel to England and signed for Northern Union clubs were James Megson, who joined Leeds in 1910, and Wilfred Mart, who joined Hull Kingston Rovers at the same time. Neither ever played for the first team at their respective clubs.

James Megson and William Mart

James Megson and William Mart are not well-known figures in either rugby code. But they both were recruited by Northern Union clubs early in 1910, and registered with the Northern Union at the same time. Megson and Mart's registrations were confirmed at the Northern Rugby League committee meeting in Huddersfield on Tuesday 25 January. Megson joined Leeds, and Mart was signed by Hull Kingston Rovers. Their reasons for coming to England are not known; whether it was for work or study, or to play Northern Union rugby.

Megson's former club or location was given as Potchefstroom. Mart was from Woodstock, a suburb of Cape Town. He did not play representative rugby union in South Africa. Mart played one first team game for Hull KR. This was on 19 February 1910 at home to Keighley. The report in the *Hull Daily Mail* commented: "Mart, the South African forward appears too light and lacks the robustness necessary. This was the first opportunity I have had of witnessing him play, and under the conditions it would be unfair to question his abilities." That seems to be the only official first team game he played for Hull KR, and he was struck off their players register on 22 May 1912.

James Megson came from Potchefstroom in the western part of what was the old Transvaal Colony. It was also not known whether he was South African or foreign born. The town is closely associated with the Great Trek, a seminal event in Afrikaner history.[7] Due to its location in the goldfields region, where various gold rushes occurred in the mid–1880s, it attracted people from all over the world. Various sporting codes, including rugby, became established in the town and the surrounding districts.

The game thrived through regular social matches and resulted in the establishment of formal clubs in the town. The pioneering Potchefstroom clubs were Potchefstroom FC, which was established in 1890 and Potchefstroom and Districts RFC, which was set up in 1907. The former, according to a respectable local historian, decided at its founding meeting to adopt the Northern Union Rules as the basis of its activities. The latter, however, adopted the rugby union rules. Both subsequently joined the Transvaal RFU and participated in its Rugby Trophy (later renamed the Pirates Grand Challenge Cup (PGCC), Neser and Country Cup competitions. Playing as a combined team in the Country Cup, they won the competition in and 1906. They also played well in the senior Transvaal competition, the PGCC. By 1907, local newspapers reported the death of the 'old' Potchefstroom club and its replacement by two new clubs, Wanderers and Crusaders. They were joined by a military club, first known as the 4th Hussars and later Cantonments. As a result of these developments, a District League was established in Potchefstroom. Megson's town was a rugby football hotbed, which must have had an influence on his decision to both enter and stay in the game.

The first mention of the name 'Megson', or 'Megsen' in an account of Potchefstroom rugby, appeared in a reference to a friendly game in August 1909 between a Potchefstroom Districts team consisting of players of the aforementioned clubs and Randfontein United RFC in Wespark. 'Megson' or 'Megsen' was one of four Cantonments players in the side that beat the visitors. The club, formerly known as the IV Q.U. Hussars, were participants in the Anglo-Boer War and were stationed in a military camp in the town. They played in the senior league, the regional association. After its departure, from 1909 they played under the name Cantonments. Maybe Megson was a British soldier who, like Alf Larard, only returned home after the war was concluded and peace secured. In fact, in the official history of the Western Transvaal Rugby Union, it says that as a result of the imminent establishment of the Union of South Africa, military activities were dramatically scaled down. By 1912, Cantonments was no more and instead, a new military club called Garrison joined the local league.

In the *Yorkshire Post* on Tuesday 18 January 1910 it was reported that Leeds had signed two half-backs, one of whom was Megson. The item reported that "Megson, though training at Headingley, has not yet turned out for either of the Leeds teams, as he has a little superfluous weight to reduce before being really fit for duty. He has played with some good clubs in South Africa." Leeds won the Challenge Cup in 1910, and finished sixth in the Northern Rugby League. As with some of his compatriots who changed codes later in the twentieth century, he may have had more chance of winning a regular first team place at a less high profile club.

4. 1919 to 1939: Wigan and South Africa

Throughout the sport's history, Wigan have been one of the 'glamour' clubs, if not the 'glamour' club of rugby league. While the town has always been a hotbed initially of the Northern Union, and subsequently of rugby league, the club have never been slow to both recruit from other clubs, and to sign international stars, both from rugby league and rugby union.

While Wigan was not the only club to have South African players between the wars, in the second half of the 1920s there was a consistent presence of South Africans in the Wigan team. Part of the reason for this was the international transfer ban that had been introduced in 1913. The sport's ruling bodies in Great Britain, Australia and New Zealand believed that the transfer ban would stop the sport's domestic competitions becoming weaker through players moving from one country to another. They were probably particularly concerned at that time about its development in Australia and New Zealand. In the latter it was very much the second rugby code behind rugby union, which was the national winter sport. In Australia, league was more established in New South Wales and Queensland, but still faced competition from rugby union, Aussie Rules and to a much lesser extent association football.

In 1923, the transfer ban was lifted briefly, but then reimposed. In June 1927 it was lifted, but there was an agreement that the 1929–30 Australian tourists could not sign for English clubs until 12 months after the conclusion of the tour.

Wigan sent club directors to seek out players in South Africa, and used recruitment agents there. During this period, Wigan Highfield were also vying for support from the Wigan public. Unlike the Central Park side, they based their playing strength on local recruitment. On 3 October 1925, the *Wigan Observer* published a cartoon of Highfield versus Wigan match with the caption: "Highfield versus the rest of the World". On 11 August 1928, the *Wigan Examiner* in a pre-season review pointed out that there were three South Africans listed in the Wigan squad: Oliver, Booysen & van Rooyen, seven Welsh players, three New Zealanders, one Scot and five Wiganers. Highfield's players were all born in Wigan except for one solitary Welshman.

The issue of how clubs tried to recruit is a recurring one throughout the history of South African players in rugby league. A report in the *Wigan Examiner* on 6 November 1926 illustrated some of the problems: "The South African correspondent of the *Sporting Chronicle* writes: "There used to be a slogan in England, 'What a hope' and one can hitch this slogan to the Wigan rugby league club, which according to one of its agents, is expecting South Africa to provide it with a scrum half-back, a winger and a centre. I question whether Wigan will get what she wants; at any rate from South Africa.

In view of the fact that Wigan got Booysen and [Attie] van Heerden from here, they may still go on hoping that this country will provide them with other talent. Personally, I think aversion in this country from professionalism in England is brought about through [ignorance]… To say the least, players do not understand professional football. Here it is regarded as a cancerous growth, and any player who deserts South African rugby for professionalism in England is regarded by the people here as an outcast.

A rugby league agent in this country is regarded as an interloper, and, to a certain extent, beneath the pale of society. This, of course, is wrong, and personally I think the people should be educated towards looking with a little more favour on the young player who is not against capitalising his skill in the football market.

I do believe that if it were not for the stand made by the public there would be many more conversions. At least from the conversations I have had with several famous players in our rugby they do not appear to be anything like as severe on the paid player as those who watch the game. A rugby league agent has to be very wary how he moves in this country – in nine cases out of 10 if he puts anything in writing it is revealed the next day in the newspapers.

Wigan's offers

For instance, it has just come to light that the Wigan agent, at present domiciled in Pretoria, is looking for a scrum-half, a winger and a centre. He got his eye on a scrum-half, Devine, of the Diggers, Johannesburg, and wrote to him. What happened? Devine, who has played for his country against Britain, and who is probably the best scrum-half in South Africa, declined to be diplomatic. He revealed the contents of the letter received by him from the Wigan agent, who, I must say, painted a lovely picture of professional football in England. In this letter the agent admits that his club is anxious for him to find three South African players, and goes on to say: "My club are prepared to offer you a lump sum of money for signing on, also to pay your rail fare and steamship passage to England. They will find you employment at your trade or profession, or give you an equivalent in wages. They also pay so much per match, win draw or lose – I think it is £5 a win, two matches a week.

I consider it a good chance to see England, and a careful man at the end of three years can return with £1,200 or £1,500 and start a nice business for himself. I consider it a chance of a lifetime for any young man to see the world."

Of course, Devine, who apparently does not understand the professional game, was so shocked on receiving the letter that he promptly had it published; at any rate, the epistle could not have appeared in print without his consent. Someday South Africa will come to realise that professional football, after all, is not the evil the ignorant would make it out to be.'" In an era when there were far fewer test matches, Daunce Devine played twice for the Springboks, once in 1924 and once in 1928. He never switched codes.

The agent's arguments to come to England and switch codes are clearly economic and to 'have an adventure' – there is no mention of what playing rugby league entailed. The average wage for a craftsman in England in 1928 was around £200 a year, so the sums mentioned are considerable. Although white workers in South Africa through segregation had a far superior position to the African or 'Coloured' workers, many did skilled blue collar jobs and would not have been able to save that amount.

However, the first notable player to switch codes actually signed for Hull Kingston Rovers. George (Gert) van Rooyen, a massive forward, went on to have a very successful rugby league career.

George van Rooyen

Gert Wilhelm [George] 'Tank' Van Rooyen was the first Springbok to move to British rugby league after the First World War. He played for three clubs, Hull Kingston Rovers, Wigan and Widnes, despite not switching codes until he was aged almost 30.

He was born in Steynesburg, and played for Johannesburg Pirates and Transvaal, as well as appearing in two tests against the All Blacks for the Springboks in their 1921 tour of Australia and New Zealand. He made his debut against New South Wales in June 1921, and on the tour played in 13 matches, including the two test matches, and scored one try. In union he played at lock-forward, but in league played in the second-row.

In September 1922 he joined Hull KR, and despite making 25 appearances for the club in his first season, missed out on playing in their team that beat Huddersfield 15–5 in the Championship final. After a further 10 games for Hull KR in the 1923–24 season, he was transferred to Wigan and made his debut on 10 November 1923 against Wigan Highfield at Central Park. However, dispute and acrimony surrounded his move. Just after signing for Wigan, a letter from him appeared in the *Johannesburg Star*. It said that he had made a mistake in coming to England and could not find work. He couldn't feed his wife and three children, and asked for support from the sporting public in South Africa for help to return home. Naturally, Hull KR were furious, and their secretary said he was not aware of van Rooyen's problems. The player himself said that he hoped that things would improve with his move to Wigan. Hull KR asked the RFL for an enquiry into the matter. The club said that they had met all their commitments in their agreement with the player. They had also agreed to help pay for his wife and children to return to South Africa because they had not settled in England.

Van Rooyen said that he had only had occasional work in the docks in Hull at 10 shillings a day. His playing terms were £3/10/0 for a win, £3 for a draw and £2/10/0 for a defeat (the average wage for a craftsman was about £3/10/0 a week). The club had found him a house, but he could not afford the rent of £1/7/6 a week. The club had also loaned him £25 which he had to pay back at £1 per match. The enquiry concluded that the club had honoured its agreement with van Rooyen, which the player accepted. It was also revealed that he had received £390 from Hull KR, an average of £7 per week, and usually earned £1/10/0 a week.

Van Rooyen was a huge man, six feet two inches tall, very strong and weighing almost 17 stone. The legendary Wigan full-back Jim Sullivan, who played for Wigan from 1921 to 1946, remembers van Rooyen as "the most fabulous character I have known in rugby league". He remembered a "great giant of a man... solid granite... the strongest man I've ever seen apart from the old music hall acts. There were times when I thought he was more than human." Some of the feats Sullivan could remember included carrying a bag of cement under each arm with ease, shifting snow from the pitch with a wooden plank 12 feet by seven inches; single-handedly lifting a horse out of manhole and hoisting a broken down van off its wheels. He was courageous as well, playing on in a match against St Helens Recs despite a gash in his cheek big enough to put his tongue through. "They can't hurt me" he said as he stayed on the field. [8]

Graham Morris described him as having "a massive frame with extraordinary strength" and that he "tore down the field like an avalanche." [9] He made 32 appearances in his first season for Wigan, scoring four tries. And honours came his way, with a Lancashire League medal and Challenge Cup winner's medal. He played in every round of the Challenge Cup, and in the final Wigan beat Oldham comfortably at Rochdale Hornets' Athletic Ground. Wigan won 21–4, and their main concern was whether the massive crowd could be kept off the pitch.

The next season he played 36 matches, scoring seven tries. Two of his tries came against the unfortunate amateurs of Flimby & Fotheringham, who were beaten 116–0 in the Challenge Cup. One further honour was selection in October 1924 for the Other Nationalities team. The side included seven Wigan players and beat England 23–17.

Further silverware came his way in 1925–26. In the Lancashire Cup Wigan reached the final, but lost 15–11 to Swinton. However, the Lancashire League was won again, and in the Championship, Hull were beaten 34–0 to set up a final against Warrington at Knowsley Road. Van Rooyen played in his first Championship Final and helped Wigan win comfortably, 22–10. The match was notable for having taken place during the General Strike, and for featuring three South African players, van Rooyen playing alongside Attie van Heerden and David Booysen.

In 1926–27 he played 40 matches, scoring four tries. Wigan lost to Swinton 23–3 in the Championship semi-final, and made little impression in the Cup competitions. In 1927–28 he was reaching the veteran stage of his career, and only made 19 first team appearances. One was in the Lancashire Cup Final, Wigan again losing to Swinton, this time 5–2. His last appearance for Wigan's first team was at Leigh on 15 September 1928. He made 178 appearances, scoring 26 tries.

But his rugby league career was not over. He moved to Widnes on a free transfer in August 1929. In more recent times Widnes became known as the 'Cup Kings', but in 1929 had only ever appeared in one final, the Lancashire Cup, in November 1928, when they lost narrowly to Wigan. The Widnes team became known as "12 Locals and a South African" as the other players were all from the town. St Helens were firm favourites to win the final, the second one to be staged at Wembley Stadium.

However, the signing of van Rooyen had an important effect on the side. A book produced as a heritage project to commemorate the club's Challenge Cup successes commented: "Widnes had rarely been in a position up to that stage to pay big wages to their players, and stood by their determination not to squander money on transfer fees but to foster and rely upon local talent. But the arrival of van Rooyen proved a success of exciting proportions. His influence on the young side was immense from the start, and the part played by the big fellow... in Widnes's great run to Wembley was significant. All this at the age of 37. Van Rooyen surprised every team in the league by his wonderful play, he was one of the cleanest players in the code and he quickly felt a part of the Widnes squad as his humorous personality shone. Even on the field he worked like a Trojan, always where the fight was thickest." [10]

Interviewed in the above book, Peter Spencer recalls that "Saints hadn't accounted for... our secret weapon, George van Rooyen. He'd come over from South Africa and played at Wigan but they thought he was past his sell by date so farmed him off to Widnes. I remember he was a tanker driver at ICI and when the fans collected to buy the ground for Widnes he got dressed up as a Zulu, wearing ostrich feathers and carrying spears. He must have made a couple of hundred pounds dressed like that." He recalls that in the final, after St Helens had opened the scoring, "Van Rooyen knocked heck out of them". [11]

Les Hoole outlines that van Rooyen "simply took control of the game". [12] Widnes won the forward battle and the scrums, and scored 10 unanswered points to take the Cup back home with a 10–3 win. There was great excitement when the team returned home. At the official welcome at the Town Hall team captain Paddy Douglas spoke, then the mayor introduced van Rooyen, who he said had been 'naturalised' as a Widnesian in London. The South African said that "I only want to tell you that there is no happier man in the world tonight than me. There has been no prouder man to play with a team like these boys and bring the Cup. Determination every time." [13]

He played 100 matches for Widnes, with the last in February 1933 at the age of 40. Sadly, van Rooyen died of cancer at a relatively young age, and only weighed nine stone when he passed away.

Van Rooyen was in many ways an exception – an experienced rugby union forward who made a successful transition to rugby league. Generally, backs have found switching codes far easier. One of the most successful at Wigan in the 1920s was another Springbok, Attie van Heerden.

Attie van Heerden

Adriaan Jacobus ('Attie') van Heerden was one of many South African rugby union players who also reached the top in another sport, in his case athletics. He was a successful hurdler, and was the South African champion in 1920 at both 120 yards and 440 yards. He was selected for South Africa to run in the 400 yards hurdles at the 1920 Olympic Games, which were held in Antwerp. He won the second heat with a time of 57.2 seconds, but did not qualify for the final.

He was born in Boshof and his rugby union career started at Stellenbosch University. He played for the Combined Universities team and the Transvaal Province side before being selected for the 1921 Springbok tour of Australia and New Zealand. He was selected for the tour despite having missed the 1920 Currie Cup competition to run in the Olympics. On tour he played in 17 matches including two tests against New Zealand, scoring a try, the Springboks' first in a test match in New Zealand. He then played his club rugby for Simmer & Jack in Johannesburg.

He signed for Wigan in September 1923, having arrived by boat in Southampton, and travelled north by train from London. A journalist reported his arrival as follows: "First impressions were extremely favourable, for the hatless figure of a 'bonny lad', carrying a small portmanteau and looking the very picture of health, was a particularly striking one, standing six feet one inch and carrying his 13 stone four pounds bulk with the ease and grace of an athlete." [14] Jack Winstanley said that he was a "colourful personality who tormented defences on the field and broke more than few hearts off it." [15]

Van Heerden made his Central Park debut on 6 October for the 'A' team and scored five tries. He made his first team debut a week later, playing on the left wing against Broughton Rangers. Wigan won 11–6, and then the following week he scored his first try at Rochdale in a 35–0 win. He was soon joined by van Rooyen. Such was the impact of these players that the RFL announced during the season that South Africans would not be considered for the British Lions tour of Australia and New Zealand at the end of the season.

Van Heerden scored consistently in his first season in rugby league. He scored four tries in a match twice, against Hull KR and Hunslet. One of his tries against Hunslet was spectacular, a length of the pitch run, beating half the Hunslet team on the way to the line.

He joined a Wigan team which was the strongest in the league. They finished top of the table with 31 wins in 38 matches. As the teams did not all play the same number of matches, the table was decided on the percentage success figures. Wigan's was 81.57; runners-up Batley were over 10 per cent behind on 70.83 per cent. However, the Championship was decided through end of season play-offs, and after beating Leigh 27–0 in the semi-final, Wigan went down 13–7 to Batley at Broughton.

However, three weeks earlier, Wigan had won the Challenge Cup, beating Oldham 21–4 in front of 40,786 fans crammed into Rochdale's Athletic Ground. The police had allowed some of the crowd onto the cycle track around the pitch, and soon thousands were moving forward for a better vantage point. Order was restored, but only with mounted policemen keeping the crowd back. After Oldham had taken an early lead through a penalty, a try from Roffey have the Central Park side a lead they would never lose. Then van Heerden scored what Les Hoole describes as "one of the most remarkable tries in the history of the Challenge Cup. Following up a cross-field kick at great speed, and, while Corsi and Knapman were waiting for the ball to roll into touch, he snapped it up from almost under the prancing feet of a mounted policeman to touch down under the posts." [16] This try has entered the sport's mythology, with other versions saying that van Heerden ran round the horse to touch down, and others moving the incident to another match altogether. Wigan won the Cup comfortably anyway.

Van Heerden had finished the season with 40 tries, and was topped in the national try scorers list only by his team mate Johnny Ring, who finished on 49. The next season was not as successful, although his 31 tries included four against amateurs Flimby & Fothergill in the Challenge Cup as Wigan ran up a 116–0 win. In the league he scored five tries in a 63–5 win over Salford at the Willows, and a hat-trick in the local derby against Wigan Highfield. Also, international honours came his way, with an appearance for the Other Nationalities side, scoring two tries.

Further honours followed in 1925–26. Wigan won the Lancashire League, and the Championship, beating Warrington 22–10 at Knowsley Road in the final, van Heerden scoring one of Wigan's six tries, set up for him by fellow South African David Booysen. Wigan also reached the final of the Lancashire Cup, losing 15–11 to Swinton at Broughton.

His final season at Central Park was 1926–27. He missed some matches, presumably through injury, and only scored 12 tries. His final appearance was in the Championship semi-final, a 23–3 defeat at Swinton on 29 April 1927. In 127 appearances for Wigan he scored 107 tries.

Attie van Heerden signed for Leigh for the 1927–28 season, and made 14 appearances in four months. He then played for St Helens amateurs Uno's Dabs before returning to South Africa. He joined the South African Highland regiment in the Second World War, becoming a lieutenant. He then worked as a security guard for Iscor in South Africa, and died on 14 October 1965.

During his time at Wigan he had made an impact on the town. Jack Winstanley says that "his flamboyancy on and off the field ensured that he would always be remembered by Wigan's sporting public. He was idolised by a host of Wigan girls who fell for his handsome masculinity (and his big powerful motorbike) and he set a fashion trend by walking round the town bareheaded at a time when nearly every man wore a hat or flat cap." [17]

The success of van Rooyen and van Heerden saw two Wigan directors visit South Africa in 1924 to find more recruits. As so often with rugby union converts, they endeavours produced mixed results. Attie van Heerden's brother Nicholas was one recruit. The *Wigan Observer* reported that he was a doctor of dental surgery of the University of Michigan in the USA and was "well known in sporting circles in South Africa. He was at one time the hurdles champion of South Africa and was Victor Ludorum of the Stellenbosch University for three years." He received his rugby training at Stellenbosch, arguably South Africa's leading rugby university and later the base of rugby supremo Danie Craven. He had represented three provinces, but was 28 years old. He only played four times for the Wigan first team, but moved to York and had a successful career there.

Another recruit who never made it at Wigan was Constant van der Spuy. The Wigan directors believed that they had signed "a player who will become the greatest scrum half-back in England." The *Wigan Examiner* said that he was "one of the foremost half-backs in the colony" and had played in most of the matches for Transvaal province since 1921. He had been picked for a representative team to play the English tourists but was injured and could not play. He played for the Simmer & Jack club, the same as Attie van Heerden and another new recruit, Carl Burger.

Wigan 1925–26: Back: J. Price, W. Hodder, R. Ilsley, F. Stephens, G. van Rooyen, J. Sherrington, T. Beetham, F. Roffey, S. Jerram; front: J. Sullivan, G. Owens, D. Booysen, D. Hurcombe, S. Oakley, T. Howley, A. van Heerden. (Photo: courtesy Robert Gate)

Left: Fred Oliver during his time at Wigan.
Right: A signed photo of Attie van Heerden.
(Both photos: courtesy Robert Gate)

Top left: David Booysen
Top right: Attie van Heerden
Left: George van Rooyen
(All courtesy Robert Gate)

Van der Spuy was 26 years old when he joined Wigan. He made a couple of first team appearances in the 1924–25 season, but in August 1925 it was reported that he had returned to South Africa for health reasons. His rugby league adventure was over.

Carl Burger joined Wigan in September 1924. He made 18 first team appearances in the 1924–25 season. He played for the 'A' team in the first half of the 1925–26 season, and was unable to win a first team place. Towards the end of the season he was even named as a reserve for the 'A' team. This was clearly a disappointment to the Wigan directors. The *Wigan Examiner* said in September 1926 that he was being placed on the transfer list and that "Burger... had the reputation of being the finest forward in South Africa when the Wigan officials who visited that country secured his signature. He played loose forward at that time and was also an excellent goalkicker. He however, figured in the second row during his appearances with the Wigan club and with such a fine marksman as Sullivan in the side Burger did not get an opportunity to kick a goal." In October it was reported that he had joined Barrow. He played 23 first team matches for the Shipbuilders that season, mainly in the second-row, but in the 1927–28 campaign was mainly in the 'A' team, only appearing twice in the first team. At the end of that season he left the club, and as far as is known did not play rugby league again.

One player who did find success at Central Park was David Booysen. Although often regarded as a utility player, he played fairly regularly for the first team from his arrival in September 1924. Heralded as the 'finest half-back ever produced by South Africa' he was the club's most successful recruit from South Africa after van Rooyen and van Heerden.

By now the international influence at Wigan was becoming very noticeable, and inevitably attracting hostility from supporters of other clubs. On 29 November 1924 'Through a Northern Window' in the *Manchester Evening Chronicle* commented on the Swinton versus Wigan match: "The Swinton crowd on Saturday said unkind things about Wigan. They described them as 'the team of nations' and one inquired if any of them spoke English. There certainly are foreigners on the side, and one of them, by the way, is a wonder – van Heerden. He must be about six feet five [inches] and he jumps accordingly. He jumped his way to a try in the first half; nothing but a few tanks and trees could have stopped him. Great man, van Heerden, whether he speaks English or not. A sportsman, withal. He reminds me of Charles Buchan – he plays the game impersonally. On one occasion after downing an opponent quite fairly, but as if opponents ought to be pushed through to New Zealand, he gently picked him up over the touch line with a smile that was charming to see."

Of course, many of the Wigan recruits were of an Afrikaner background, and English would not have been their first language.

David Booysen

David ('Davie') Booysen signed for Wigan RLFC in August 1924. He arrived in Wigan in October 1924. After a couple of matches in the 'A' team to become acclimatised to a new game and a new country, he was in the first team.

A cartoonist's look at four of Wigan's South Africans in the 1920s:
Van der Spuy, van Rooyen, Burger and van Heerden.

Left: Attie van Heerden. Right: George van Rooyen.
(Both photos: Courtesy *Rugby League Journal*)

Booysen is overshadowed by van Rooyen and van Heerden in the history of Wigan RLFC and is often seen as a utility player, maybe a 'squad' player in today's terms. But as Jack Winstanley points out "It was said that he never fulfilled his potential at Wigan, yet he played more than 150 games and scored nearly 50 tries in a four year stay." [18]

Booysen made his name on the rough and tumble rural rugby scene of the Western Province Country Districts on the outskirts of Cape Town. He lived in the wine producing town of Paarl, a few kilometres outside Cape Town, joined the local rugby club at an early age and soon made a name for himself as a half-back. As a member of a rural club in the Western Province Rugby Union of the South African Rugby Football Board (SARFB), he played his rugby in the various Country Cup competitions organised by the Country Conference or Country Districts subcommittee of the provincial union. At a time that individually owned motor vehicles were the privilege of a small minority, the club honoured its match commitments by travelling by lorry or goods train to neighbouring towns. Reimbursements of legitimate travelling expenses by the provincial union to its various clubs in time became a serious bone of contention. Furthermore, due to the large distances involved, country clubs only played a handful of matches annually, much to the frustration of the sport's fans.

Despite the drawbacks of being a country rugby union player, Booysen soon made a name for himself. In the 1920s, following a string of consistent performances, he won representative honours when he was selected for the Western Province Country Districts XV for a tour of Rhodesia. Remarkably, this was achieved despite being a member of a team with mediocre and inconsistent results. Playing at this level provided him with an opportunity to display his talents on a bigger stage and begin the process of building a reputation beyond his home base. He grabbed this chance with both hands and proved his worth as a player. His presence was, however, not enough to establish his side as a rural rugby powerhouse at the end of the 1922 season. Lack of player commitment combined with growing employer dissatisfaction because of rugby-related work absenteeism caused by the need to travel long distances for matches, left the club with the prospect of imminent collapse and a non-start for the 1923 season.

Assisted by a comprehensive newspaper campaign exhorting the young men of the district not to abandon the game, coupled with real hard-nosed lobbying on behalf of the country rugby fraternity, slowly but surely, began to turn the situation around. Under new management, a committed Country Districts sub-committee and a larger pool of players, the Paarl RUFC began to be successful on the field. Booysen continued to blossom and remained competitive at Country Districts level. Playing in a pivotal position, and being a regular scorer, meant that the club's success also were his. The results of the 1923 season were particularly pleasing. Paarl RUFC won the Country Cup and Booysen was a regular member of the districts team when the opportunity arose. Paarl's players had a lot to look forward to in the 1924 season.

That season was, however, a watershed in Booysen's rugby career. With the aid of the local newspaper, the *Paarl Post*, interest in the club remained high and a good crop of new players arrived. With the pending British Lions tour of South Africa high on the agenda, the players looked forward to a game between the tourists and the Combined Country Districts, an opportunity for further representative honours. Issues at committee level, however, remained unresolved and seeped back into the club structures with the issue of the reimbursement of travelling expenses the main point of dispute between country clubs and the urban-based provincial union. Throughout, this matter was emphasised as a key to the survival of rural rugby. Despite the intensity of these debates, great care was taken not to confuse matters. It was made it clear that the matter was about the reimbursement of clubs and not payment of players. Away from boardroom issues, Booysen was elected as vice-captain of the senior team for the coming season.

Despite its previous success, internal problems were however just under the surface. Halfway through the season, many players left the Paarl club, much to the detriment of its most talented players. Booysen became the first team captain. This was, however, only for a short time because of his recruitment by Wigan in August 1924. When the news broke, starting with the matches on 30 August, Booysen was barred from playing for the club in the Country Cup. The town's sentiment was, however, far from negative, judging from the following report in the *Paarl Post*:

David Booysen – Professional
"As all country footballers know, Davie Booysen has signed on as a professional for the Wigan club. It is not generally known, however, that Booysen sails for England next Friday to commence his duties for his new club. Whilst we do not view professionalism with any friendly eye, we in common with all sporting Paarlites have a real affection for Booysen whose sporting qualities have made him one of the most popular sportsmen in Paarl. Booysen has served the Paarl Club well through thick and thin, and he displayed his sporting worth when, in the face of practically insuperable difficulties at the commencement of this season, he assumed the responsibilities of Captain of the Paarl Club to its present successful position in country football. Booysen gave Paarl of his best unstintingly, and we would be very poor sportsmen did we not show our appreciation of those services. Wigan Club is fortunate to secure so fine a sportsman, and Paarl's loss is Wigan's gain. We shall miss Booysen tremendously on the football field, on the cycle track and in all branches of sport, but we wish him every success in his new career, and a safe return to South Africa again in a few years time and he has our assurances that he will always be remembered in Paarl whenever rugby and cycling are spoken of. We hope that he will not altogether forget his old friends when he is on the other side, and that he will let us know how he is progressing from time to time." [19]

At a farewell event in the Central Hotel in town on 24 September, Paarl greeted its favourite son and presented him with a gift of a travelling rug and a walking stick. With these pieces of a town's devotion, Booysen launched his rugby league career with a try, next to fellow South African Attie van Heerden, who scored a hat trick, for Wigan in the local derby against Wigan Highfield, won by Wigan 58–0.

Booysen played his first two matches at half-back, and the local paper said that he was "proving [to be] a valuable asset to the side." He was then chosen at centre for a friendly with Huddersfield, but his next first team match was on 14 February against Flimby and Fothergill in the Challenge Cup. He scored a hat trick of tries as Wigan ran in 116 points against amateur opposition. He scored another try at Hunslet the following week in a 16–3 win, and the *Wigan Observer* said that he had "made a rapid improvement recently". Previewing the next match, against Leeds, it said that Booysen "was picked up quite by accident, as it were, when the Wigan 'Expeditionary Force' was [in South Africa] has come on wonderfully well lately, and seems to have a clear-cut future in the game." But he was dropped after that game, and returned to the 'A' team, partnering fellow South African van der Spuy at half-back.

On 17 March 1925 he returned to the first team, this time at centre, against Bradford Northern. Wigan won 15–0, and, having received the ball from a scrum near the line, "cut towards the right wing and then swerved inside to score a brilliant try." He kept his place at centre for the rest of the campaign. At Huddersfield he "delighted the crowd with a thrilling run" and at Craven Park in the Championship semi-final "was the pick of the threequarters, though he is still impetuous." The *Sporting Chronicle's* reporter felt that "He would do better by steadying himself more and by making sure he has the ball before commencing to swerve." His 14 appearances had yielded eight tries.

The next season saw his first honours in his new code. Wigan won the Championship and Lancashire League and were runners-up in the Lancashire Cup. Booysen was ever-present, but while making 35 appearances at centre, made 12 at half-back. For much of the season his partner on the wing was Attie van Heerden.

His progress was shown by the *Observer's* report of Wigan's 14–10 win at Central Park against Warrington in the Lancashire Cup: "The outstanding player in the Wigan team was Booysen. He is fast developing into a brilliant centre, and requires a lot of holding when on the attack. He gave a glimpse of his abilities last season at Huddersfield, where he created a good impression. He is a sound grafter and plays with determination the whole of the 80 minutes. On present form he is certain to retain his inclusion in the senior team. The two tries which he procured were the outcome of brilliant manoeuvring, whilst he also took part in the movement when Sherrington got over for a try."

Other reports confirm his consistent form for Wigan. In February he played for the Other Nationalities team against England at Whitehaven. England won 37–11, but Booysen scored a try. At Warrington at the end of March, Wigan won 34–4, and the *Wigan Examiner* reported: "Booysen loves a dry ground and he was in his happiest mood on the sandy turf... The South African was a continuous source of worry to the home brigade, who were puzzled by his movements." In the Championship semi-final against Hull he scored two tries, and was "the outstanding player on the Wigan side." In the final Wigan beat Warrington 22–10. Booysen did not score, but had touched down 14 times in the season, the best return of his Wigan career.

Having become established – more or less – at centre, Booysen opened the 1926–27 season at half-back. Wigan didn't reach the heights of the previous season. They finished third in the Championship and made little impact in the cups. In October, the *Examiner* said that Booysen played better at half-back than centre. After a 35–2 win at Widnes, the paper said that "Booysen... beat the opposing halves time after time, and had advantage been taken of these fine efforts the score would have reached half a century. The South African, I am convinced, is far better at outside half than at centre." A month later, despite a defeat in St Helens against the Recs, it was reported that Booysen "responded with many brilliant bursts. He was undoubtedly the most prominent half of the match."

However, by March the paper was critical of Booysen's form at half-back, although three weeks later he "gave a much improved exhibition". By the end of the season he had played 42 matches, missing only two first team games; 38 of his appearances were at half-back.

In 1927–28, Booysen again played regularly at half-back, despite the *Examiner* proclaiming in September that he "is not a scrum half-back." But four weeks later he was "outstanding" at outside half, and his touch-finding from free kicks was "exceptionally good".

Wigan finished eighth, a sharp decline on the previous season, but once again reached the Lancashire Cup Final, narrowly losing 5–2 to Swinton. Booysen made 43 first team appearances, missing only four matches, and only played once at centre. His 13 tries included a hat-trick against Warrington on 18 April, when fellow South African Fred Oliver also scored three tries.

Booysen started the 1928–29 season in the first team, but Wigan's regular half-back combination became Syd Abram and Arthur Binks. Booysen played occasionally, usually when one of the half-backs was injured. On 29 December he played at Headingley in a 19–10 win over Leeds. The *Examiner* said that "Booysen ... played a splendid game, opening out play cleverly and doing grand work on defence," and that he "played one of his best games for a couple of seasons. His reputation for handling on a wet ground is not good, but I think he missed only one pass on Saturday."

On 15 January the paper included a letter about Booysen: "At Leeds [Booysen] had the better of the duel with a man who many consider the finest half-back in the league. In the Wakefield match two perfect passes of his were missed by one of the centres. ....Wigan need a class outside half-back, a man who can think in terms of football. They have one in Booysen and in this respect it would pay them to hold on to what they have got."

However, his last first team game was on 5 January 1929, a 23–5 defeat against Swinton at Central Park. He was put on the transfer list at £400, and continued to be selected for the 'A' team. There is no record of him playing rugby league after the 1928–29 season.

Overall, he played 158 games for Wigan, 50 at centre and 108 at half-back. In three seasons he only missed six first team matches, before losing his place early in the 1928–29 season. He scored 47 tries – almost one every three games.

Some of the South Africans signed by Wigan in the 1920s made little impact, and either returned home or moved to other clubs. Booysen was a regular member of the first team for three seasons, played for the Other Nationalities side and clearly adapted well to rugby league. He missed out on the club's 1929 appearance in the first Challenge Cup Final at Wembley, but as Jack Winstanley said, he "made a real and lasting impact".

According to Winstanley, Booysen was also a "leading South African cyclist", married a Wigan girl and set up a business as a Scotch draper. It is not known if he stayed in Wigan after he retired from rugby league or returned to South Africa.

A South African rising rugby union star signed for Wigan in January 1927. W.F. (Fred) Oliver was described as one of the Rand's best rugby footballers. For the past two or three seasons he had played on the left wing for Diggers, and had played for Transvaal in the Currie Cup and other provincial games. He had completed his apprenticeship as fitter just before coming to Wigan. He was aged 21.

Sadly, Fred Oliver never really fulfilled his potential in rugby league. The write-ups given to some of Wigan's recruits, no doubt to justify the signing on fees and other costs of bringing them to the club from South Africa must have put enormous pressure on them to succeed. In some cases, and Oliver arguably is one of these, they would have been better off joining a less eminent club where they would have been given more chance to adapt to a new country, new climate and new code of rugby.

W.F. (Fred) Oliver

Fred Oliver represented Diggers RFC in the Transvaal Pirates Grand Challenge Trophy competition. During the last seven years of his rugby union career, in contrast with former years, Diggers did not once won the coveted challenge trophy. They did, however, won the Lilienfeld Challenge Trophy in his last season, 1926. Despite not being among the trophy winners in this period, Oliver, a useful and fast winger was still part of a club with a strong winning culture, highly competitive character and illustrious past.

On the back of a series of strong and consistent performances, Oliver made his Transvaal debut in 1925; a year after R. Cove-Smith's British Lions visited South Africa. Not being part of the representative provincial set-up yet, Oliver missed selection for the Transvaal and Witwatersrand teams that played the tourists. As a seasoned senior club player, he finally made his break into the representative team with the start of the Currie Cup season. Also, he played in a series of provincial friendly games. Although they won five of their eight senior games, 1925 overall was not a good season since Western Province defeated the Johannesburgers in the final to deny them Currie Cup glory.

Since the next season was a non-Currie Cup season and with no prospect of any international teams coming to visit, provincial players such as Oliver had to be contend with the usual staple of inter-province friendlies. To provide their players with a bit more of a challenge, the Transvaal union entered their team into a Northern Competition for sides in the northern part of South Africa. This was no real alternative for ambitious players such as Oliver, who by the end of the domestic season decided to cross over to rugby league with

Wigan. Jack Winstanley, in the *Illustrated History of Wigan RLFC* says that "Oliver was the leading try scorer in South Africa's Currie Cup competition."

Oliver made his debut for the 'A' team, and the Wigan local paper said that: "He seems just the type of threequarter who will do well at Central Park. A strongly built man, he should strengthen a position that has not been filled to the club's satisfaction for some time." On 8 February 1927, it said that against Broughton, Oliver had few opportunities, but showed he was a "strong and speedy runner."

A couple of weeks later, against amateurs Pemberton in the Challenge Cup, the report said that Oliver's "try early on in the cup tie demonstrated that he is a wing threequarter who will be very dangerous. I like his style of running. He has a delightful action, and what is more, he possesses a most effective swerve. Oliver had a great reputation as a wing man in South Africa, and his pace was such that he was asked to train as a sprinter. If he handles the ball often enough he will score many tries. At present Oliver seems to be rather slow in making up his mind what to do when the ball is loose. Perhaps the new rules are troubling him a little and probably experience is all that is necessary to enable him to develop into a threequarter of all-round excellence."

On 12 March 1927, the paper reported that at Salford: "Oliver could not handle the slippery ball, and lost two glorious openings in the first half. He showed great dash and swerve in a fine run after the interval. Oliver is still weak on defence and ought to have saved one of the tries..." It was clearly taking him time to adapt to his new code, and probably life in Wigan, but on 2 April the report of the match against Hull said that "...Oliver gave his best display since the Pemberton match. He handled far oftener than he had done in any previous games with Wigan and proved that, if given possession, he will make a very good attempt to reach the line. His defence, too, was better than it has been hitherto, though on occasions he was badly beaten by accepting the 'dummy' pass." A week later, in the return at Hull, Oliver "...scored two fine tries... also tackled much better than he had done previously." Towards the end of April, the paper said, maybe optimistically, that "Oliver has also shown great improvement in his running and I think he will make one of the best wing threequarters in the rugby league." In his first season he had a run of 13 consecutive matches in the first team, always on the left wing, from 5 February to 16 April, scoring seven tries.

Early on in the 1927–28 season, after defeats to Hull and Hunslet, the paper commented on the club's recruitment efforts: "Up to the time of the South African visit of the Wigan directors in search of players – a tour that may be counted a failure – no club in the Rugby League had had such great success with imported players.... Some of the exponents of whom big fees have been paid lately, however, have not justified the expense involved in their signing."

Oliver had started the 1927–28 season well, with four tries against Wigan Highfield and a hat-trick against Rochdale Hornets. But the signing of New Zealand winger Lou Brown added to competition for places, and Oliver usually played on the right wing, where he contended for a place with Johnny Ring. He played 22 games overall, 18 on the right wing and four on the left. His 19 tries included the four against Wigan Highfield and three hat-tricks. In an end-of-season rout of Warrington, fellow South African David Booysen also scored a hat-trick.

On 10 December 1927 the *Wigan Evening Post* columnist had said that: "I am glad to see that Oliver is being given a trial at centre today in the 'A' team. A man who can score tries like Oliver gained against Hull KR does not deserve relegation to the second team and if he displays anything like an aptitude for the inside position, Oliver ought to be given a chance with the first team. Oliver's positional play has not always been altogether good and it may be that he will find centre threequarter strange. Some men seem to be able to adapt themselves to almost any position however, and Oliver may do well at centre." However, Roy Kinnear provided further competition at centre in the first team.

Oliver scored two tries against Wigan Highfield in his first match in the first team in the 1928–29 season, on 8 September. Four days later, he scored a hat-trick against Barrow. The *Post* said of his display against Highfield: "Oliver believes in taking the short cut to the line when there is a chance of scoring and his exhibition of diving was greatly appreciated." He kept his place for a 6–2 defeat at Leigh, but then played three matches for Batley before returning to action for Wigan at Warrington on 20 October, when four Wigan players were playing for Glamorgan. *The Post* commented: "Oliver … was not a success on the left wing". A few days later, the paper's columnist wrote: "Oliver has been a most disappointing player. At times he has shown excellent form but at others he has been very poor. At Leigh, for instance, he never seemed to be able to get going and it was the same on Saturday. It is true that in the first half he did not get a chance and that after the interval he handled on very few occasions, but twice he had opportunities which a speedy wing threequarter ought to have turned to account."

That was his last match for the first team. He played a few games for the 'A' team, often with David Booysen, whose Wigan career was coming to an end, and even George van Rooyen on occasions. In January, all three were on the transfer list, Oliver at £300. Winstanley comments that "His pedigree was good, but he found it tough going at Central Park…"

It is not known if he returned to South Africa or stayed in Wigan. In the club's heritage list, he was number 324 to play for the first team. Had he joined a lower-profile club, and had more opportunity to gradually establish himself in his new sport he may have done better. As it was, his rugby career was effectively over in his early 20s.

In June 1927, the transfer ban was lifted. Now English clubs could target Australians and New Zealanders who already had experience in rugby league, rather than invest in South African rugby union players. In 1937, the ban was reimposed, but by then there was little interest in trying to recruit South Africans. The English and Welsh rugby union scenes offered more potential for successful recruitment to rugby league.

5. 1945 to 1956: A handful of South Africans

In 1941, the transfer ban had run out, not that anyone really noticed because rugby league was just about surviving in the third year of the Second World War. The sport returned to full strength in the 1945–46 season. Some Australians and New Zealanders who were to become some of the sport's greatest names came to England. Brian Bevan joined Warrington and was later joined by compatriot Harry Bath after he initially joined Barrow; Wigan recruited Ces Mountford from New Zealand and Arthur Clues joined Leeds having played against the 1946 Lions for Australia. Pat Devery, Johnny Hunter and Lionel Cooper all joined Huddersfield and contributed much to their post-war success.

With tried and tested rugby league players available until the ban was reimposed in August 1947, there was little interest in South African rugby league players. Even after the clubs were stopped from signing rugby league players from Australia and New Zealand, rugby union players could still be recruited from 'down under', although that was also stopped in December 1951. Of course, Welsh rugby union, as always, provided rich potential for rugby league, and at some clubs half the first team were Welsh.

A handful of South Africans did play in English rugby league in the first decade after the war. Ian Clark and Ken Morrison were at Huddersfield from 1948 to 1955. As with some of the players Wigan recruited in the 1920s, they may have been able to win a regular first team place at a less high profile club. Huddersfield were very successful in this period, but both players found it difficult to secure a first team place. They had come to England in February 1948, to study engineering.

Clark made his first team debut in March 1948, but only had a regular place in 1950–51. Playing mainly at centre he made 35 appearances and scored six tries, but this was because Pat Devery was injured for much of the season. He also played for the Other Nationalities team against France in December 1950, and was in the Huddersfield team that won the Yorkshire Cup in 1950–51. The international make-up of the Huddersfield team was shown in a Yorkshire Cup match in 1948–49. Six nationalities were represented in the Huddersfield team – the four home nations, Australia and South Africa – by Clark. Overall, he made 54 first team appearances and scored 11 tries. In an article about the two players, the *1955 Fartown Rugby League Year Book* said that Clark's career had been "held up by illness".

Ken Morrison, who was born in Scotland, but had emigrated to South Africa, played in the second row. In seven seasons he played 21 first team games and scored three tries. He played in the 1950 Championship Final at Maine Road, which Huddersfield surprisingly lost 20–2 to an under-strength Wigan team. The *Year Book* said that he had problems with recurring shoulder dislocations in the latter part of his stay at Fartown.

Both players played for the 'A' team for three seasons after their last first team appearances and made over 70 appearances for the 'A' team. Coincidentally, both scored 19 tries. The *Year Book* said that "they were useful members of the team during their stay and both … expressed their appreciation of the treatment they received at Fartown." It said that both had married English girls; Ken and his wife sailed for South Africa in May 1955, and Ian was planning to go there with his wife as well.

The most successful South African in this period was Jack Pansegrouw. Initially signed by Leeds, he found more success when he moved to Halifax, and played in the 1949 Challenge Cup Final.

Jacobeaus (Jack) Pansegrouw

Jack Pansegrouw started his provincial rugby career in 1945 just as the Second World War entered its final stages. Playing for Crown Mines RFC in the Pirates Grand Challenge and President's Cup of the Transvaal Rugby Union, the miners' club faced formidable opponents in the form of Diggers, Rand Leases and Johannesburg Police. These encounters stood him in good stead since the end of war also brought battle-hardened soldiers back home and onto the rugby fields of South Africa.

As the country slowly started to normalise itself after being an active participant in the War, the Currie Cup competition was reinstituted in 1945 after a six year suspension. Transvaal played 10 provincial games and won nine of them. This was a most satisfying return to competitive provincial rugby. For Jan Pansegrouw, his debut year was a learning period and opportunity to gain experience while his province was rebuilding. Playing opportunities were spread among a larger group of players, so he did not have a regular place. More gratifying was his club's formal admission into the Pirates Grand Challenge competition and its recognition as a worthy and competitive opponent.

The 1946 season, when Transvaal played 15 representative games – seven Currie Cup games and eight friendlies – gave Pansegrouw more top-level experience. Playing together with Okey Geffin and Duimpie Coetzee, future rugby league pioneers in South Africa, the team and player had another satisfying season.

A consistent performer, Pansegrouw made it back into the provincial side for the 1947 season. In the Currie Cup, Transvaal won five matches to reach the final, and faced a strong Western Province team. They also gave a good account of themselves in seven friendlies. Pansegrouw, however, was omitted from the XV for the Currie Cup Final on 27 September 1947. The season's hard work, however, came to nothing when Western Province won 16–12. This brought Pansegrouw's rugby union career to an end.

Pansegrouw signed for Leeds during the 1947–48 season. Described as 'an enormous second-rower' by Halifax historian Andrew Hardcastle, he played four matches in the second row for Leeds towards the end of the season, scoring one try. There was strong competition for places in the second-row at Headingley, including Australian star Arthur Clues. Pansegrouw was given a free transfer by Leeds in January 1949, having failed to make a first team appearance in the 1948–49 season. He was immediately signed by Halifax, and made his debut for the Thrum Hallers at Rochdale in a 5–0 defeat on 22 January 1949.

He won a regular place at Thrum Hall, in the second-row, and only missed two games for the rest of the season, scoring one try. His arrival coincided with Halifax's best Challenge Cup run for a decade, and he played in all the Challenge Cup matches, including a desperately narrow 11–10 win over Huddersfield in front of 64,250 fans at Odsal.

Left: Jacobus (Jack) Pansegrouw
(Photo: Courtesy Dave Makin)

Below: The 1948–49 Halifax team that reached the
Challenge Cup Final. Pansegrouw is on the far right in
the back row.
(Photo: Courtesy Robert Gate)

Wembley, however, was an anti-climax. Bradford Northern won comfortably 12–0 in front of a sell-out 95,050 crowd.

Pansegrouw kept his place at the start of the 1949–50 season, including four appearances in the front row. He made his final appearance for the club on 15 October at home to Hull. He subsequently returned to South Africa. He was involved as a coach when professional rugby league started in South Africa in 1962, and was also a recruitment agent, helping various players switch codes.

One player who deserves recognition for perseverance if nothing else is Dave Knopf. Often described as a South African, he was, in fact, born in Australia, but came to Wigan in 1950 from Johannesburg, where he had been playing rugby union. In March 1950, he signed as an amateur for Wigan, as a stand-off. He had arrived in Hindley to stay with friends and asked for a trial at Central Park. He was 19 years old and was working as a labourer in a Wigan cotton mill. Wigan coach Jim Sullivan said he "made a good impression." The *Rugby Leaguer* said that he had been working in the stock exchange in Johannesburg, "but his ambition lay in England." Middlesex cricketer Jack Robertson had considered bringing Knopf to England after he had been coaching in Johannesburg, but thought he was too young. He had made his mark in rugby union with Old Forestonians. He had written to Bradford Northern asking for trial, but they had advised him not to travel overseas because rugby league was a tough game and they feared he might not be a success. However, he "was not discouraged" and a friend who worked in Wigan realised his potential. In August 1950 it was reported that he left Central Park without having played for either the first team or the 'A' team. He played for Wigan cricket club and was working as a warehouse clerk in Manchester. He had signed for Salford, but injured his leg while training and was out of action for seven months. He then played three games for Salford's 'A' team, scoring three tries and kicking seven goals, but then returned to Johannesburg. However, he was still determined to make it in rugby league.

In 1953, on the recommendation of Birmingham City FC centre forward Ted Purdon he joined Halifax, but could not win a regular first team place. He was described as having "pace and plenty of courage". The club offered to play his fare back to South Africa. Instead, he signed for Bradford Northern. Their manager, Dai Rees, said: "Old friends at Halifax whose judgement I respect have told me that they believe Knopf has more in him than was evidenced during his trials at Thrum Hall. Knopf himself is convinced that there is a future in rugby league and so we are giving him a chance to prove himself." He had come to England at the start of the season, but played only half a dozen games for Halifax, three of which were in the first team. Rees knew that Northern's regular left winger, Jack McLean, was almost certain to return to New Zealand when his contract expired at the end of the season.

Northern's right winger, Bob Hawes, was also coming to the end of his career. In January 1954, the *Leaguer* reported that Knopf played against York for Northern's first team but "Did not greatly impress". He played again and scored two tries, in place of injured Hawes. The report said that "Knopf has readily learnt some of the tricks. He still has many more to brush up; but, obviously, he is the type of player who will expand should first team games continue his way. Indeed, it may be that Northern have found an almost ready made successor to Bob Hawes... with the coaching of Dai Rees and Trevor Foster he may be a star next season. He is a powerful runner on the burst and against Castleford he must have impressed many by the manner in which collected passes with one hand." By the end of the season Knopf had played 15 first team matches and scored 16 tries.

He won a regular place in the 1954–55 campaign, with 37 appearances, but in a less successful Northern side only scored 10 times. Following an injury, he returned to South Africa in October 1955. The *Rugby Leaguer* reported that "Bradford Northern's 24 year old right winger has played his last game for the club. Tomorrow he and two Bradford men will begin a 10,000 mile journey from Yorkshire to ... Johannesburg ... It is almost exactly two years since this speedy San came to Odsal from the Halifax club which had bought him to England... Although he never reached the McLean standard he soon made his mark at Odsal and was a welcome replacement for Bob Hawes when he returned to New Zealand. Many at Odsal will regret his departure, but he, too, will miss Yorkshire because his leaving will mean the end of his rugby career. There is no rugby league in South Africa and he is banned from playing rugby union again."

Another player who was involved with English rugby league in the early to mid–1950s was Gene Forster, who in the 1960s was involved in setting up rugby league in South Africa. He played for Bradford Northern, but there is no record of him playing for the first team.

By 1957, the supply of rugby union players from South Wales was slowing down. There had been some recruitment from Scottish rugby union, including Great Britain star Dave Valentine. While clubs could still sign English union players, the better players were often based in the south, from a middle class background and had little incentive to switch to rugby league. So the more prosperous northern clubs once again started looking at South African rugby union to recruit their international stars. One of the biggest movements of players into rugby league internationally was about to begin.

Left: Ronnie Colin (Photo: Courtesy *Rugby League Journal*)
Right: Fred Griffiths (Photo: Courtesy *Rugby League Journal*)

Ronnie Colin (right) in action for Hunslet.

6. 1957: The new wave starts

South African players, particularly but not exclusively backs, made a major impact on English rugby league in the period from 1957 to 1968. Every year there was at least one South African in the top 20 try scorers. On five occasions the top try scorer was a South African, with Tom van Vollenhoven, Trevor Lake and Len Killeen leading the way. Four times in 11 seasons, the top points scorer was South African, Freddie Griffiths once, and Killeen three times. In 1965–66, there were five South Africans in the top 20 try scorers.

There were South Africans at most of the game's top clubs. However, as with other 'rugby migrations' from Wales, Australia and New Zealand, players tended to join their compatriots at particular clubs. Wakefield Trinity, Wigan and St Helens usually had at least one South African in this period; other clubs did not sign any. Some of the smaller clubs also recruited from this 'new' pool of potential rugby league talent, also with varying degrees of success.

Of the 11 Challenge Cup Finals from 1958 to 1968, at least one South African played in eight of them; 1958, 1964 and 1967 were the exceptions. The clubs in the latter two matches, Widnes, Hull KR, Featherstone and Barrow did not do much, if any recruitment of South African players. The 1958 final was at the beginning of the growth in South Africans in English rugby league and neither Wigan nor Workington Town had any South African recruits at that time. Similarly in the Championship finals, in every one of the nine matches from 1959 to 1968, at least one South African took part. In 1963 and 1964, the Northern Rugby League ran with two divisions, so there was no championship final.

The new players arriving in England faced various issues. For a player coming from Wales to the north of England, they could be moving to a similar community to the one they were leaving behind; and sometimes stayed with the same company. Certainly up to the mid–1980s, when the industry started to decline more rapidly, coal mining linked South Wales and many of the rugby league strongholds in Yorkshire and Lancashire. They were used to the weather, and spoke the same language. Their extended family were often a three or four hour train or car ride away. Rugby union players would not have played rugby league, but they may have watched it on television, or seen the game live. Those who did National Service, which lasted in Great Britain until 1962, may have mixed with rugby league players in Armed Forces rugby union, and played with them. [20] Some may even have initially been approached to switch codes while doing National Service!

Australian and New Zealand rugby union players would have probably watched rugby league, and may even have played it while at school. Certainly in New Zealand, the barriers between the codes were less rigid than in Great Britain. And the New Zealand climate was not that different, at least in the winter, from England.

South Africans faced more barriers. They did not necessarily speak English as a first language. The climate was very different from what they would experience in England. Moving from one of South Africa's leading cities, such as Cape Town, Johannesburg or Durban to the north of England would have been a huge change. But the white players were also coming from a society legally segregated in every aspect of its life, where the white minority, even if doing blue collar supervisory jobs, usually had a privileged lifestyle compared to the African majority community and the 'coloured' mixed race community. Having an African maid to do the housework would not have been unusual for many of the players who came to England. While the Afro-Caribbean community was still fairly small at this time, there were black players in rugby league, and for the South Africans to play both with them as team-mates and against them must have been a new and unusual experience for them.

The players who had won Springbok honours also had a privileged position in South African society. While rugby union there was amateur, undoubtedly their status will have helped them secure jobs and other positions in society. Rugby union was the leading winter sport for the Afrikaner elite, although the players who came to England in this period were from both English and Afrikaner South African backgrounds.

From February 1957, when Ronnie Colin signed for Hunslet, to the end of the 1958–59 season, at least 17 South Africans came into English rugby league. Seven of them had won full Springbok honours. Nine of the 30 English rugby league clubs, which at that time were only based in the sport's three traditional counties of Lancashire, Yorkshire and Cumberland, brought players over. St Helens led the way with four; Wakefield Trinity and Leeds three each; Hull, Hunslet, Huddersfield, Whitehaven, Wigan and York made up the rest. Blackpool Borough signed Ted Brophy from St Helens after he had failed to win a regular place there.

Of the players who came in this period, only Ivor Dorrington and Ted Brophy were forwards. Two were scrum-halves, the rest were backs. Of the 17 players, eight could be judged to have been a success – to have won something in the game, or to have stayed for more than one season and won a regular first team place.

One who was a success, albeit for just over two seasons, was Ronnie Colin. He was signed by the south Leeds side in January 1957, and arrived at the club in early February.

Ronnie Colin

As Ludwig Japhet of the Transvaal National Sporting Club in Johannesburg started to finalise arrangements for the introduction of rugby league in South Africa in 1957, Ronnie Colin left Cape Town and Gardens RFC for a career in rugby league. He became the only South African player in England in the 1956–57 season.[21] Playing at centre; he was adjudged as a steady player "with a fine turn of speed." [22] Unfortunately his playing career in both the Western Province Grand Challenge and Town Challenge Cup competitions coincided with that of high profile and established provincial and national players such as Gert Rheeder, Alan Skene, Dawie Ackerman, Ivor Dorrington, Tommy Gentles, Rudi Hasse and Jan Lotriet. These players were household names in the province and first-choice selections for Currie Cup and Board Trophy competitions. Despite playing for Gardens RFC, one of the oldest clubs in Cape Town and a prolific producer of both provincial and national players over the years and which offered opportunities to play against these opponents, Colin struggled to attract the attention of the provincial selectors. Stellenbosch University also dominated the local rugby scene in 1956 to 1957 which made things difficult for non-student players such as Colin. So when John Hastie, the Springbok association football full-back and former Leeds

United player, recommended him to Hunslet RLFC, Colin, aged 25, was ready to give up his job as compositor at a printing company in Cape Town for a career in the 13-man code.

Colin made his first team debut for Hunslet on 2 March 1957, in a home win over Bradford Northern. Only four more first team appearances came his way that season, but he did finish with a hat-trick of tries in the last match of the campaign, a 30–7 win at Dewsbury.

Now settled into his new code, he was ever-present for Hunslet in the 1957–58 season, playing 33 matches on the left wing and eight on the right. He scored 29 tries, including a hat-trick in Hunslet's memorable derby win over Leeds on 12 October at Parkside. He finished 15th in the top try scorers' table, his team finished a respectable 11th in the league.

In 1958–59, he missed the first half of the season, and seems to have stayed in South Africa where he was involved in recruiting players for other clubs, but returned to action on 20 December. He finished the season with 24 appearances, mainly on the right wing, and 18 tries. Hunslet had finished third in the league table, with 57 points, and reached the Championship final after winning 22–11 at Wigan in the semi-final. There they faced a rampant St Helens side in front of 52,560 fans at Odsal. Hunslet led 12–4 after 17 minutes, but then St Helens took control, and his compatriot Tom van Vollenhoven scored a hat-trick of tries in their 44–22 win. Despite the scoreline, Graham Morris comments that "Hunslet contributed hugely to an entertaining match". [23]

During his return to Cape Town for a holiday in 1958, Colin played a central role in recruiting new players for rugby league. He was linked with the recruitment of Jan Lotriet his former Gardens team mate; Alan Skene, Ivor Dorrington and Tommy Gentles. He was publicly criticised by past Springboks such as former captain Hennie Muller. In order to prepare his recruits for their new challenge, Colin took them through the basics of the 13-man code on Green Point Common in Cape Town following their banning from all rugby union facilities. [24]

After his short stint in British rugby league, Colin returned to South Africa at the beginning of the 1960s. He worked at a Cape Town printing firm and – banned from rugby union – he joined the Camps Bay Association Football Club, incidentally also the sporting home of Hugh Gillespie after his stint in rugby league. [25] He later assisted with the recruitment to rugby league of Louis Neumann and Goolam Abed. [26] With the launch of rugby league in South Africa at the beginning of 1962 he joined the operations of Rugby League South Africa. With Tommy Gentles he worked to form a rugby league structure in and around Cape Town and to find playing venues for the code. [27] His recruitment efforts on behalf of RLSA, interaction with local players and clubs became a major cause of concern for rugby union circles. Union had already faced recruitment attempts by Jan Pansegrouw [28] and in 1957 by Japhet and his collaborators to play an exhibition game in Bellville. [29]

When Hamiltons, a local rugby union club, played Camps Bay with Colin in its team in a social football match in 1961, some union administrators demanded punitive action against Hamiltons. [30] This dispute, which also reached the board room of the South African Rugby Football Board, created huge divisions in the Western Province rugby fraternity and coincided with the national effort to establish and consolidate a significant rugby league presence in the country. [31]

Despite these problems, the code was formally launched and by February 1962, Colin, as an interim coach, attended the first public training session of the Johannesburg Spartans and a yet to be named rugby league football club at the Cecil Payne grounds in Maraisburg in Johannesburg.[32] However, in March 1962 he switched his allegiance from RLSA to the National Rugby League and a newly-established Cape Town-based company called the Western Province Rugby League (Pty.) Ltd. with Tommy Gentles as one of its directors.[33]

Colin along with Hugh Gillespie and Ivor Dorrington, also recruited players for the new club for the NRL. This incident, together with other differences, helped derail the early talks between the two rival bodies to form one national rugby league organisation.[34]

But by August 1962, now for the RLSA, Colin formed part of the playing and coaching staff of Johannesburg City in their matches against Vaal RLFC[35] and Southern Suburbs. The RLSA's match programme listed him as their player-coach.[36] He was listed as a try scorer in the Vaal match. He maintained his involvement throughout the first season and the announcement of a planned merger between the rival bodies under the auspices of the RFL. With the collapse of the code by September 1963, the dream of people like Colin, who devoted their best years to the promotion of the 13-man code, finally came to an end.

After retiring, Ronnie and his wife lived for a time in the USA, raising money for AIDS-HIV projects in South Africa. They subsequently returned to South Africa, and Ronnie died of cancer on 2 February 2015.

Fred Griffiths

When the influx of South African players started in 1957, Wigan were one of the few clubs who had a history of signing players from the country, with Attie van Heerden and others having played for the club in the 1920s.

Griffiths signed for Wigan on 28 November 1957. He was born in the Eastern Cape and was of Welsh descent. He first played rugby union at Marist Brothers College in Uitenhague, near Port Elizabeth, and played for the local club and for Diggers in Kitwe in Rhodesia in 1957. He also represented Eastern Province and Rhodesia in the Currie Cup, and was seen as a future Springbok when he signed for Wigan; injury had spoilt his chances of selection on the Springboks' tour of Australia and New Zealand. He was also an accomplished water polo player, and worked as a fitter in a copper mine before his move to Central Park. A school teacher from Wigan working in Rhodesia put him in contact with the club, and, as he said in an interview published in 2000 in *Rugby League Journal*, he had always wanted to go overseas on a working holiday, so signed for Wigan for five years, accepting a £2,000 signing on fee.

Interviewed soon after his arrival at Wigan, he said that he had thought that the game looked 'tough' when he first watched it, and this was borne out by his experience! He said "I'm getting used to it now, and also to the increased pace of the game." He found that playing full-back in league was different to union: "[in league] one is expected to attack at every opportunity, and in the rugby union ... the role is almost purely defensive. Soon after I arrived I was told that a full-back who kicked the ball 'got the bird'. Consequently I have been careful to avoid doing what was one of my main functions of the union game. It might be worthwhile, however, after longer experience, to attempt to find touch occasionally with long kicks which could gain say 40 or 50 yards." He said that he felt fitter since coming to Wigan, although he "trained very hard in South Africa". Overall, he "found the rule on playing the ball after a tackle rather difficult at first. I am sure that the rugby league game is much more spectacular than that of rugby union, and the forwards here handle the ball much better than those in the union game. The opportunities for open play are greater. Where a run of 60 or 70 yards would be talked about for a long time in South Africa, it is not unusual in rugby league."

Griffiths had the nickname of 'Poensie', nothing to do with rugby, but one his grandmother had given him. He made his debut on 14 December 1957 against Widnes.

Griffiths had been lined up to replace Jack Cunliffe, who was coming to the end of his career. However, it took him time to adjust to rugby league and Cunliffe kept his place for the 1958 Challenge Cup Final against Workington. However, in 1958–59, he became a regular in the side. He kicked six goals as Wigan retained the Challenge Cup, beating Hull 30–13. He had played – and scored – in every round of the Cup run. His goalkicking, regarded as the best since Wigan legend Jim Sullivan, helped him to top the national points scorers chart for the season, with 394 points. His 176 goals was a Wigan club record.

Further success followed in 1959–60, when he again kicked six goals in a final, this time in the Championship, as Wigan beat Wakefield Trinity 27–3. In 1962 he experienced defeat for the first time in a rugby league final. He scored all Wigan's points in a 12–6 defeat to St Helens in the Challenge Cup. He played twice for a Rugby League XIII in 1961–62, against the New Zealand tourists and against a French XIII. In June 1962 he played as a guest for Wakefield Trinity on their tour of South Africa.

He left Wigan in November 1962, having completed the five years of his original contract. A few months before, he had wanted to renew his deal with Wigan, but was looking for another signing-on fee, which the RFL by-laws did not allow. He recalled that "I went over with my solicitor to Leeds to see Bill Fallowfield (then secretary of the Rugby Football League). He said to me 'Well look, you're almost 30 years of age now. It's the by-laws of the game that are restricting this, not free trade. If you take us to court we'll put you out of the game for two years, and by the age of 32 nobody will know Fred Griffiths. So why don't you go to North Sydney?" [37]

Wigan had indicated that they would not stop him moving to Australia, so he played his last game for them on 24 November at Hull and arrived in Sydney in January 1963 to join North Sydney. In 161 games for Wigan he scored 43 tries, 663 goals and 1,455 points.

He soon made an impact with his new club. Andrew Moore says that he "proved [to be] an experienced and inspiring captain-coach under whose tutelage the Bears made two semi-final series in 1964 and 1965. In three years they did not lose one game at North Sydney Oval. Griffiths was worth every penny, his game flawed only by a certain fragility in defence."[38] Moore also points out that Griffiths was the first player to join Australian rugby league from Great Britain and bring his family with him.

During his first season with Norths, Griffiths achieved international honours for South Africa. His club released him to play for the South African tourists, and he made five appearances, including a test match against Australia when he kicked five goals. He also captained an Other Nationalities side against New South Wales Colts in 1964.

Griffiths continued his points scoring success in Australia. He was the season's leading points scorer from 1963 to 1965, with 136 points, 154 points and 177 points, the latter being a club record. Alan Whiticker and Glen Hudson say that he was "cool under pressure and a good defensive full-back" and a "thorough professional in his four seasons as captain-coach and a prolific point scorer to boot."[39]

In 1967 he left Norths to captain-coach Griffith in the Wagga local competition. They won the Group 20 competition. He then moved to Nowra. He lived in Australia for the rest of his life, and settled in Perth, where he died in 2000, aged 65. Looking back in the interview published in *Rugby League Journal*, he reflected that when he grew up "it was the time of apartheid. It was just part of your life then and you weren't aware of any alternatives until all the good things that have gone on in more recent years in the country."

1958 Boland, Western Province and South West Districts team, four of whom later played rugby league: Dawie Ackerman (back row, far right); Hugh Gillespie and Alan Skene (middle row on left); and Tommy Gentles (front row, centre). (Photo: Courtesy Boland Rugby Union.)

7. 1958: Three Springboks

Of the nine players who came to England in 1958, four found success and five failed to make a major impact on rugby league. Ernie and Ossie Deysel signed for Leeds, before returning home after a few months in England, their rugby careers effectively over. Both had won rugby union honours in Rhodesia. One was a centre, the other a winger. Ernie was aged 21 when he joined Leeds, his brother was a couple of years older.

The first arrival in 1958 was Ted Brophy. Although not one of the great rugby league players, he is remembered by players and supporters alike as a great character. After initially joining St Helens, he could not win a regular place there, but found more success at Blackpool and then Leigh before returning home in 1962.

Ted Brophy

During her rugby union heyday, Rhodesia produced a significant number of players who represented their country with distinction in the tough world of Currie Cup rugby. As a South African affiliate, its players were eligible for selection for the Springboks, and the country indeed contributed a small number of players, including one national captain, to the Springbok side. Although flanker Ted (or Ed) Brophy never became a Springbok, he represented his country with distinction on Currie Cup level during the 1956 and 1957 seasons.

As a Bancroft RFC player in the copper-producing Northern Rhodesia (now Zambia), he regularly played against clubs like Nchanga RFC and Inyanzura, who often included notable South African players who were working in the region's mines. Among his team mates were Tom van Vollenhoven and Fred 'Poensie' Griffiths. In the Currie Cup he faced the best of South African and Rhodesian rugby. Rugby in the northern territory was an important social activity for the white community. Representative rugby in these areas often consisted of matches between regional and sub-national combination teams such as Copper Belt and Midlands. These were played at events such as agricultural shows and Founder's Day meetings.

Brophy made his national debut for the Rhodesian senior side in 1956 when some of the leading players were not available. As part of a 17 member squad led by Attie Botha, he went with the team on a four match Currie Cup tour of South Africa. They lost the first match against Transvaal 18–3, but won a friendly against the same opponents 25–11 at Krugersdorp. According to a *Sunday Express* reporter, "De Klerk, Roebert and Brophy were outstanding. Never before have I seen better jumpers for the ball." They beat Eastern Transvaal in the next Currie Cup game 21–6 in Springs. Brophy scored his only try for his country, following good interplay between backs and forwards. Rhodesia, however, lost 11–0 to Northern Transvaal in their last game on a tour which was the last of Brophy's rugby union career. The team, according to team manager, Fred Jamieson, returned "that much wiser but no nearer to winning the coveted Currie Cup". Brophy had been, in his assessment, the most consistent player on tour.

Left: Ted Brophy in action for Leigh.
(Photo: Courtesy *Rugby League Journal*)

Given the periodic nature of Currie Cup and the infrequency of international tours, Brophy missed out on selection for the national side against touring teams that visited Rhodesia. Among these were the 1953 Australian Wallabies and 1955 British Lions tours, which were just prior to his national debut and the 1958 French tourists after he played his last rugby union match.

In the 1957 season, with only regional representative matches against a visiting Oxford-Cambridge touring team and a three match Currie Cup campaign, Brophy as part of an outstanding pack, contributed to his team's two wins and one defeat. This season, coincidentally the only season that 'Poensie' Griffiths played for Rhodesia, brought the curtain down on Brophy's rugby union career.

On 22 March 1958, Ted Brophy signed for St Helens. He was almost 28 years old, having been born on 14 April 1930. However, he made little impression at St Helens, and only played two first team matches before joining Blackpool Borough. His debut was against Borough, on 29 March 1958, and his final match was at the start of the 1958–59 season, at home to Widnes.

Blackpool were one of the game's smaller clubs, far removed from the giants at Knowsley Road. But the move did give Brophy a chance to learn his new sport under less pressure than with St Helens. He made his debut for the seaside club on 8 November 1958 in a 46–7 thrashing at Widnes. In his first season he played 18 matches, mainly in the second-row. Blackpool finished 24th out of 30 clubs, with 15 wins from 38 games. The following season he played nine matches, again split between the front-row and the second-row before Leigh signed him. A history of the club, published in 1971, says he was the "major signing" for the club that season. He made his debut in a 19–0 win at Huddersfield, and by the end of the season had played 20 games, with nine at prop and 11 in the second row. Again, he did not make one spot his own. The next season he played 17 matches, all at prop, but did not appear after 26 November.

He was joined at the club by four of his compatriots. Tom Moodie was signed in January, but only stayed until April, and never played for the first team. Towards the end of the season, Ken Boonzaier, Piet Botha and Chris Landsberg were recruited. Leigh had had a relatively successful season, finishing sixth. The next season the club dropped to 17th, with the chairman blaming the new recruits for the lack of progress. This was a disaster for the club, as it meant they would play the 1962–63 season in the newly created Second Division.

Brophy played 24 matches in the 1961–62 season, again switching between prop and the second row. He also won his only representative honour this season. On 12 October 1961, a

Rugby League XIII lost to a French XIII 21–20. The RFL used these games – there had been a similar fixture against the Kiwis the previous month – to give their South African stars the chance of representative rugby. Four South Africans had faced the Kiwis, and against the French, all the backs were South African, and Brophy played at prop. Also, this match clashed with county championship matches, which involved many of the sport's leading English players.

In June 1962, Wakefield Trinity toured South Africa at the invitation of the National Rugby League. Trinity took some South African guest players with them, including Ted Brophy. Described as a "rough and rugged" forward in a preview of the tour in the *Johannesburg Star*, he played regularly for Trinity, who won all the matches comfortably, and even scored a couple of tries.

Brophy's final season at Leigh was 1962–63. He played nine more matches, to bring his total for the club to 70, with one try. His last match was on 1 December 1962, an 18–15 win at Salford. He left the club quite suddenly, and sailed for home from Southampton.

The statistics and records cannot do justice to Brophy's time in rugby league. Known as a 'character', stories and myths about him, often related to alcohol, and his time as a nightclub doorman in St Helens, abound. One that is true is that he saved the life of St Helens and Great Britain star Dick Huddart, who recalls: "We'd been playing Leigh and were out drinking after the game. After I came out of Stan Owen's pub I found the battery flat in my little van which was parked on a slope. I tried to clutch start it rolling down the hill. It was pitch black, and there was a canal right at the bottom... whoosh! The van and I were suddenly in the wash. I couldn't get out of the door, but next thing I saw Ted Brophy, one of the Leigh players, bobbing about in the water. He got the door open and me out. It was a lucky escape – happy days." Apparently Brophy got a bravery award for this feat. The story sometimes appears on websites as Huddart rescuing Brophy!

Austin Rhodes played against Ted Brophy for St Helens, and with him towards the end of his time at Leigh. In his autobiography, *A lad from Donkey Common*, Austin recalls: "One of the biggest characters was the South African forward Ted Brophy, who had come over to join St Helens a few years before. He would never claim to be the greatest forward ever. He had no pace as such, but he was great for team spirit and absolutely nuts. Ted lived above a chippie in Westfield Street near St Helens town centre and once jumped in the Manchester Ship Canal from the Railway Bridge at Widnes with Alan Winstanley. I saw Ted the day after he did it, funnily enough. I went upstairs to his place in Westfield Street. I said "What on earth have you been doing?" Ted lifted his shirt and he was black and blue from his neck to his backside. He must have turned over and hit the water full on with his back. Perhaps it was a drunken dare, but Ted didn't need drink to do that – he was just daft. I also saw him do a dive at Southport pool off the top board. They cleared the pool for him to do it and there he was just like Johnny Weissmuller.

Ted was actually very light on his feet and worked at a club in Frodsham which I think was called the Mersey View. We used to go there with the Mylers. He would always be asking us if our glasses needed to be filled. He would come over with our refills and more often than not they would be half price. The music would come on and he would do a soft shoe shuffle. Marlene says that he invented the *Moonwalk* before Michael Jackson. He was a very entertaining man and the life-and-soul of the party.

In those days, there were a lot of players who turned out for teams and they didn't have much ability, particularly in the forwards. In the bad weather, ankle deep in mud, they didn't need too much ability. Side-stepping, swerving and stuff like that were not needed. Grit, determination, size and fitness were the keys to success. They also needed to tackle.

Despite Ted Brophy's uplifting presence, Leigh were pretty ordinary performers in 1962–63. We finished the season in seventh place in the Second Division, winning 14 from 26 matches."

The well-known rugby league broadcaster and journalist, the late Keith Macklin also had problems with Brophy, but not of the player's making. Macklin was covering a fog-bound match at Craven Park between Hull KR and Leigh. Struggling to identify the players, he had to make a man-of-the-match award at the end of the game. He nominated Brophy, only to find later on that he had not actually been playing!

Ted Brophy died on 4 December 2000, aged 69, in his native South Africa. Bill Robinson, the then chairman of the Leigh Past Players Association, and a former team-mate of Brophy's commented: "Lots of fans will be sad to hear of Ted's death. He was well thought of in the town."

In July 1958, Huddersfield signed Athol Brown, a 25-year-old engine driver from Rhodesia. He made his debut on 16 August 1958 against Warrington. He was a winger, who was five feet 10 inches tall, and weighed 12 stones. In his first season at Fartown, he played 11 times and scored 5 tries before a leg injury at Whitehaven finished his season. The *Fartown Year Book* for 1959 said that he had "shown promise in his early games".

In 1959–60 he played 16 times for the first team, and 15 for the 'A' team. He played three matches early in the season, then won his first team place back early in February and was a regular for the rest of the campaign. Against lowly Doncaster he scored twice on Easter Monday and then four tries the next day against the hapless Dons. Overall, he scored 11 tries in the season. In 1960–61, he played fairly regularly until 7 January 1961, making 19 appearances with seven tries.

He usually played on the right wing, but did play one game at stand-off, and scored two tries. On 29 October, he played in the Yorkshire Cup Final against Leeds at Headingley. Huddersfield lost 16–10 to Wakefield Trinity. It was the club's last appearance in a Yorkshire Cup Final. Overall, he made 46 first team appearances and scored 23 tries. He was not on Huddersfield's retained register for 1962, but appeared on it again the next year. He was finally removed from the club's register in June 1964.

Not satisfied with having Tom van Vollenhoven on one flank, St Helens returned to South Africa to recruit another Springbok flyer, Jan Prinsloo, who joined the club in October 1958.

Johannes Albertus (Jan) Prinsloo

St Helens initially approached Jan Prinsloo in the spring of 1958, but were rebuffed because Prinsloo was keen to be capped by the Springboks before he considered a switch to rugby league. Realistically, achieving international honours in union put him in a stronger negotiating position with any rugby league suitors. His international honours concluded a union career that had seen him appear 32 times for the Transvaal side.

Prinsloo duly won his Springbok honours, appearing twice against the French tourists in July and August 1958. He was born on 18 May 1935, and was a Detective Sergeant in the South African Police when he accepted a £4,000 offer from St Helens. At six feet tall and 14 stones, he was large for a rugby league winger, but was very quick. He was a good enough athlete to compete in top level sprinting in South Africa. A press report from South Africa which Saints received as part of the correspondence leading up to him signing for the club said that he had run the 100 yards in 9.6 seconds.

He signed for St Helens on 14 October 1958, having been advised by a Mr Timms in South Africa, one of the numerous agents who helped clubs recruit South African players at this time, who was also Fred Griffiths's brother-in-law. He marked his debut against Rochdale Hornets on 8 November with two tries, and by the end of the season had scored 27 tries in 29 matches, including hat-tricks against Salford and Blackpool. He took over the left-wing place in the Saints line up from Frank Carlton, although coach Jim Sullivan did consider moving van Vollenhoven into the centre to accommodate Prinsloo.

Honours soon followed. He missed out on the Lancashire Cup Final, which Saints lost to Oldham, but was part of the team that beat Hunslet 44–22 in the Championship Final at Odsal on 16 May. Saints had finished top of the table with 63 points from 38 matches, and had beaten Oldham 42–4 in the semi-final to reach the final. The winger opposing him for Hunslet was fellow South African Ronnie Colin. Tom van Vollenhoven was Saints' star, with a hat-trick, as they came back from 12–4 down to demolish Hunslet, but Prinsloo claimed one try, finishing off a six-man move just before half-time.

Saints were less consistent in 1959–60. Prinsloo got a runners-up medal in the Lancashire Cup, when Saints lost 5–4 to Warrington. He scored 29 tries in 38 appearances, enough to finish ninth in the national try scorers list for the season. The influence of South African backs is shown by Tom van Vollenhoven and Alan Skene both finishing ahead of him. His tally for the season included four in one match against Liverpool City.

Prinsloo won one more medal for Saints. He was part of the team that beat Swinton 15–9 in the Lancashire Cup Final at Wigan in October 1960. But in January 1961, Saints paid a record transfer fee of £11,000 to Wigan for Great Britain winger Mick Sullivan. St Helens recouped part of the fee by transferring Prinsloo to Wakefield Trinity for £9,000. However, Saints historian Alex Service points out that Prinsloo "had a formidable record of 76 tries in 91 games, which certainly compared favourably with Sullivan's scoring feats at Wigan. Moreover, no opposing winger had managed to score against him since the start of the season." His final match in a Saints shirt was against Warrington on 7 January 1961. Despite the change of clubs, he still managed 22 tries in the season.

St. Helens Rugby Football Club Ltd.

Ground—Knowsley Road.

Patron :—The Right Hon. The Earl of Derby, M.C.

Ref.:—

Telephone : Ground 3697

Home Telephone : 6301

All communications to be addressed to B. LOWE, Secretary, Knowsley Road, St. Helens.

AGREEMENT MADE BETWEEN JAN PRINSLOO AND ST. HELENS RUGBY FOOTBALL CLUB LIMITED.

I, JAN PRINSLOO hereby agree to sign the necessary application forms provided by the Rugby Football League to become a registered player of the St. Helens Rugby Football Club Limited which binds me to play Rugby League Football for the St. Helens Rugby Football Club as long as the Club require my services, this being an agreement which can only be terminated by consent of the Club, and in consideration therfor the Club hereby agrees to give to the player the sum of £4,000 (FOUR THOUSAND POUNDS) as a signing fee on receipt of his signature on the said application forms.

The Club also agrees to provide suitable living accomodation to be rented by the player for the period that the player is retained by the Club, and to provide Air Passage Money for the player and his Wife from South Africa to England.

The Club also agrees to pay a minimum playing wage for the period the player is retained by the Club subject to his fitness to play.

The Club agrees to use all endeavours to obtain suitable employment for the player.

WE authorise Jack Pansegrouw to sign this agreement as agent for and on behalf of the St. Helens Rugby Football Club Limited.

....

H. B. Cook.   Chairman.

....

Jan Prinsloo.

....

Jack Pansegrouw.

Jan Prinsloo's letter of agreement to join St Helens, with Jack Pansegrouw acting as their agent.
(Courtesy Alex Service)

When he had moved clubs, in an interview with Derek Marshall, Prinsloo had said that "I am really pleased to join Wakefield. I have been told they may want me to play on either wing. Wherever it is will be alright with me." In his first full season in West Yorkshire, he scored 30 tries for Trinity in only 25 appearances. But did not appear in any of the finals the team reached. He was injured against the New Zealand tourists, and missed six games, including the start of the team's successful Challenge Cup run. He only appeared once in Trinity's run to Wembley, at Blackpool in the second round when they won 16–4. One highlight during the season was scoring six tries against Bradford Northern at Odsal. Another was his selection, along with fellow South African club mates Colin Greenwood and Alan Skene, for a Rugby League XIII to play a French XIII.

In June 1962 he toured South Africa with Wakefield, and was one of the former Springboks whose presence was used to promote the tour. However, in the first half of 1962–63 he was in dispute with Trinity, and wanted to return to play in South Africa. He returned home in December 1962 "without clearance" meaning he could not play rugby league in South Africa.

In Mike Rylance's comprehensive history of the club, he says that the *Wakefield Express* reported that "the desire of Prinsloo to return to South Africa has been a talking point ever since he failed a fitness test for the Wembley final in May." Rylance adds: Prinsloo finally took the matter into his own hands in late December when he, his wife and two children suddenly left the country, their departure hastened by the death of his father-in-law and illness of his mother-in-law. In an interview given at the airport, Prinsloo said: 'There has been bad feeling on both sides since I received a groin injury last October. I have played only eight games out of 16 this season because of this injury. I've tried to get away for six months but the club said I had a life-long contract. This is nonsense. I signed nothing when I joined them. I don't think the trouble I've had will stop me playing in South Africa.'" [40]

Wakefield Trinity historian John Lindley, in his club history *100 years of Rugby* said that "Prinsloo played only 48 games for the £9,000 fee Trinity paid to St Helens, but he scored 45 tries – a ratio of success greater than any other player the club has had. A great pity that his career with Wakefield was not of much longer duration." On the Saints Heritage Society website, Dave Dooley commented on his time at Knowsley Road: "Jan Prinsloo had the daunting task of wearing the Saints number five jersey at the same time as Tom van Vollenhoven was setting the whole game on fire on the other wing. His record and strike-rate demonstrates what a fine finisher Jan Prinsloo was in our game."

Prinsloo died on 28 July 1966 at the young age of 31 in Wellington in South Africa. He had been playing rugby union, despite being banned because of having played professional rugby league. He collapsed after a match and died from a heart attack. Newspaper reports mentioned that he had experienced rheumatic problems when playing for Wakefield. The year before he died, the Somerset West club had been warned for playing him in rugby union matches because he was banned. When he died he was working as a sales representative and was engaged to be married. His death was front-page news in South Africa. Had he stayed in British rugby league, he could have found further success, having scored regularly for two of the game's leading sides.

Not wanting to be outdone by their local rivals, Wigan also sought some new South African talent. Both the players they signed were – maybe not surprisingly – high profile. In 1957, Fred 'Poensie' Griffiths made a major impact on his new code. The other signing, current Springbok scrum-half Tommy Gentles, did not. His recruitment by rugby league was seen as a major blow for rugby union, but the defensive demands on a scrum-half in league were very different then from those in union, and however skilful and willing he was, Gentles was not big enough to be an effective rugby league player.

Tommy Gentles

Tommy Gentles is one of the smallest players ever to have worn the coveted Springbok jersey. Despite his slight built, he was recognised as an agile and nippy scrum-half with proven experience in the rough-and-tumble of Western Province's Grand Challenge and Town Challenge competitions. He represented his province in the Currie Cup as well as playing for the Springboks. Born on 31 May 1934, Gentles made his debut for Western Province (WP) at the tender age of 20 in 1955. Although the season was a non-Currie Cup season because of the British Lions tour, there were still opportunities for him to become established on the provincial and international scene. The provincial friendlies were an important opportunity for players like Gentles to hone their skills and to display their prowess.

In July 1955, prior to the arrival of the British Lions, Tommy Gentles together with Dawie Ackerman and Wilf Rosenberg was selected for the Junior Springboks, coached and managed by Danie Craven for a short tour of South Africa and Rhodesia. The idea was to use the junior team (later known as the Gazelles) as a tool to develop future Springboks. The basis for selection set in 1955 according to one source was: "A player must be a prospective Springbok and must be young. Once a Junior Springbok he should become a Springbok, all things being equal." [41] During the tour the team played three matches; against Natal, Central Universities and Rhodesia.

Although Gentles did not play for WP against the British tourists, he represented his province in the eight games, of which they won five and drew one. Among his team mates were Dawie Ackerman, Ivor Dorrington, Rudi Hasse, Gert Rheeder, Hennie Van Zyl and Allan Skene. Despite his limited first-class experience, Gentles grabbed the opportunities on offer to impress the national selectors and won a place in the Springbok team for the test against the Lions on 6 August at Ellis Park. At a height of five feet three inches, Gentles became the shortest Springbok ever. With his lack of experience, he had an inauspicious start and failed to impress. He was dropped for the third test, but following an equally unimpressive performance by his replacement, was recalled for the fourth and decisive test.

Although Gentles was included in the touring party to New Zealand and Australia in 1956, his form was indifferent at best. He got his first start in the third tour match, against NSW Country on 22 May. He did not contribute any points in a 15–8 victory. Furthermore, his relative lack of international experience coupled with inauspicious performances in midweek games denied him a place in the test team. Overall, he played 14 matches on tour, including 11 in the New Zealand leg of the tour. He scored against the Nelson Combined XV and Southland. To compound matters, 1956 was not a vintage season for WP which also limited his development.

The next season, 1957, which was a Currie Cup one, was more successful for the men of Cape Town. They beat Transvaal in the Board Trophy Final at Newlands 12–5; and toured the Northern provinces for three games. As result of his good form, Gentles won back the selectors' favour and kept his place in the provincial side for the WP Jubilee season in 1958.

When the French team arrived for their first-ever tour of South Africa in 1958, Gentles together with Hugh Gillespie, Dawie Ackerman and Alan Skene was selected for a combined WP-Boland-South Western Districts Combined XV against the tourists in Wellington on 30 July. The match was won by the home side 38–8 with tries by Gillespie, Skene and Ackerman. As a result of this victory, eight members of this team, including Gentles (who was awarded with the vice-captaincy), were selected for the second test at Ellis Park on 16 August 1958. They were, however, not up to the challenge. South Africa lost 9–5 and the series 1–0.

Gentles also represented WP against the visiting British Barbarians in a 12–10 win, and in three provincial games. At the end of the season, after six test matches and 18 international games, Gentles decided that his future lay in rugby league, and signed for Wigan.

The risks involved in switching from rugby union to rugby league are graphically illustrated by the experiences of Tommy Gentles. In November 1958, Wigan paid their biggest ever fee for an overseas player when they signed the 24-year-old Springbok scrum-half. He was a big loss to the Springboks, but sadly made little impact on rugby league.

Why the Wigan directors decided to sign him is a mystery; they already had five scrum-halves on their books. But at five feet three inches tall, weighing just 10 stones and wearing size four boots, Gentles was always going to find the going tough in rugby league. Apparently Wigan chairman Bill Gore exclaimed 'What have we done?' when he saw the tiny figure of Gentles, wearing glasses, at London Airport.

Jack Winstanley recalls that "Gentles scored two tries in his 'A' team debut against Swinton – and was a very genuine young man – [but] he clearly wasn't ready for the sometimes cut-throat rigours of rugby league football." Gentles made his first team debut against Salford at Central Park on Christmas Day 1958, but only made one more first team appearance that season, scoring one try. In the 1959–60 season he played a further five first team matches before a move to Leeds. There is a story about his time at Wigan that may be a myth: when there was a snowfall, someone rolled a giant snowball on the pitch, which was taller than Tommy Gentles.

Gentles moved to Leeds, but never played for the first team. Ken Dalby comments that for Leeds "The fact that no less than 10 different half-back combinations had been tried since August pinpointed the need for real authority and skill at the base of the scrum. To that end, the management recruited not one, but two, international scrum halves immediately before the Cup deadline, Tommy Gentles … being signed for a comparatively modest fee, purely as an insurance against a possible breakdown in the negotiations to obtain the services of Colin Evans, who had played for Wales at Twickenham only a fortnight earlier." Evans made his first team debut on 6 February, and went on to have a successful career with Leeds. Gentles returned to South Africa with his wife Jean, who he had met in Wigan. He was involved in the rugby league competitions in the country in the early 1960s as a coach and director, but did not play.

He became a successful insurance broker back in South Africa. He died in Johannesburg on 29 June 2011, aged 77. The obituary in *www.rugby365.com* recalled that his time in rugby league was "... a miserable experience and one that cost him dearly in days when rugby union treated league players as pariahs. He was not allowed to wear Springbok colours or coach a club side in South Africa and once, when he went to Villagers to have a drink with some of the players from his 1958 champion side, he was required to leave the Villager clubhouse...". He had also, apparently, according to Paul Dobson, coached rugby union under an assumed name. His son Ian played rugby union for Transvaal Schools.
(Tommy Gentles photo: Courtesy *Rugby League Journal*)

Wakefield Trinity were one of the top English clubs at this time, and one who had a regular South African presence until the early 1970s. However, their first signings were disappointing. Ivor Dorrington, despite having a reputation as a powerful forward in South African provincial rugby, could not adjust to rugby league. He came to the club in November 1958, along with a centre or winger, Jan Lotriet, who only made three appearances for the Yorkshire club before returning home the following season.

Ivor Dorrington

In *Donaldson's Sporting Encyclopaedia of South Africa*, Ivor Dorrington has an entry including leisurely pursuits such as tennis, ballroom dancing, 'jitter bugging' and cricket as well as being a provincial rugby player. He comes across as a man of leisure and probably one of South African rugby's first 'men-about-town'. Dorrington was born on 25 June 1926 in Port Elizabeth in the Eastern Cape, and completed his high school education at Grey High.

He represented his high school in both rugby and cricket as well as indulging in wrestling and boxing at the local YMCA. He was a member of Walmer and Claremont Cricket Clubs at home and later in Cape Town. Upon his arrival in the Mother City, he joined the Gardens RFC, an affiliate of the Western Province Rugby Union and one of the oldest local clubs having been established in 1882. He played in the Grand Challenge and Town Challenge competitions. From 1936 to 1948, the club took the honours in the senior competition seven times and also produced a fair quota of both provincial and national players. After its 1948 Grand Challenge victory and elimination from the Town Challenge, the club, despite being very competitive, somewhat lost its momentum.

So by the time Dorrington joined Gardens, it was well versed in the art of playing hard, uncompromising and winning rugby. This helped him win a place in the 1952 Western Province (WP) side, the start of a career of 52 representative matches for his union. In a season of mixed fortunes, the WP side was eliminated at the semi-final stage of the Currie

Cup by a rampaging Boland side which denied Dorrington an early opportunity to taste championship glory.

After a satisfactory debut at provincial level, Dorrington kept his place and played his first international match against the touring Australians at Newlands on 25 July 1953. They lost 11–3. This minor setback did not discourage Dorrington and by the 1954 Currie Cup season, he was part of a strong team including Alan Skene, Gert Rheeder and Dawie Ackerman. In the final against Northern Transvaal, in front of 40,000 fans, he and Ackerman were tasked with isolating the dangerous Pretoria half-backs, especially their Springbok fly-half, Hannes Brewis. This directly contributed to WP's 11–8 victory.

When the British Lions arrived in South Africa in 1955, Dorrington was among the 28 players that represented the province in friendlies. He, however, failed to make the team for the match against the tourists at Newlands which hampered his chances of staking a serious claim for a place in the national side. But he did make a significant contribution to victories in five of their eight friendlies that season.

At the start of his fifth senior season in 1957, aged 30, Dorrington continued to hold his own among the best of WP rugby. He not only assisted his province to victory in the Board Trophy competition through hard and uncompromising play, but also stood up to the equally rough treatment meted out by the opponents in the season finale at Newlands. Joining him in the 24-man squad were Rudi Hasse, Dawie Ackerman, Tommy Gentles and Jan Lotriet, all of whom were destined for rugby league.

Despite the inevitability of advancing age, Dorrington continue to push hard for recognition during a season which saw WP celebrate its Diamond Jubilee, the arrival of the British Barbarians and the first French team to visit South Africa. Although he represented WP that season, he was overlooked for the select combination of Boland-Western Province-South Western Districts which played the French at Wellington. The 1958 season was Dorrington's last season of competitive representative rugby union, because, along with Jan Lotriet and Alan Skene, he switched to rugby league and joined Wakefield Trinity.

Wakefield Trinity had some very successful South African recruits in the late 1950s and 1960s. However, their first major signing, Ivor Dorrington, was not one of them. It has always been more difficult for forwards to switch codes, and sadly, Dorrington's experience bore this out.

He was probably not helped by being described as the "Iron Man" of South African rugby union by Ronnie Colin, who although playing for Hunslet helped Trinity sign him. He was actually the second South African to sign for Trinity, but arrived before centre or winger Jan Lotriet, who came by ship to England rather than fly.

On 8 November 1958, the *Wakefield Express* reported Ronnie Colin, the Hunslet winger and agent who had arranged the move saying that "Everyone wants a Vince Karalius in their team, well here is a tougher South African version." The report went on to say that "Let it be admitted at once that in certain circles Trinity's capture has been criticised on account of the fact that he has reached 28 years of age. [Actually 32!] It must be confessed that it might seem a bit steep to plunge out with £2,000 for a possible three-year contract, but is that a fair way to assess the value of an untried commodity of such high repute?" Would Trinity have signed him if they had known his real age?

Dorrington was reported to be six feet one inch tall and to weigh over 15 stone. Colin claimed that "The only reason he hasn't played for South Africa is because if he gets pushed around, he does something about it." He also said that Dorrington was known as one of the fittest players in the country, and that he "...is a must for rugby league."

The *Express* also quoted from a 'Sportsman of the week' feature in a South African newspaper: "Dorrington is a natural sportsman who would have been as good at tennis or golf as he is at rugby, had he concentrated on them instead. In fact, his father (a representative cricket and water polo player) was keen that as a youngster, Ivor should concentrate on golf and forbade him to play rugby lest he hurt his hands. Ivor used to smuggle his togs out of the house in those early days when he was a fast-moving centre threequarter. His father, who was a scratch golfer himself, relented when he saw the keenness Ivor had for rugby and he was temporarily content with his golfing ambitions for his sons when Rick, Ivor's elder brother, reached the final of the South African amateur championship some years ago."

At this time, Wakefield were one of the strongest teams in the country. Dorrington made his debut in a televised match against Hunslet at Belle Vue on 29 November, although fog apparently undermined the coverage. It was the first time a match had been televised at Belle Vue. He played in the second row, and kept his place for the next two matches. He returned to the team on 24 January, and played a further seven games, the final one being on 14 March.

The next season, Trinity won the Challenge Cup and reached the Championship final. But Ivor Dorrington only made a couple of appearances early in the season. He scored his only try for Trinity in the second match, a 27–17 win over Leeds at Belle Vue on 26 August. Overall, he made just 12 first team appearances.

His compatriot, Jan Lotriet, was released by Trinity in October 1959. At the end of the month, the *Wakefield Express* reported that Dorrington was also going home at the end of December. The report said that he "had enjoyed his time here" and when questioned about whether he would be a scout for Trinity in South Africa, said that "if he saw any players he considered worthwhile he would certainly recommend them to Wakefield. He stressed that he would recommend only young players, particularly in the case of forwards, for they would require about four years to settle down into the rugby league code. Speaking of his own experience, Dorrington commented that, after 12 years in the amateur game, it was expecting too much for a player to fit in properly." He was, however, pleased with the club: "I am highly satisfied with the way Wakefield have treated me and the players, well, they are great chaps." At a farewell do arranged for him by the supporters club, he also commented on the 'grand comradeship' he had found at the club, and regretted that he had not made the move earlier. To switch codes effectively at the age of 32 was beyond him

Left: Alan Skene.
(Photo: Courtesy Robert Gate)
Right::Ivor Dorrington
(Courtesy *Rugby League Journal*)

Eddie Waring, in a feature on international players in British rugby league, quoted Dorrington as saying he was "too old and too cold" and said that "one can sympathise with him."

The third player Wakefield signed at the same time as Lotriet and Dorrington, Alan Skene, was one of their most successful recruits from South Africa. As with Jan Prinsloo, who would later join him at Wakefield, Skene had won one cap for the Springboks, who lost another highly promising back to rugby league.

Alan Skene

It was Ivor Dorrington recommended that the club approach Alan Skene. Skene was born on 2 October 1932, and played for Villagers and Western Province before playing for the Springboks against France on 16 August 1958. He had made 50 representative appearances for Western Province. He was supported by Ronnie Colin in South Africa after deciding to switch codes.

He signed for Trinity on 6 December 1958, and made his debut on 25 December at Castleford. A pen portrait of him in a booklet commemorating Trinity's Challenge Cup triumphs said that he "immediately settled to [a] new code under weather conditions hitherto completely alien to him."

He played in the centre for Trinity, and was fortunate that his centre partner was Neil Fox, who was starting a career that would last for two decades. His partnership with Fred Smith made a very strong right wing. In 1959–60 they scored 73 tries between them, with Skene scoring 35. Smith's 38 was a new club record. Skene finished sixth in the season's national try scorers list. His compatriot Tom van Vollenhoven topped the list with 54; Smith and Neil Fox also finished ahead of him, Fox notching 37, although his tally also included tries for Great Britain and Yorkshire.

Two of Skene's tries came in the Challenge Cup Final, when Trinity beat Hull 38–5 at Wembley. The following weekend Trinity had the chance of the League and Cup double, but Wigan overwhelmed them 27–3. But two medals in his first full season was a good return. Trinity had also won the Yorkshire League.

The next season brought another medal – Skene was part of the Wakefield team that beat Huddersfield 16–10 in the Yorkshire Cup Final. Further success followed in 1961–62, when Wakefield again reached the Championship and Challenge Cup Finals. Trinity triumphed again at Wembley, Neil Fox scoring all the points in a 12–6 win over Huddersfield. But the Fartown side got their revenge the next week, winning the Championship Final 14–5 at Odsal. Trinity also won the Yorkshire League.

Earlier in the season, Skene had scored his first try in a Cup Final, when Wakefield beat Leeds 13–9 to win the Yorkshire Cup. And he won his first international honours, playing twice for a Rugby League XIII, against France and New Zealand. He scored 24 tries, but was only the fourth highest South African in the season's list, van Vollenhoven, club-mate Jan Prinsloo and Workington's Piet Pretorius were all ahead of him. He also played for Wakefield Trinity on their 1962 tour to South Africa.

Alan Skene left Wakefield in November 1962, having played 136 games, scoring 69 tries. In four years he had played in six major finals, and won three medals for the Yorkshire League. After a break in South Africa, he followed some of his fellow countrymen to play rugby league in Australia, and joined South Sydney. He only played for one season with Souths, scoring two tries in 16 appearances. However, he was a member of the 1963 South African team that toured Australia and New Zealand, and played in both tests against Australia.

Alan Skene died on 13 August 2001 in George in the Western Cape, aged 69.

8. 1959: The Flying Dentist

Only four new players came to English rugby league from South Africa in 1959. Again, South African rugby union lost a prominent Springbok when Wilf Rosenberg signed for Leeds, and went on to win a Championship medal with his new club. The other three players, Hugh Gillespie, Percy Landsberg and Tony Forster, had less success in their new code.

Wilf Rosenberg

Wilf Rosenberg's story could be hard to believe if it was a novel. Except in Israel, the professional football codes have attracted precious few Jewish players over the years. And for the son of a Rabbi to play professional sport was remarkable. To find success thousands of miles from home, in a game he had never played at a senior level before turning professional was even more notable. And to play while studying to be a dentist – a rare example of an academically highly qualified man in professional rugby league – seems almost to be entering the world of fantasy. But all this was true of Wilf Rosenberg.

He was born in Cape Town on 18 June 1934. His father, Phillip Rosenberg, was from Poland, his mother was Lithuanian. Fleeing repression in Eastern and Central Europe, some Jews who did not head for Great Britain or the USA ended up in South Africa. When Wilf was three years old, the family emigrated to Australia, where his father had been appointed as Chief Rabbi in Sydney. He first played rugby union at the age of six, and by the age of 14 was being tipped as a future Australian international. He attended the Sydney Grammar School, and was coached by former Australian rugby union international Ron Rankin. Interviewed for this book, he recalled in 2011: "I had a wonderful childhood. I achieved first class metric, and generally did well academically and was offered scholarships. In my youth I was better at cricket than rugby. I was also a junior boxing champion.

His family returned to South Africa when he was aged 15, after his father accepted a post as a Rabbi in Johannesburg.

Although his parents followed the 'Orthodox' strand of Judaism[42], Wilf's father allowed him to play rugby on Saturdays, the Jewish Sabbath, but never saw him play. Asked about this many years later, when he was emigrating to Israel in 2010 to live with his family, he said that his father believed that "My son was born with a God-given talent. Who am I to argue with God?"

Wilf went to Wits University in Johannesburg to study medicine. His performances for the University team saw him selected for Transvaal at the age of 17, and the Northern Universities side. He recalled: "There was a lot of press publicity when I was selected for Transvaal, which was the most powerful provincial side, and then when I was chosen for the Springboks."

However, a serious knee injury saw him miss the whole of the 1954 season. Despite concerns over his tackling ability – no one doubted his attacking skills – he was selected for South Africa to play against the British Lions in 1955. Last minute coaching on his tackling paid off, because he tackled the Lions centres out of the game and scored two tries. He won five test caps for South Africa, three against the British Lions, one against France in 1958 and one against the All Blacks, on a 1956 tour to New Zealand when injury restricted him to just two appearances. Wilf recalled in 2011 that he was one of 10 Jews who had played for the Springboks, and a well-known artist, Ritchie Ryall, did a painting of them. Wilf said that Danie Craven was superstitious, and believed that the Springboks would win "if there was a Jewish boy in the side." Morris Zimmerman was one of the selectors and was very close to Craven. For the first test against the Lions the selectors did not chose him, believing that the British threequarters would be too strong for him to handle, but he was then chosen for the second test. Wilf remembers being in the cinema on a Saturday night when the team was announced and realising that he was going to make his debut for the Springboks in Cape Town at Newlands. "I was very proud, I was only the fifth Jewish Springbok."

Interviewed in 2010, Rosenberg recalled how he "hated politics" and avoided political activity in the 1950s, attracting criticism from fellow Jew Helen Suzman MP, a well-known opponent of the apartheid regime. However, he also upset the Government foreign minister on his test debut, as he ran towards the stands for the African and Coloured supporters to acknowledge them, getting a cheer for his efforts.

It was through his father that he switched codes and followed other South African players into British rugby league in the late 1950s, signing for Leeds in February 1959. Apparently agents for Leeds met his father at the airport on a trip to Britain, and offered £6,000 for his son to join Leeds. His father signed the forms on his son's behalf, and then telegrammed Wilf, who was on his honeymoon in Durban, to let him know what he had done! Wilf later recalled that he "knew about rugby league growing up in Australia, but I never had any dreams of playing the game until my father made it a fait accompli." He had played rugby league at school in Australia, but had no plans to turn professional, although his wife was pleased to have the opportunity to come to England.

Wilf initially played as a centre in his new code, and signed up for a four year dentistry course at Leeds University, despite having done four years of medicine at Wits. The medical school he applied to in Leeds to continue his studies said that they "had never heard of Wits" and told him that he would have to start from the beginning to do medicine. So he switched to dentistry.

He had been registered with the club a couple of days before the deadline for playing in the Challenge Cup, but the RFL refused to accept the form his father had signed on his behalf. His career started slowly with Leeds, until, as Ken Dalby recalls he "suddenly clicked into action in the very last match of the season, selling a classic dummy in his own '25', skating at speed over a midfield morass, and then accelerating round Pimblett, the Widnes full-back, to bring down the house with a sensationally spectacular dive for the touchdown."[43]

It became clear that he would make a better winger than centre in rugby league. Centre play in union is quite different to league – and his partnership with Great Britain international Derek Hallas on the right flank meant that his speed could be used to full effect. Eleven tries in nine matches towards the end of the 1959–60 season promised well for 1960–61.

Despite being one of the most prestigious clubs in the game, with a magnificent ground, Leeds had never won the Championship. The 1960–61 season finally saw the Headingley club crowned as champions, and Wilf Rosenberg, now known as the 'Flying Dentist' made a major contribution to their triumph.

He scored tries regularly as Leeds finished top of the table with 30 wins from 36 matches. In those days the championship was decided through a playoff system, the top four teams meeting in semi-finals, with the final deciding who would be declared the Champions. Leeds faced St Helens, who had finished fourth, at Headingley. His first try, from a Dennis Goodwin pass, gave him a post-war club record 43 in a season, beating Drew Turnbull's 42 in 1954–55. His second, taking him to 44, saw him beat three defenders to score from 40 yards out and make the match safe for Leeds. He recalls that one supporter told him after the game that the Jewish people were "so proud" of him.

Sadly, that was the last try he scored for the club. Leeds won the final 25–10 against Warrington in front of over 52,000 fans at Odsal. But early the next season, he broke his jaw in a very physical derby match at Parkside against Hunslet. Reluctant to play in the 'A' team, he asked for a transfer, and moved to Hull in December 1961. He had scored 73 tries for Leeds in 81 matches. Phil Caplan and Peter Smith, in their book on 100 great Leeds players, recall how he returned to the club for a dinner to celebrate the 40th anniversary of the championship win: "His alluring smile lit up the room and brought back a host of golden memories to his still-adoring fans." [44]

Hull paid £5,750 to bring Wilf to The Boulevard. He recalls that "Ronnie Teeman got me a good deal at Hull. And the fee they received was a record for Leeds at that time." He made his debut, against Bramley on 9 December 1961, scoring two tries. But his efforts were overshadowed by a young trialist on the other wing who scored a hat-trick. Clive Sullivan was the other winger, who went on to be a legend in Hull. But one of his tries, a "thrilling dash to the line" according to the *Hull Daily Mail*, showed his new fans his potential.

He finished the season with 15 tries in 21 matches, including a hat-trick against a struggling Bradford Northern. But he broke his jaw again in the close season, while playing as a guest for Wakefield Trinity on their tour of South Africa. Luckily it was only a hairline fracture, and he returned to action for the new season. But then a cartilage operation meant he missed more matches. Hull were not particularly strong at this time, and finished bottom of the league in 1963–64, when he only scored nine tries in 27 matches.

His dental studies completed, Wilf retired from rugby league and returned to South Africa in December 1964. His last match was against Leeds, a 23–3 defeat. He had played 86 matches for Hull, scoring 42 tries. He said that he could not risk damaging his hands playing rugby, which would have finished his career as a dentist. The club agreed to release him from the rest of his contract.

Sadly, his dental career was cut short by a major stroke in 1971. He then became involved in property development and promoting boxing. He also wrote about rugby union for the *Sunday Times* in South Africa, and was a television commentator for SABC. Although the stroke left his right side weak, he ran six 'Comrades Marathons' in the 1980s and 1990s. He was also a good cricketer and squash player.

Wilf Rosenberg scoring a spectacular try for Leeds. (Photo: Courtesy *Rugby League Journal*)

He never played rugby union again, but was involved in two television programmes, *Rugby on the edge* and *Wilf's whistle*, about the game. He says that they were controversial, and that people sometimes came to the SABC offices looking for him. He wrote about the game for the South African *Sunday Times* for over 20 years. Through boxing he met President Nelson Mandela, who was a great enthusiast for the sport.

His success in rugby was recognised when he was inducted into the Jewish Sportsman's Hall of Fame in 1997, and the Leeds Rugby League Hall of Fame in 2002. Another unusual honour came from the South African Jewish Museum, who as part of an exhibition on 'The Glory of the Game' in 2009 identified the 10 Jewish players who had played for the Springboks as the 'Springbok Minyan', including Wilf.[45]

His wife died in 1989, and with two of his children living in Australia, he emigrated to Israel in 2010, attracting considerable media coverage, to live near his daughter and her family.

He visited Leeds in 2011 to attend a 50th anniversary dinner celebrating the club's 1961 Championship success. He said that there was a lot of publicity when he arrived in Israel. "The press found out I was there, and were phoning me. It was all over the Israeli newspapers. Even a television show was interested." When he visited Leeds, there was coverage of his visit in the local and rugby league papers, and his exploits are still fondly remembered in Leeds and Hull.

Hugh Gillespie

In South African rugby union it was far more difficult for players based in the rural areas such as with the Boland Rugby Union to achieve recognition. Caledon, in the picturesque Overberg region, 90 minutes' drive from Cape Town was Hugh Gillespie's home. He was working as a sales representative for an oil company in 1958 when he burst onto the provincial rugby scene.

Gillespie, playing at centre, made his debut for Boland in 1958, a non-Currie Cup year with the first French tourists in South Africa. Players such as Gillespie therefore had to show their worth to challenge for national honours in inter-provincial friendlies. His province was also in contention for league honours. In a mediocre season, Boland played six matches, but won only three. Gillespie played in all six fixtures. He also impressed in a 6–3 victory over Western Province, Boland's illustrious neighbours after the former beat the touring British Barbarians a week earlier. He was also selected for a Combined Select XV of Boland, South Western Districts and Western Province players to play the French at Wellington. Playing with Alan Skene, Tommy Gentles, Chris Koch and Dawie Ackerman, Gillespie scored a try in their 38–8 win. Eight members of the team were chosen for the national team to play the French in the second test four days later. Significantly Skene, Gillespie's midfield partner was among them. Gillespie then became a victim of the Boland selectors' inconsistency and was relegated to playing club rugby. He rejoined Hamiltons RFC.

In 1958, with Ronnie Colin's return to Cape Town, Gillespie actively pursued the possibility of a rugby league career. As rumours about his pending defection reached the local media, the SA Rugby Football Board suspended him, Tony Forster and Alan Skene. He appealed against his suspension. After a relatively short wait, his suspension and those of his co-accused was finally lifted in December 1958 only for them to accept offers to switch codes. Their actions prompted the local media to question the purpose of preventative suspensions since they had not stopped behind-the-screens negotiations.

Gillespie signed for York at the beginning of 1959, and made his first team debut at centre in March 1959. York finished 11th in the league that season and were not one of the sport's leading clubs. Gillespie had been paid £2,000 for a three year deal. He played three matches in his first season, without scoring a try. However, he won a regular first team place on the wing in the 1959–60 season, scoring 20 tries in 34 matches. He was the club's top try scorer. Despite his efforts, York dropped down the table to 21st place. Much to York's annoyance, he then returned to South Africa, breaking his contract. York subsequently tried to take legal action against him, but could not enforce the judgement because South Africa had left the Commonwealth and were outside the jurisdiction of British courts. Gillespie played association football when he returned to South Africa, but returned to rugby league in 1962 when he played in the National Rugby League.

Photo: Hugh Gillespie (Courtesy Hendrik Snyders)

Another of Gillespie's colleagues who had been suspended joined Whitehaven. Tony Forster was 23 years old when he signed a three year deal with the Cumbrian club in January 1959. He got a £1,000 tax-free payment, but, according to Harry Edgar in *Chocolate, Blue and Gold*, his history of the club "just didn't make it in rugby league". He was groomed to take over at full-back from club stalwart John McKeown. He kept his place for the second half of the 1958–59 season, but when McKeown rejoined the club lost his spot and was restricted to playing for the 'A' team. Whitehaven tried to find him another club, and he had trials at Leeds, Bradford Northern, Leigh and Blackpool. The club agreed to release him from his contract and even paid his fare back to South Africa. He made less than 20 first team appearances.

In October 1959, St Helens signed Percy Landsberg. He was born in Kitwe in Northern Rhodesia, and had been playing rugby union for the Nchanga club in Rhodesia, the Transvaal under-19 side and Rhodesia. With his compatriots Tom van Vollenhoven and Jan Prinsloo holding down the winger positions, and veteran Duggie Greenall at centre, he found it difficult to win a regular first team place. He made his debut on 7 November 1959 against Liverpool City, and played the last of his 22 first team matches against Whitehaven almost exactly a year later. He scored two tries, kicked 11 goals in the first team, and returned to South Africa to play association football.

In January 1963, St Helens wrote to the National Rugby League in South Africa, trying to arrange a player-exchange for Landsberg. Their letter said that he was "an excellent goalkicker and an outstanding ball handler. During his stay in this country he played regular first team rugby for St Helens and can now be classed as an experienced rugby league player." Saints had noted that Jan Prinsloo was trying to play in South Africa, and were pointing out that they held Landsberg's registration.

Photo: Tony Forster (Courtesy *Rugby League Journal*)

9. 1961: Arrivals and departures

In 1960, although various South Africans continued to play for their clubs, there were no new arrivals until Tom Moodie signed for Leigh in December, although he only arrived in January 1961. This was reported as Leigh's first deal with for a Commonwealth rugby union player. Moodie played at second row or loose-forward. He was 22 years old and came from Lusaka in Northern Rhodesia, where he played for the Harlequins club. He had scored 50 tries in a season and a half, was 6 feet 2 inches tall and weighed 13½ stones. He worked as a chartered secretary and had made representative appearances for West and East Transvaal.

However, Moodie never played for the first team at Leigh, although he was joined there by three of his compatriots. Ted Brophy was also at the club, having signed from Blackpool in 1959.

The best player to join English rugby league from South Africa in 1961 was undoubtedly Colin Greenwood. He signed for Wakefield Trinity in July 1961. Earlier in the year they had signed Jan Prinsloo from St Helens, Alan Skene was still at the club and they later recruited Gert 'Oupa' Coetzer. Trinity were one of the game's top clubs at this time, and their great sides of the 1960s usually contained at least one South African.

Colin Marius (Col) Greenwood

Colin Greenwood was another Springbok who won one cap before switching codes. He played against Ireland in Cape Town in May 1961, and signed for Wakefield Trinity a month later, becoming the fifth South African since 1958 to join the club.

Greenwood was born on 25 January 1936 in Cape Town. He played for Northerns and Western Province, and had been in the trials for the 1960–61 tour of Great Britain and France, and was considered unlucky not to be selected. He joined Trinity for a signing on fee of £4,000, a club record for a rugby union recruit. He came to Trinity as a result of the club chairman's scouting trip to South Africa in March 1961.

Greenwood made his debut for Trinity against York at the start of the 1961–62 season. He played at centre in union, but at Wakefield became a utility player, at times finding it hard to establish a regular place in one of the strongest sides in English rugby league at the time. A profile of him in a booklet produced to mark Trinity's cup wins in the early 1960s said that "He was left centre in Trinity's record breaking 1st round Yorkshire Cup win over Bradford Northern; stand-off half against the 1961 New Zealanders – and on the left wing in the Yorkshire Cup Final against Leeds." [46]

That Yorkshire Cup Final, a 19–9 win against Leeds, was his first honour in rugby league. He played in the first round of the Challenge Cup, but did not appear in the competition again that season as Trinity went on to win it. However, in 1962–63, he played in the first round, a 15–3 win over Bradford Northern, and then did not play again until the Final, when Trinity beat Wigan 25–10 at Wembley.

On the international scene, he played for a Rugby League XIII against a French XIII in October 1961, when six of the team were South African, including all the backs and Ted Brophy in the pack. In 1963 he played for the South African tourists against Australia and New Zealand and scored two tries against Australia in a 54–21 defeat.

Overall for Wakefield Trinity he played 75 matches, scoring 32 tries. He then joined his compatriot Fred Griffiths at North Sydney. He also took his family to Australia, like Griffiths, and according to Andrew Moore, was "an enterprising figure both on and off the field. Within a fortnight of arriving in Sydney he had moved out of the motel room the club had provided for him because he considered it too expensive, and found himself a house to buy... as well as a job and a car." [47] Greenwood made 77 appearances for Norths, scoring 24 tries. He became captain-coach in 1968, which ended in controversy. Despite many innovations introduced by Greenwood, the team struggled. Moore comments that "He had moved swiftly to overturn the more lackadaisical methods of his immediate predecessors. Special pre-season training sessions for backs and forwards were introduced to enhance stamina and strength. These were followed by iced fruit juices rather than beer. He had moved to standardise 'moves' within the club so that player substitutions would not be unnecessarily disruptive. Detailed statistics were maintained about tackles, moves and penalty counts."[48]

The club introduced the English coach Roy Francis to take over from Greenwood, initially as a 'guest' for six weeks. Not surprisingly, Greenwood was upset. The issue was further complicated as Francis was black, and had been the first black player to play for Great Britain in 1947. Moore points out that Greenwood was not consulted about the change, and was aggrieved because his requests for a goalkicker to the club management had been turned down earlier in the year on financial grounds, yet now they could afford Francis.

Francis hoped Greenwood would stay at the club as player in 1969, but that was never really possible. Greenwood took court action against the club, and denied any animosity towards Francis, writing him a supportive letter in February 1969. He denied any element of racism in his refusal to work with the new coach. This incident took place at a time when international concern was growing about the apartheid regime. The England cricket tour to South Africa had been abandoned following the selection of Basil D'Olivera by the MCC in 1968. The opposition to tours by the South African rugby union team was developing. It would be surprising if Greenwood was not influenced by his upbringing and background in South Africa, although many of the South African players who came to Great Britain did play with black team-mates, seemingly without problems.

Greenwood moved on to Canterbury Bankstown in 1969, played a couple of games there and returned to South Africa in 1971. In 1995, after the election of the first democratically elected government, led by President Nelson Mandela, he wrote to Andrew Moore saying that he believed there was a "fashionable bandwagon of bringing politics into the picture particularly in the South African context. Many of us have acquired a tolerance for the naivety of foreigners who have absolutely not the slightest grasp of the complexity of our problem in South Africa, and who either identify with a particular Populist viewpoint or have the audacity to solve our problems." [49]

Greenwood's son played rugby league in South Africa when the game was relaunched in 1989. Colin Greenwood died on 3 October 1998 in George in the Western Cape, aged 62.

Rugby league's attention was now drawn to potential recruits among the Coloured and African (then known as 'Bantu') rugby players. Rugby union was a popular sport among the Coloured community in the Western Cape. It also had a significant following in the African majority population in areas such as the Eastern Province and Transvaal, although association football was their main winter game.

In a rigidly racially segregated society there were few opportunities for players from either community to progress. Playing for the South African Coloured XV or Bantu XV respectively was the height of their aspirations. There was no racially mixed sport allowed, so the possibility of playing for the country's best clubs, provincial teams or national side was firmly barred to them.

Signing for an English rugby league club for a white player gave them the chance of overseas travel, to earn something through their rugby skills and to maybe put some money by to use when they returned home. For a Coloured or African player, the stakes were much higher; the opportunity to play a sport at the highest possible club level, and to be part of a society where – while there was certainly racism – would treat them more equally than ever seemed possible at that time in South Africa.

Some players adjusted to these opportunities more easily than others, as will become clear later in this book, but for all of them it was a huge opportunity.

Among the first to leave, on the eve of receiving his fourth national cap for the South African Coloured Rugby Football Board (SACRFB) team, in 1961 was Goolam Abed, accompanied by Louis Neumann [50] of Thistles Rugby Football Club, Western Province and the City & Suburban Rugby Union. Their deal was facilitated by former Springbok Louis Babrow and Jim Windsor, a Yorkshire bookmaker. As unknowns in the white mainstream media, but armed with the recommendation of a former white Springbok, both players were offered a guaranteed paid return trip and a stint as amateurs, but with no guarantee of a professional contract [51] with Leeds RLFC. In contrast, their white counterparts based on their reputations (and possibly even race) were able to secure such contracts even before leaving South Africa.[52] Playing as amateurs, meant that the rookies still had to prove their worth before being considered for a more substantial and professional contract.

In *Forgotten Heroes* by Abdurahman Booley, Abed is described as a "...well-built fly-half [with] all the ingredients to make him a player of class. Goolie was a devastating runner of the ball, and with his high jinks, always difficult to tackle." The profile also says that his first love was cricket, and he played with Basil D'Olivera for the South African Coloured team.

After his debut match against Hunslet, Abed, a back, struggled to establish himself in a very competitive environment. Neumann, on the other hand, had far less problems as a forward and was able to make his mark right from the outset. Ironically, within the Leeds set-up both players find themselves as equals to their white compatriot and former Springbok centre Wilf Rosenberg. After a bumpy start as a trialist and with the assistance of Rosenberg,[53] Abed sufficiently impressed the scouts and was offered a five year contract worth £1,000 per year as a centre and wing by Bradford Northern (now the Bradford Bulls).[54] Northern had been one of the sport's leading clubs after the Second World War, but since the mid–1950s had been in a gradual spiral of decline. The club eventually collapsed in

December 1963, only to be re-launched the following year and rejoined the Rugby League for the start of the 1964–65 season.

During his three year stint at the club, he played in 46 first team matches, scoring five tries and 55 goals.[55] This was followed by a further two seasons with Batley RLFC where he continued his good form and played 36 first team matches, with four tries and 44 goals, before his eventual retirement as a result of an injured shoulder.[56]

Interviewed later about his experiences in England, Abed remarked: "I left South Africa because I was restricted there and could not develop further. Although there was racial prejudice on the part of spectators at the time, in Britain I tasted freedom and far less restrictions than in South Africa. It was difficult at times when players on other teams made comments about colour and nationality. But I usually ended up having a drink with them and becoming firm friends" [57]

Having experience the folding of his first rugby league club, Abed diversified his interests and used the full range of his capabilities. As an accomplished cricketer, he developed a parallel cricketing career in the summer outside the then professional rugby league season. Retirement from rugby in 1967–68 signalled the beginning of a professional cricket career with Rochdale Cricket Club in the Central Lancashire League. Based on a successful spell at his first club, he secured further spells, both as a professional and amateur with Castleton Moor, Balshaw (Bolton Cricket Association) and Nelson cricket clubs. In addition to this, as a qualified printer engraver he established and developed a printing and engraving business in Rochdale. He successfully combined his professional career with various community-orientated roles on and off the field of play. Through this civic-orientation, he earned the respect of all and was honoured by his community as the "cricketer who broke down the racial barriers." [58]

In 2010, Abed, now living in Cape Town, joined an elite band of sporting stars when he was awarded the Order of Ikhamanga for his contribution to South African sport. He received the accolade from the South African president, Thabo Mbeki, at a ceremony in Johannesburg.

After his successful Leeds debut, Neumann fully established himself in his new code and went on to play 158 first team games for Leeds. He scored 16 tries and kicked a goal for a total of 50 first team points. Arguably, he was one of the most successful South African forwards in English rugby league in this period.

In 1967 he left Leeds having secured a contract with the Australian club, Eastern Suburbs (later the Sydney Roosters) where he stayed for four seasons, 1967 to 1971. During this time, he made 81 first team appearances for the club. In addition, he earned further accolades by becoming their player-coach during a difficult 1969 season, a mere two years after moving to Australia and added another 22 matches as coach, albeit with mixed successes, to his league record.[59] Having made his name with one of Australia's foremost clubs,[60] he obtained a new contract with Orange RLFC in New South Wales.[61] Louis Neumann stayed in Australia and died in 2003.

Top left: Louis Neumann.
Top right: Goolam Abed.

(Both photos: Courtesy Robert Gate)

Bottom right: Duncan Pikoli.

71

Abed and Neumann, along with Noor 'Gubby' Daniels – who joined Barrow – were the first players from the Coloured community in South Africa to switch to rugby league, the first player from the African community also came to England in 1961, when Andile (Duncan) Pikoli joined Barrow. He was accompanied by Daniels, who never played for the first team, but Pikoli did go on to establish himself in rugby league.

Pikoli joined Barrow from the Butcher Birds club in May 1961. He had also played for the Port Elizabeth Eagles, and been 'capped' for the South African Bantu team. He joined Barrow when the club was declining from the heights they had reached in the mid–1950s. He made his debut at Doncaster on 19 August 1961, and played 16 matches in the first team that season on the wing, scoring three tries. He also worked as a nurse at North Lonsdale Hospital. In May 1963, having not played in the Barrow fist team for a year, he joined Liverpool City, initially on loan. He made a handful of appearances for them in the 1963–64 season before retiring from rugby league. A pen-picture of him in the Liverpool City programme for their match against York on 7 December 1965, said that Pikoli was five feet eight inches high, weighed 11 stones 11 pounds and was a "clever and speedy winger".

Pikoli was a political activist with links to the then banned African National Congress (ANC); and did not place all his hopes on a rugby league career. As a committed and proud South African, it was his hope to play an active role in freeing his homeland and to bear witness to the demise of apartheid. This stance and open support for the banned political movements, led to the refusal of the apartheid government to issue him with a new passport in 1982 and resulted in his formal political exile. Unable to return home, he enrolled for a degree in social work at Middlesex Polytechnic. Upon graduation, he set up home in Surrey and embarked on his chosen career with the City of Westminster. When he became eligible for British citizenship, he refused on political grounds to apply for it. [62] He had told his son that he was 'a proud South African' and had hoped to return home permanently one day.

Duncan Pikoli died in 2004, still living in England. He had lost touch with his family in South Africa after his last visit to them in Port Elizabeth in 1995. He had said that he wanted to be buried in South Africa, and arrangements were made to bring his body home.

Another player from the Coloured community to come to England was Salie Schroeder. He signed for Doncaster. The south Yorkshire club had only joined the Northern Rugby League in 1951, and generally had struggled on and off the pitch. Schroeder coming to England to play rugby league was to end in tragedy.

Salie Schroeder

Salie Schroeder played rugby union for the Rosslyn club in Cape Town, and represented the Western Province Coloured team. He was in his early 20s when he joined Doncaster in the summer of 1961, and made his debut at the end of August against Hull KR, when he scored a try. He only played three more games for the first team, the last at Salford on 23 September. He broke his wrist and did not play for the first team again, although he did return to the 'A' team before the end of the season. He played both at centre and on the wing. However, he was popular with the Doncaster supporters and was seen to have potential in his new code.

Negotiations for his transfer had been held up because a Paarl Moslem girl alleged he was trying to leave without providing for her. She said he had married her in a Muslim ceremony. The Doncaster club paid him a signing-on fee of more than £500.

However, tragedy struck in July 1962. He had fallen in love with a local 19-year-old girl, Margaret Stephanie Raynes. Her father owned a smallholding near the club's ground. In June she broke off the relationship, saying that there was something in his 'love life' in South Africa which made it impossible for them to marry.

The *Johannesburg Star* reported that Schroeder had told a friend: "My life is over now. I don't want to play rugby again and I don't want to work. Stephanie meant everything to me. The club have told me to take a holiday and try to forget the girl. They say that if I make any trouble they will send me back to South Africa." A police spokesman said Schroeder called on a friend in London a few days ago and asked where he could get a revolver. The friend said he could not help.

The club history records that "Schroeder was besotted by the girl and to attract her attention he once tried to throw himself under a bus on Arskey Road. However, her wish not to continue the relationship upset Schroeder, a devout Muslim, and after finding she was seeing another man, he bought a gun with the money the club had given him to take a break back in his own country and murdered her in the doorway to Berry's Ballroom in Printing Office Street. Schroeder then turned the gun on himself and committed suicide." Just before the shooting, Schroeder had been in a friend's office in Doncaster, and had been talking about a girl he had met while on holiday in Paris. [63]

It was rare for a South African player to stay long enough in England to be given a testimonial, which were normally only awarded after 10 years service to a club. One who did was Johnny Gaydon.

Johnny Gaydon

From the players' perspective, the period 1960 to 1964 was a bad one for those ambitious South Africans and Rhodesians eager to progress in rugby union. With the Springboks due to play both overseas and at home against touring sides, the domestic season for four years had no Currie Cup rugby. With opportunities to play representative rugby at a premium, young players had to show their mettle in domestic competitions. Emerging talented players, such as Johnny Gaydon, who played on the wing or in the threequarters, therefore had to make do with either playing in the regional Clark Cup competition as a member of Northern Rhodesia teams or the odd match against visiting select teams, such as the Northern Transvaal Districts XV, that visited Rhodesia. Occasional visits also came from the other side of the border by the East African Rugby Football Union – today the Kenya RFU. As a player with Mufulira RFC in the north of the country (today part of Zambia), Gaydon's club played in the local club league competition against affiliates to the Rhodesia Congo Border RFU.

Rugby in the northern territory (or the 'Copper Belt'), as mentioned elsewhere, was an important social activity. Representative rugby in these areas was often special games between regional and sub-national combination teams such as Copper Belt XV and Midlands

XV. Competitions included the Raymond Brookes Cup and Werner Cup. Also, Northern Rhodesia came second to the south in most team sports which further constricted representative opportunities.

Despite these limitations, Gaydon made an impression and was chosen for the Rhodesian XV to face Colin Meads' All Blacks at Nkana, the copper-mining section of Kitwe, in June 1960. The Rhodesian side in the 1959 Currie Cup competition was not 'particularly impressive', so the team needed some new talent. Gaydon, one of 11 Northern Rhodesian players in the side, like many of his team mates, failed to really grasp the opportunity to make his mark. The game was described by contemporary rugby writers as the 'poorest display' by an All Black touring team since 1953–54 when they played California on their way home from Great Britain. The home team, however, was complimented for having 'tackled with spirit and gave a good account of themselves at forward'. Although they lost 13–9, they emerged with a measure of credibility. Gaydon, however, failed to shine and was dropped for the second game against the tourists. The Northern Rhodesian side, however, performed well in the Clark Cup and twice beat their Southern counterparts 18–8. Thanks to solid performances on the domestic scene, Gaydon showed his undoubted talent and ability despite the lack of opportunities. As a result of the impact made by fellow Rhodesian-based players like Tom van Vollenhoven, Freddie Griffiths, Athol Brown and Ted Brophy, at the end of the 1960 season John Gaydon went in search of further opportunity and ventured into rugby league.

Gaydon became another South African recruit for St Helens. However, his opportunities on the wing at Knowsley Road were very limited. On one flank was Tom van Vollenhoven, on the other Great Britain international Mick Sullivan. He made his first team debut on 18 March 1961, at Halifax. In front of 12,000 fans Saints won 19–12, and he marked his debut with a try. He scored in his next match, at Barrow and then touched down twice against Salford in a 45–2 win at Knowsley Road, so had scored four tries in his first week in the first team. Although he played a further six matches that season, and four in 1961–62, scoring one try, he was never going to win a regular first team place on the wing. His last match for Saints was at Whitehaven on 7 October 1961. He was again on the winning side, but then signed for Widnes, joining former Saints Alan Briers and Jim Measures there.

Widnes supporter Phil Fearnley reflects on his time at Naughton Park: "For Widnes fans of a certain age, South African Johnny Gaydon, is held in deep affection. He was known to the fans on the terraces simply as Johnny. His arrival at Naughton Park cost £3,000, a tidy sum for the time, on a five year contract. Rumours of his arrival circulated for some time before it happened in 1961. Joe Egan, the club's coach, looked to add pace to the team and neighbours St Helens were overloaded on the wings with Tom van Vollenhoven and the formidable Mick Sullivan.

Details in the press and match programmes of the day tended to describe him as both South African and wearing a beard as if it was some medical attachment. Nearer the mark was a modest and unassuming man with a ready smile who proved to be tremendously loyal to the Chemics. He gave yeoman service to the men in black and white for over a decade. This was reciprocated by the club and its supporters with a testimonial in 1972. He was 5 feet 10 inches tall and weighed in at 11 stones 10 pounds. He was aged 23 when he made his Widnes debut. Between 1961 and 1971 he played 314 times for the first-team, scored 116 tries and kicked four goals (all in the 1966–67 season). Overall, he scored 356 points for the first team.

After a satisfactory first team debut in a 10–5 win at Barrow, curious local fans provided a slightly larger crowd than could be expected for the visit of Liverpool City's second string for his home debut. Widnes won a poor match 16–6 with Gaydon providing the only flashes of excitement with two late tries that would be his trade mark. He had a distinctive running style of chin-up, a flurry of arms and legs, a swerve and side-step across the pitch before a final straightening-up burst to finish. On his day he was one of the most entertaining players in the 1960s.

From memory, two tries stand out: a third round Challenge Cup tie at home against Hull Kingston Rovers beginning on the halfway touchline and ending under the posts; and a length of the field effort against Featherstone Rovers. French visitors Cavaillon conceded a hat-trick of tries in May 1968 in the new era of limited tackles.

But none of his tries was as crucial as the one he scored in a 1964 Challenge Cup quarter-final second replay against champions and cup favourites Swinton witnessed by over 21,000 at Wigan with a midweek afternoon kick-off. One spectacular run ended inches from the line before being slammed into touch. A few minutes later he roared under the posts to score after a Ray Owen break and Arthur Hughes carry. Widnes had booked their place in the semi-finals against a talented Castleford team and Wembley fever spread throughout the town. Johnny played in a 7–7 draw before 25,000 at Station Road, Swinton but following a fitness test on an injured thigh lost his place to Billy Thompson for the replay at Belle Vue, Wakefield. Thompson's opportunist kick and chase from half-back saw him score the decisive try but note was also made of his strong defence. On this basis, Thompson who had not been a first team regular, took the wing berth at Wembley in front of Johnny. Despite this huge disappointment as the Chemics took the cup from Hull Kingston Rovers, his loyalty never wavered.

This flying winger had contributed greatly on the road to Wembley starting in the first eight of nine ties. It took a record number of gruelling games for Widnes to reach the final. The 1964 Challenge Cup produced more draws and subsequent replays than any other year until the introduction of extra time and golden point made replays obsolete.

His final game for the Widnes first team was at Headingley on 12 October 1971, a 33–6 defeat to Leeds. He had played the first 16 matches of the season, and also made 9 appearances for the 'A' team that season. His testimonial match was at Widnes on 4 June 1972. It was his misfortune that Widnes did not build on their 1964 Challenge Cup Final triumph, and he never played in a cup final in any competition for the club. Widnes's great days were just around the corner.

Gaydon won international status on South Africa's tour of Australia and New Zealand in 1963. He turned out at centre against the Kiwis in Auckland, when South Africa won 4–3 in a mud bath and against the Kangaroos in Brisbane on the wing, a 34–6 defeat. He scored three tries on the tour. He was also selected for a Rugby League representative side against a Paris XIII in May 1966 at the famous Parc des Princes stadium. The French side won 20–0.

NAUGHTON PARK :: WIDNES

JOHN GAYDON TESTIMONIAL MATCH.

JOHN GAYDON XIII

v

WIDNES-BORN TEAM

Sunday, June 4th, 1972

SOUVENIR PROGRAMME 2p

Left: The cover from the match programme for John Gaydon's testimonial match at Widnes.
(Courtesy Phil Fearnley)

Right: Johnny Gaydon
(Photo: Courtesy Robert Gate)

Never too proud to play for the 'A' team, he turned out in 24 matches scoring 11 tries. He is remembered as a speedy try scoring winger, and an excellent ambassador for the club off the pitch. He was a model professional in an era of part-time players, lighting up dull, winter afternoons in the monochrome 1960s of a heavy chemical town."

When John Gaydon retired from rugby league he returned to South Africa and lived in Johannesburg. In 2009, he moved, with his wife Jean, to Vermont on the Western Cape. On his return he played rugby union for a junior club. Interviewed by Dennis Glynn in 2012 for *Rugby League Journal*, he said that he supported rugby league in South Africa, but believed that the code faced an uphill struggle to become established there. He is still in contact with George Nicholls, who he believes is the hardest and most skilful forward from his time in the game. He says that his most fearsome opponent was Billy Boston.

Gaydon is proud to have been considered a success in English rugby league, and said that his career in England was a hugely enjoyable adventure, despite the disappointment of not playing in the 1964 Challenge Cup Final.

Another club to sign South African players at this time was Workington Town. The club had only joined the Northern Rugby League in 1945. In the 1950s the club had been successful under the direction of Gus Risman, but in the last two seasons of that decade had dropped down the table. They hoped that their new recruits, Piet Pretorius and Japie Ferreira, could revive their fortunes.

Jacobus 'Japie' Ferreira and Pietrus (Piet) Johannes Pretorius

In 1961, Workington Town signed two South African backs, Japie Ferreira and Piet Pretorius. They found some success at the game's most northern professional club, but only completed two years of five year contracts. As with some other South Africans, the bitter cold of the 1963 winter was too much for them.

In his rugby union playing days, from 1957 to 1961, Japie Ferreira, like so many of his Vereeniging RFC contemporaries, never had the honour of lifting the coveted Pirates Grand Challenge Cup of the Transvaal Rugby Union. Neither was his club a prodigious producer of provincial players for the Transvaal Currie Cup side. On his debut in 1957, Ferreira became only the seventh Vereeniging representative in the Transvaal provincial side. Similarly, after Felix Du Plessis, he became only the second Vereeniging player to play against an international team when he represented a Transvaal XV against the New Zealand All Blacks in 1960.

The Springboks 1956 overseas tour meant that the Currie Cup competition that year was severely weakened, with many key players away. Provincial players therefore looked with great anticipation towards the 1957 season as one that would offer real competition rather than friendly provincial matches. That season, Ferreira's debut year under the captaincy of Natie Rens, Transvaal played nine matches and after a string of good performances, played against Western Province for the SA Board Trophy. Ferreira, however, did not make the team for the final on 28 September at Newlands, Cape Town and was spared the disappointment of a 12–5 defeat.

The 1958 season saw the arrival of the British Barbarians and the French touring teams. Although Transvaal fielded both a senior side and two combined sides against the visitors, Ferreira did not make it for any of these matches and therefore could not accumulate any experience against international opposition. He did, however, maintain his place in the senior team that over the course of the season played seven friendly games.

At the Annual General Meeting of the Transvaal Rugby Union in 1959, all clubs were warned about liaisons with rugby league agents intent on recruiting players to turn professional. Against this background, Transvaal embarked on the second leg of the Currie Cup competition which saw Ferreira yet again an integral part of the team. Following a string of solid performances, he made it into the last – and deciding – match of the competition in September 1959 at Ellis Park. Western Province, coming back after trailing and a prolonged period of high-intensity battle, secured an 11–11 draw and the championship to deny Transvaal and Ferreira a taste of Currie Cup glory.

The 1960 season was the beginning of a decade of rugby in which 13 international touring teams visited South Africa. This gave Ferreira his first taste of international matches when he was selected for the Transvaal XV instead of the senior side against the New Zealand All Blacks. Playing at fly-half in combination with Landsberg of Westfield RFC, he opposed his Auckland counterpart Nesbitt in a match that the home side lost 9–3. With 1960, however, not being a Currie Cup season (postponed until 1964), Ferreira lost the opportunity to play in more representative games and could therefore not really challenge for national honours. With only short tours by Ireland and the Australian Wallabies and a limited number of games against select rather than provincial combinations, Ferreira's competitive career effectively came to the end.

Although Vereeniging RFC had a much lower profile than Diggers and Pirates in the Transvaal Rugby Union's premier competitions; it contributed a number of talented players to the provincial side. Other than Japie Ferreira, Vereeniging also groomed Piet Pretorius for life in the Pirates Grand Challenge and for the tough SA Rugby Football Board Trophy and Currie Cup competitions. A speedy winger, Pretorius played with and under the captaincy of high profile Springboks like Natie Rens and Manntjies Gericke, stalwarts in the Johannesburg-based provincial outfit. He also had to compete for a place against Springbok speedsters Jan Prinsloo (Police), Michael Antelme (University of Witwatersrand) and Hennie Van Zyl (Diggers).

His representative provincial debut came in 1959, a Currie Cup year. Diggers continued to dominate Transvaal rugby with back-to-back wins in the Pirates Grand Challenge competition. Pretorius therefore had his work cut out to keep his place in the provincial team. During the season, the team played several provincial friendlies as well as its Currie Cup matches. Pretorius played in many of these encounters. After a successful season, he kept his place in a star-studded team that included at least seven national players including Ackerman, Van Zyl, Rens, Pelser and Mickey Gerber to face Western Province in the last match of the series on 5 September, to decide who won the Board Challenge Trophy. Opposing them was a Western Province team that included Colin Greenwood and Charlie Nimb. In front of 24,000 fans, the two teams played out a hard-fought 11–11 draw. This did guarantee Western Province the trophy based on their first round performance in 1957.

Two weeks after the Board Final, the two sides, with Pretorius in the mix, faced each other again, this time for the Currie Cup. Despite playing at home, Transvaal lost 12–8. This again denied Pretorius a championship victory, but personally it capped a satisfactory season. This final was the end of Currie Cup rugby up to 1964 because of international tours. This made it harder for young players such as Pretorius to progress.

The 1960 season saw the All Blacks tour South Africa. This tour offered Pretorius and his peers an opportunity to sample international rugby. Although he missed out on selection for the senior Transvaal side for their match against the tourists, he was chosen for the Transvaal XV for their match at Ellis Park on 3 September 1960. This match, coming at the end of the tour against a relatively young and inexperienced side, was described by some rugby scribes as an 'anti-climax' and supposedly a 'swansong' and tension-free match'. Aiming to take revenge for the defeat of their seniors, the young Transvalers gave it their best. They were, however, defeated 9–3 after a hard-fought match in which Japie Ferreira and Landsberg also played. With no representative Currie Cup matches for the next four years, this match was effectively Pretorius's swansong and the end of his rugby union career. On the eve of the 1961 rugby union season, Pretorius signed for Workington Town RFLC, and left for the north of England to embark on a career in rugby league.

Ferreira and Pretorius joined Workington Town, and made their debuts against Hull KR in a 31–4 victory at Derwent Park in the first match of the 1961–62 season. Pretorius had signed for the club in March. Pretorius only missed three games in the season, playing on the left wing, and scored 28 tries from 37 matches. He was not, however, the club's top scorer. Workington legend Ike Southward scored 32 tries from the right wing. Japie Ferreira found it more difficult to win a regular place, and made 16 appearances, mainly at left-centre in a partnership with Pretorius.

Piet Pretorius scoring for Workington Town. (Photo: Courtesy *Rugby League Journal*)

Japie Ferreira. (Photo: Courtesy *Rugby League Journal*)

He scored three tries and kicked 30 goals, but was competing for the left-centre spot with Eddie Brennan, the team's regular goalkicker. The team ended the season in fifth place, an improvement on the previous season's 10th spot.

The following season, 1962–63 saw the Northern Rugby League split into two divisions for the first time since before the First World War. Workington started well and won the Western Division competition, a new initiative to provide more local fixtures to make up for the reduction in league fixtures. Workington had won all their eight fixtures, and in the play-offs beat Wigan before beating Widnes in the final after a replay. Pretorius played in both the final and the replay, and scored a try in each match.

The second half of the season was disrupted by dreadful winter, with only a handful of matches played between Boxing Day and the second week of March. Joe Holliday reflects in his history of the club: "...the early season successes were not to be repeated when the hard frost subsided, it seemed that the long lay-off had affected the fitness levels of some of the older players and the two South Africans had decided to go home away from the cold climate with winger Piet Pretorius only appearing in one match after the season restarted on 2 March 1963 and Jappie Ferreira failing to gain selection. Before the freeze, Pretorius had scored 16 tries in 17 matches, but played his last game on 2 March. Ferreira never established a regular place, and his 13 games included seven at full-back, two at right-centre and four at left-centre.

A newspaper report said that Pretorius was going home at the end of April and that Ferreira would probably go with him. He said that he had no quarrel with the club, although they had failed to find him an "acceptable" job and had "paid him a weekly wage for doing nothing". He also said that his wife "had not liked the long, cold winter" and that she was anxious to return home because her mother was unwell. He indicated that he would consider playing rugby league in South Africa, but Workington Town chairman Jim Graves said that he had signed a five year contract and would want a transfer fee for him.

Interestingly, Pretorius's efforts for Workington Town are not forgotten. In 2012, Joe Holliday, who wrote the club history, included him in his greatest ever Workington Town selection. He wrote in the *Workington Times & Star:* "South African-born Piet was a winger who only needed half a chance to leave defenders grasping at fresh air.

He crossed for 28 tries in his first season for Town and a further 16 in only 18 appearances the following term before deciding the harsh winter weather in West Cumbria was not to his liking and returned home. Had he stayed, I'm sure he would have gone on and scored many more tries and become a household name in the history of rugby league."

Three more players signed for Leigh in 1961, who are covered in the next chapter. One other South African recruit was Johannes de Klerk, who joined Huddersfield in July 1961. He found it difficult to win a first team place at one of the sport's top clubs, and only made his league debut in February 1962, having played in a pre-season friendly. He scored a try against Liverpool City, but did not play for the club's first team again. He made 11 appearances for the 'A' team, but was not retained by the club at the end of the season.

10. Trouble at Leigh

Since 1906, the Northern Rugby League had operated as one division. But for the 1962–63 season, it was agreed to split the league into two divisions, a First Division of 16 clubs and a Second Division of 14. This made the 1961–62 season a very competitive and important one.

On paper, Leigh should not have had any great concerns about making the cut for the top flight. In 1960–61, the club had finished sixth, just two points away from fourth place and the end-of-season play-offs which decided the Championship. Towards the end of the season they had signed Bev Risman from rugby union. Risman, a British Lion, went on to have a great career in rugby league.

The club also decided to look to South Africa for more recruits. They already had Ted Brophy in their ranks, and in January 1961 had signed Tom Moodie. In April three more players arrived; Kenneth Robert Boonzaier from Witwatersrand University, Pieter Johannes Botha from the Railway club in Bloemfontein who had played for the Orange Free State and Christoffel Hercules Landsberg from Westonaria in the Transvaal. The Leigh match day programme in January 1961 said that there was "Tremendous enthusiasm in the town for the South African signings." All of them seemed to have good credentials – Boonzaier was described as being six feet tall and weighing 13½ stones, was 22 years old, the top scorer in the Transvaal with 130 goals and could run 100 yards in 9.8 seconds. Piet Botha, who was 24 years old, was reputedly one of the top goalkickers in South Africa. The club had paid them both close to £4,000 to sign.

They had little chance to make much impact in the 1960–61 season. Ken Boonzaier played four matches, and scored two tries in a 46–11 win over Rochdale Hornets. Piet Botha played twice, in the final two games, and kicked eight goals in each. Landsberg also played in the last match of the season.

However, Leigh dropped down the table in the crucial 1961–62 season, and finished 17th – one place and four competition points from a place in the new First Division. It seems hard to blame Piet Botha for this decline – he played 31 matches and kicked 82 goals, putting him in the national top 20 goal scorers and points scorers. Ken Boonzaier also played regularly, and made 24 appearances, but only scored three tries – curiously a hat-trick against Batley. Chris Landsberg only played six matches, and scored once. Moodie never played for the first team. Michael Latham and Mike Hulme, in their club history, express their disappointment at the players' performances as well. They say that Leigh fans saw "little of that sort of speed" from Boonzaier who had run 100 yards in 9.8 seconds, and that Chris Landsberg was "another spectacular failure". They conclude that Leigh had "their fingers and pockets burned" through signing the South Africans, although they do not include Ted Brophy in this, who they say gave the club "loyal service".[64]

Comparing Leigh's records with the previous season, it is immediately noticeable that they only scored 72 tries, compared to 122 the previous year. Their top scorer was Gwyn Davies with seven tries, the previous year three players had reached double figures, with Mick Martyn scoring an impressive 22. Of the players the club signed, Danny Harris from Cardiff rugby union played nine games, Derek Fieldhouse from Salford RLFC played three matches and Stan Walmsley from Tyldesley RUFC played 23 matches. However, some of the club's more established players missed matches through injury.

In June 1962, the *Johannesburg Star* reported that a 'Storm' was brewing in League. Botha and Boonzaier had played in the first National Rugby League game for Vikings, without permission from Leigh. Apparently Leigh were expecting Botha to return, but the club said that Boonzaier had left the club without "saying a word". Leigh were considering taking legal action, and the players' appearances had wider implications for the National Rugby League. They would find it difficult to be recognized by the sport's authorities if they fielded players already registered with an English or Australian club. The report noted that Landsberg and Moodie had been removed from Leigh's register of players.

The next day, 29 June, the paper reported that Botha said ": "I saw Leigh officials when I was in London recently and everything seems to be sorted out." NRL official Gene Forster added: "We do not wish to damage our chances of recognition in England and I will immediately get in touch with them again. In any event, Botha will play as a guest player tomorrow."

However, this was not the end of the matter. On 15 August, under a headline 'South Africans caused club's woes', the *Star* reported that Leigh RLC chairman Jack Harding, who flew out to sign four South African players in 1961 at an estimated cost of R20,000 [£10,000] had placed the chief blame on them for the club's slide into the second division. In his annual report to shareholders, Mr Harding said that easy excuses could be found, such as repeated injuries, but the main reason was some inept performances by the team as a whole and the South Africans in particular. "It has to be admitted that the South African venture has been a complete failure" he said. "The players did not settle down in spite of every effort to make them comfortable. All were found good accommodation and jobs" he commented. "They might have settled down eventually but their wives were always homesick and wanting to return home." The four players were Tom Moodie, Chris Landsberg, Piet Botha and Ken Boonzaier. Ted Brophy was not blamed for the club's performances.

The next day, the paper reported Boonzaier's response, under the headline "'Never felt wanted at Leigh' says Boonzaier." The report said that "The submission by the Leigh RLC chairman Mr Jack Harding, that the chief blame for the club's slide into the Second Division could be placed on their former South African players, has brought an immediate reaction from one of them, Ken Boonzaier, who said today that the South Africans' hopes and beliefs were never fulfilled.

According to Boonzaier, the South Africans were promised jobs and houses that never materialised, and for 16 months had to contend with jealousy, even from their own team mates, who regarded them as interlopers, taking the bread out of their mouths.

Boonzaier alleges that for two months he walked Manchester looking for a job and a house, after he and his wife were initially billeted in a single room. When he appealed to the directors, he was told that the club was not a charitable organisation. He had been offered a job at R16 [£8] a week and his wife one for R7 [£3.50]. In the end he had to buy a house with his signing on fee.

Leigh team at Wigan September 1961. Ken Boonzaier is on the front row far left, Piet Botha third from left, Chris Landsberg fifth from left. (Photo: Courtesy Michael Latham)

Boonzaier denied that the South Africans' poor form caused the club's slump. "At one time they had eight first team players injured and they had no option but to bring in Piet Botha (the former Free State full-back) and myself. Botha was so bad that he scored threequarters of the club's total points tally, and finished seventeenth highest scorer in the league. I wonder what more they expected of him." He concluded: "I challenge the fact that the club did everything to help us settle down. We never felt wanted the whole time we were there.'"

With many rugby union players switching codes, both to play league in South Africa and England, no doubt this was good news for that code's followers. The dispute does illustrate the problems facing rugby migrants – to set up home and find work in a new country very different from home; to hope that their families also settled; and to learn a new code of rugby when there were great expectations of them because of the fees paid to sign them. The latter point was often one that caused resentment among established rugby league professionals – seeing new recruits to the code given large signing on fees, when young rugby league amateurs were not given such rewards.

Although the movement of players to England was now starting to slow down, there is no evidence that the experience of the Leigh players discouraged others from moving. In fact, with rugby league tenuously being established in South Africa, the possibility for English clubs of signing players who already had some rugby league experience was becoming apparent. However, while some players had been successful in England, others had either failed to make the grade or had returned home prematurely. So the clubs did become more careful from 1963 onwards with their Southern African signings, and the regular flow of players which there had been from 1957 to 1962 dropped off to a trickle.

Ken Boonzaier played for the Rugby League South Africa side in all three matches against the British Lions in August 1962. However, he was not in the South African squad that toured Australia and New Zealand in 1963.

RUGBY LEAGUE XIII

(Colours — Red Jerseys and White Shorts)

1. **F. GRIFFITHS (Wigan) — Captain**
   Full Back

2. **T. VAN VOLLENHOVEN (St. Helens)**
   Right Wing

3. **A. SKENE (Wakefield T.)**
   Rt. Centre

4. **C. LANDSBERG (Leigh)**
   Left Centre

5. **B. BEVAN (Warrington)**
   Left Wing

6. **B. RISMAN (Leigh)**
   Stand-off

7. **B. SHILLINGLAW (Whitehaven)**
   Scrum-Half

8. **A. THOMPSON (Swinton)**
   Front Row

9. **L. McINTYRE (Oldham)**
   Hooker

10. **E. BATE (Widnes)**
    Front Row

11. **D. HARRIS (Leigh)**
    2nd Row

12. **L. GILFEDDER (Warrington)**
    2nd Row

13. **H. DUFFY (Salford)**
    Loose Forward

Left: The match programme showing four South Africans in a Rugby League XIII who beat the New Zealanders 22–20 at Manchester's White City Stadium on 20 September 1961. Alan Skene scored a try and Fred Griffiths kicked five goals.

Three weeks later, on 12 October, six South Africans played for a Rugby League XIII who lost 21–20 to a French XIII at Parc des Princes in Paris. Griffiths was at full-back, the threequarters were van Vollenhoven, Skene, Greenwood and Prinsloo and Ted Brophy played at prop.

Below: 1961 South Africa rugby union team versus Ireland. Charlie Nimb (back row, far left), Colin Greenwood (back row, second in from right), Martin Pelser (middle row, third from left) and Hennie van Zyl (middle row, fourth from left) all subsequently switched codes.
(Photo: Courtesy SA Rugby Museum)

11. 1962: Len Killeen and Trevor Lake

The launch of professional rugby league in South Africa in the summer of 1962 to some extent cut across the flow of players to England. Players now had a choice if they wanted to play rugby league – they could certainly earn more and play in a more high profile version of the sport if they came to England; but if they did not want to leave South Africa – and probably a relatively comfortable lifestyle, good climate and their homes and jobs, they could now play rugby league there.

The establishment of the National Rugby League and Rugby League South Africa also raised the possibility of English clubs signing players who had already played rugby league. Mike Brown and Charlie Nimb both moved to England in 1962 from South African rugby league clubs.

However, of the eight players who came to English rugby league clubs in 1962, the two who made the most impact were Len Killeen and Trevor Lake. They both went to Lancashire, Killeen to St Helens and Lake to the other side of Billinge, where he joined Wigan. Both were wingers and both had a major impact on their new sport.

Leonard Michael Anthony (Len) Killeen

Eighteen months after letting Jan Prinsloo move to Wakefield Trinity, St Helens signed Len Killeen, which meant that again Saints fielded two South African wingers. Unlike some of his compatriots who moved to rugby league in this period, he had not won Springbok honours, but arguably achieved more than most in rugby league. He was one of a handful of South African players to be successful both in England and Australia.

In South Africa he played union for Uitenhague Swifts and Eastern Province. He was the second Uitenhague player to switch codes, the other one being Wigan's Fred Griffiths. The agent who arranged the move was Griffiths's brother-in-law. Killeen had played on the wing for Uitenhague, but at full-back and on the wing for the Eastern Province side. He was a multi-talented sportsman, having won South Africa honours at basketball and played baseball.

Killeen worked as a locomotive fitter for South African railways before joining St Helens for a reported £4,000 signing-on fee, aged 23. He arrived at St Helens in June 1962, having recently married his wife Cathy. The Uitenhague local newspaper reporter said about his departure that "I have always felt that this young railway artisan was the most talented rugby player in our midst since Gordon Jordaan … I am confident he will do well in rugby league … There were opinions in certain rugby circles that he was the obvious man for a place on the next Springbok touring team to New Zealand as a utility player."

St Helens had made contact with Len Killeen through Albert Timms, who lived in Uitenhage. St Helens had to apply for Ministry of Labour permits (now a work permit) for Len and his wife Cathy. Club secretary Basil Lowe's letter to the Aliens Department of the Home Office said that "…we are prepared to employ him on the ground staff of this club …

We consider that the employment of an alien is reasonable as it is not possible at the moment to obtain first class wing-threequarters in this country..."

The work permit was agreed in September 1962, initially for one year, with Killeen being employed as an assistant sports instructor at St Helens College. Permission was also given for him to play professional rugby league. Killeen was given an initial £2,000 signing on fee, with a further £400 after playing six first team games.

After playing against Liverpool City in a pre-season match, he made his debut against Salford on 18 August. Alex Service in *The march of the Saints* said he was a "speedy, elusive runner with a fine pair of hands" and "proved he had all the credentials to make himself a big hit with the fans".

Killeen replaced Mick Sullivan in the Saints line-up, who had been transferred to York. He scored 25 tries in 27 matches in his first season, and was only beaten by van Vollenhoven, who finished on 33. He missed out on the Lancashire Cup Final, as Sullivan was still with the club. In 1963–64 he was less successful with only 13 tries in 29 matches, but did win his first medal in rugby league, helping Saints beat Swinton 10–7 at Central Park to win the Western Division Championship. [65]

The appointment of Joe Coan as coach at the start of the 1964–65 season saw a great period of success for both Saints and Killeen. He took over the goalkicking from Kel Coslett, and with 140 goals and 26 tries was the sport's top points scorer for the season with 358. One particularly memorable try came against Warrington at Knowsley Road. He gathered the ball behind his own line, burst through a gap in the Warrington defence and scored under the posts in the last minute of the match. He was too shattered to attempt the conversion.

His consistency contributed to Saints winning the Lancashire Cup, Lancashire League and the League Leaders Trophy. But the Championship did not end up at Knowsley Road. Sixteen clubs were allowed to enter the end of season play-offs that decided the title, and seventh placed Halifax proved too good for St Helens in the Final at Swinton, winning 15–7. Killeen scored all the Saints' points with a try and two goals.

Killeen really came to the fore in 1965–66. With Tom van Vollenhoven's scoring starting to decline, with only 18 tries, Killeen ended up as top try scorer and goalkicker in the game, with 32 tries and 120 goals from 44 appearances for 336 points – 22 less than the previous season. Saints missed out on the new BBC2 Floodlit Trophy; Killeen's kicking failed for once as Castleford won 4–0 in the Final.

However, in the Challenge Cup it was a different story. St Helens beat Hull KR with a controversial try from Alex Murphy in injury time at Knowsley Road in the third round, but it was Killeen's conversion that clinched their 12–10 victory. In the semi-final, Saints faced Dewsbury, whose captain was Mick Sullivan, the man Len had replaced at Knowsley Road. He scored all Saints' points – two tries and two goals – to give the Knowsley Road side a 12–5 victory. One of his tries was a 90-yard run following an interception near his own line.

At Wembley Saints faced the old enemy – Wigan. In a match memorable for allegations of dubious tactics by Saints, taking advantage of Wigan's lack of an experienced hooker to win penalties, Killeen scored a try, three penalties and two conversions – 13 of Saints' 21 points in their 21–2 win. And he missed the conversion of his own try, a fantastic piece of handling to touch down Bill Benyon's kick through. His second penalty was a remarkable effort – from five yards inside the Saints half and six yards from the right hand touchline.

Killeen won the Lance Todd Trophy for the man-of-the-match, telling the BBC's David Coleman that it was "just fantastic" to achieve his ambitions of winning the Challenge Cup and Lance Todd Trophy in one go. The *Rugby Leaguer's* headline for their match report was "Wonder-goal Killeen gets Lance Todd Trophy". He was only the second overseas player to win the trophy, after Ces Mountford, the first winger and the first South African.

A week later, Saints faced Halifax in the Championship Final. The league and cup double was secured with a 35–12 win over their conquerors the previous season. Killeen's contribution was a hat-trick of tries and six goals.

Killeen's final season at the club was 1966–67. Saints found little success in the cup competitions, but once again reached the Championship final. A 5–5 draw with Wakefield Trinity on 6 May was followed by a replay four days later at Swinton. A crowd of 33,537 saw Wakefield win their first Championship, beating Saints 21–9. Killeen kicked two goals, finishing with 148 and 19 tries for the season, a total of 353 points from 44 matches.

Much to the regret of St Helens supporters, 'Lenny the Lion' moved to Australian rugby league, joining Balmain in Sydney for a transfer fee of £4,500. In 187 appearances he had scored 115 tries, 408 goals and 1,161 points and finished as the sport's top scorer for the third consecutive season. In recognition of his achievements, he was later elected to the St Helens RLFC Hall of Fame.

In his book on 100 St Helens greats, Alex Service wrote that Killeen was "an unorthodox footballer and a brilliant entertainer. He could beat opposing defenders with sheer pace, a mesmerising body swerve, or kick over a helpless full-back and regather on his way to the try-line." Service also adds that he "was also one of the sweetest kickers of a rugby ball Saints' fans had ever seen."

His success continued in Australia. He played for Balmain until 1971, scoring 36 tries and 278 goals (including 8 drop-goals) in 78 appearances. He was part of Balmain's Premiership winning team in 1969, establishing a club record with 207 points from 9 tries and 90 goals, including six drop-goals. His Australian career concluded with 8 matches for Penrith in 1972, with two tries and 15 goals. He then retired and returned to South Africa. In 2009, Killeen and his wife Cathy were invited back to Balmain to attend a 40th anniversary of the club's memorable 11–2 victory over South Sydney in the 1969 final. Killeen had contributed two goals to help give Balmain a shock win. The club's press release said that Killeen headed the guest list at the event which was held at the Sydney Cricket Ground, the 1969 final venue.

At the time of writing, Len Killeen is the only South African winner of the Lance Todd Trophy. He is a member of both the St Helens and Balmain Halls of Fame. He died in Port Elizabeth on 31 October 2011.

Trevor Lake

Just as Fred Griffiths's Wigan career was coming to an end in November 1962, the club signed two new players from Southern Africa. One was full-back John Winton, who spent two years at Central Park before being sold to Oldham; the other was winger Trevor Lake.

In some ways it was a surprising signing, as Wigan already had Billy Boston and Frank Carlton as their wingers, but the Rhodesian flyer went on to make a major impact during his four years at Central Park.

Lake was born in Umtali in Rhodesia, and played rugby union as a flank forward at school. However, more success came when he switched to the wing. He played for Old Miltonians, the Matabeleland province side, Rhodesia and the Quagga team – a South African select team similar to the Barbarians. He also had three trials for the Springboks before being approached to join Wigan. Someone from Wigan who worked for the Rhodesia Iron and Steel Corporation approached him on behalf of the club, and he signed a four year contract with a £5,000 signing on fee.

He made his debut at Central Park on 3 November 1962, and scored two tries against Oldham in a 14–14 draw, with compatriot Winton missing with six kicks. Wigan skipper Eric Ashton recognised his talent: "He was a good finisher. You never had to look for him. If you broke, he'd be with you. He was a great talent." [66]

Lake had refused to play a trial for Wigan, and had made his debut only a few hours after arriving at the club. The supporters soon recognised his talent. Jack Winstanley wrote that "Lake was a winner in his five year career with Wigan. A sort of latter-day van Heerden without the compelling physique but the same sort of twinkle-in-the-eye charm, Trevor Lake was a no-nonsense, straight-talking individual who survived a high speed collision with a giraffe in his young days and later conquered the effects of a horrific works accident that snapped both his legs." [67]

He played 17 league matches in the weather-disrupted 1962–63 season, scoring 10 more tries to add to the two on his debut. But he did not feature in Wigan's Challenge Cup run, which took them to Wembley and a 25–10 defeat against Wakefield Trinity. Lake was a reserve on the big day, but went on to make two Final appearances during his time at Central Park.

Wigan finished runners-up in the first Division in 1963–64, but made little impact in the cup competitions. But for Lake it was a magnificent season, with 43 tries from 40 appearances. Even then he was not the top try-scorer in the game, Swinton's Johnny Stopford finished with 45. However, in 1964–65 he made up for the disappointment of missing out on the Challenge Cup Final in 1963. He played in every match on the way to Wembley, scored a try in the first round against Barrow and then got two against Swinton in the semi-final.

In the final Wigan faced Hunslet, and won 20–16 in one of the greatest finals of all time. Lake scored two of his team's tries. His first helped consolidate Wigan's lead in the first half, for his second he was put in by Ray Ashby and, according to Les Hoole, "swallow-dived in at the corner for a spectacular try." [68]

He also topped both his club and the national try scorers list with 40 from 34 appearances. Along with Gert Coetzer, Lake played for a Commonwealth XIII against the New Zealand tourists at the start of the 1965–66 season, although South Africa had left the Commonwealth in 1961. Wigan returned to Wembley for the Challenge Cup Final, this time to play local rivals St Helens. He missed the first round win over Halifax, but played in every other Challenge Cup match, including a four try haul against Whitehaven in the second round. But the final was an anti-climax, with Wigan lacking a regular hooker, they were unable to win possession at the scrums and lost 21–2. In the Championship they had finished third in the table, and lost in the semi-final to Halifax. He scored 32 tries in the season, once again topping the Wigan try scorers list, and finishing joint top with Len Killeen in the national list.

Wigan had last won the Lancashire Cup in the 1951–52 season. With only a few weeks left on his contract, and the club refusing to pay the £3,000 Lake wanted to extend it, his last act for Wigan was to help them win the long-elusive Lancashire Cup. He scored in the first round win at Leigh, missed the narrow win over St Helens in the second round, but then returned for the semi-final and final. His last match was the final, a 16–13 win over Oldham at Swinton. In four years at Central Park he scored 132 tries in 140 appearances, and was top try scorer for the club in the three full seasons he played.

He then signed for St George in Australia, following Fred Griffiths, Colin Greenwood and others to the ARL. He received a reputed £12,000 signing on fee, but the move was not a success. He only played eight matches in two years, scoring four tries. A knee injury in 1968 finished his career in Australia, and he returned to South Africa in 1969. He went on to develop a successful business career.

However, that was not the end of his involvement in rugby league. He attended the meeting in 1988 that Dave Southern and Tony Barker organised to re-establish the game in the country. He helped form the SARL, and became its president. However, along with Dave Southern, he left the organisation in 1993 to help form Mini-League. He still supports the game in his home country, and visits Wigan on occasions, where, according to Ian Morrison "fans still talk about his speed, his defensive work and, above all, his sporting nature." [69]

One of the qualities needed by any rugby winger is speed. In 1996, Ray Hewson produced a study of speed and rugby league players. He said of Trevor Lake: "Lake was… rather slim of physique for the rigouts of League rugby but lacked nothing in guts. Looking back, Lake was probably underrated by many in terms of speed which he possessed in abundance and coupled with the most elusive running style which was augmented by a long striding gait, he took many confident defences by surprise for, once away, he was virtually uncatchable." [170]

On Monday 24 September 1962, the *Johannesburg Star* reported that Mike Brown had been sold by National Rugby League club Johannesburg Celtic to Halifax for 8,000 Rand. Gene Forster, a Celtic director, said that "This money will be invested to enable us to buy more players. We know who we want and now we are in a position to approach them."

Brown was described as "a promising centre", who received only a "token percentage" of the signing-on fee (this was not actually correct), was under contract for four years – three with Halifax and a fourth back with Celtic. "He can stay in Britain longer, but then the fee increases," Forster explained. He said that Celtic had become a "sister club" of Halifax and it was their intention to exchange players in the off season. Celtic particularly wanted British forwards, as that was where the weakness in the South African game lay.

Mike Brown

Although the Simmer & Jack RFC do not exist anymore, the legacy of the once competitive and proud club with outstanding players like former Springbok and Wigan legend Attie van Heerden and centre Mike Brown continues to exist through the Germiston Simmer RFC today. An affiliate of the Transvaal Rugby Union (now the Golden Lions Rugby Union) in Johannesburg, the club in its heyday were the Pirates Grand Challenge Champions in 1921, 1922 and 1933; and the winner of the Survivor competition in 1919.

It also produced a significant number of players for the Transvaal province team as well as for the Springboks. Centred on the Simmer & Jack gold mine, the club attracted a lot of young rugby-loving men in search of employment. The mining company still exists today.

Brown played for the club in the late 1950s and early 1960s and was part of the setup when they lost the 1961 Grand Challenge Trophy by one point. With the advent of rugby league in South Africa, he joined Johannesburg Celtic and the ranks of the 13-man code. According to club sources, Simmer & Jack lost around 20 players to the new code and only Diggers RFC probably lost more players to rugby league. Similarly, the Germiston club suffered from the exit of key players as a result of the establishment of rugby league. This saw the two clubs to pool resources and to reconstitute themselves as Germiston-Simmer.

Johannesburg Celtic, affiliated to the National Rugby League (NRL), played in the newly-established competition, the NRL Cup. This pioneering competition kicked off on Wednesday 23 May 1962 at Milner Park with the match between Celtic and the Boksburg Vikings with Jakkals Keevy as referee. Brown played in this competition for the first NRL season and impressed sufficiently to win a contract with Halifax RFLC. He therefore became the first league transfer from a South African to a British club. In addition, according to the *Sunday Times* of 23 September 1962, a player exchange agreement between the clubs during their off-seasons was planned.

Halifax rugby league historian Andrew Hardcastle reflects on Mike Brown's time in England: "For English rugby league clubs in the early 1960s, the excitement of recruiting an overseas player had been largely denied to them. A ban on signing Australian and New Zealand rugby league and rugby union players had been in force since 1951. Halifax had been one of the last to get a deal through when they acquired the services of Kiwi centre Tommy Lynch, and he was a huge success – he is now a member of the club's Hall of Fame.

So, when in 1962 the directors heard of a South African centre called Mike Brown, their excitement was aroused. Could he be the player to bring back their glory days of the 1950s? Another Tommy Lynch? 'Two sources brought Mike to our notice,' wrote Secretary-Manager Bill Hughes in his programme notes for a match on 29 September, "and the recommendations were so strong that no time was lost by the chairman of our Football Sub-Committee in flying out to South Africa to clinch the deal." One of the sources was Ronnie Stansfield, a Halifax man and former local league player who had moved to South Africa and was refereeing in the newly-formed professional league. He had sent a programme for the Johannesburg Celtic versus Pretoria Vikings match, stressing how well Brown had played.

The Halifax directors were clearly intrigued by this new league, and discussed at boardroom level the idea of sending out some of their players during the summer to help establish the game. Club minutes show that a deal with Mike was quickly agreed, with £2,500 paid to him for a three-year contract – around £45,000 in today's money, so it was a large outlay for a rugby league club at that time.

He arrived in Halifax on Sunday 7 October, and met club officials and the press at the Thrum Hall ground the following day. He told them he was match fit, having played for Johannesburg Celtic during the summer and had trained since he signed for Halifax.

In those days it was the directors who selected the team, so it was no surprise that he was thrust straight into first team action. Halifax were in Division One of the newly created two-division system – the equivalent of today's Super League – and had a tough match on the Saturday against Hull Kingston Rovers. The *Halifax Courier* rugby league correspondent Roland Tinker was maybe more realistic than the directors. He reported in his match preview that "Brown has been moving well in training, but I reckon he is going to find his first senior game much more arduous than anything he has experienced before."

He was picked as centre partner to Halifax's legendary winger Johnny Freeman in a team that was missing a few regulars through injury. And it was Rovers who came out on top, recording their first league win at Thrum Hall since the Second World War, 19–11. No blame was attached to the newcomer. "Brown didn't get much of the ball," wrote Tinker. "However, he need not be disheartened, for he was as good as a lot of the more experienced players."

He kept his place for the following Saturday's trip through the Lake District to unbeaten Workington Town. Playing directly opposite him was John O'Neill, a proven top rugby league centre who had scored three tries against Wigan the previous Monday and already had 13 tries that season. O'Neill scored two more as Workington won comfortably 39–12 to leave Halifax bottom of the table, but again no blame was attached to the South African in match reports.

What he needed, though, was to gain some experience in the second team. The *Halifax Courier* reported on 26th October that "Mike Brown, who has not accustomed himself to our sort of weather or football, will play for the 'A' team at Huddersfield." Less harshly, the match programme explained that "Colin Dixon takes over the left centre berth from Mike Brown, who after his baptism in two strenuous matches, plays in the 'A' Team. He should be able to find his feet quicker in Yorkshire Senior Competition football than in the hurly-burly of the Fist Division." It added: "Mike, incidentally, starts work on Monday. His work permit is now complete. Once he settles down to his new life we are certain he will fulfil all expectations."

With those original expectations sensibly moderated, Mike did indeed settle well. After four games with the second team, he won back his place with the seniors, playing initially on the wing, but later often at centre. By the end of the season he had made 25 appearances, scoring seven tries. The team had quickly recovered from its shaky start to finish well clear of the relegation places.

Halifax 1963–64. Mike Brown is sitting on the far right in the middle row.
The trophy is the Yorkshire Cup. (Photo courtesy Andrew Hardcastle)

The 1963–64 season saw Halifax fare well. They finished in the top half of the table, and also won two significant trophies, the Yorkshire Cup and the Eastern Division Championship. Now usually on the wing, Mike played in 20 matches, scoring five tries, but missed out on selection for both finals to Duncan Jackson, a Yorkshire county representative player. Post-match celebration photographs from the Yorkshire Cup Final show him with the players, holding his winners' medal, so he was probably first reserve in those days before substitutes. He also played a few games for Halifax's powerful second team, who easily won their league that season, but missed their Championship Final too, having played so many games for the first team.

The following season brought the reappearance in rugby league of Bradford Northern, who had folded in December 1963. They were on the look-out for new players, and Halifax agreed to release Mike and scrum-half Bryn Jones, who both moved down the road to Odsal for a knock-down joint fee of £1,000. Mike was a regular with them for two seasons, and played on into 1966–67. He scored nine tries for Bradford in 57 appearances, and played an important role in re-establishing the club in professional rugby league.

He had proved himself to be a sound and reliable player, well able to hold his own at the top level of the English game. He was never a blockbusting powerhouse centre, nor a speedy, spectacular winger, but he was always worth a place in the team. As Bill Hughes wrote in his Halifax programme notes in January 1964: "We are very fortunate in having two wings like Mike and Duncan for one position. Both fill the bill admirably."

The other player to come to England with experience of rugby league in South Africa was Charlie Nimb, who made his debut for Hull on the same day as Brown made his for Halifax, 13 October 1962.

Charles Frederick (Charlie) Nimb

As the battle between the Springboks and the British Lions moved into its last phase during the week of the 3 to 10 September 1938, Charles Frederick (Charlie) Nimb was born in Paarl in the Cape Province. His birthday on the 6th came three days after a dramatic 19–3 Springbok victory and four days before an equally momentous 21–16 Lions victory to conclude the last international series before the Second World War.

After enrolling at Voortrekker High school in the Cape Town suburb of Wynberg, the skills required to become a first-class rugby player was further honed. His 21st birthday in 1959 found him at South Africa's second oldest club, Villagers and playing first-team rugby as a fly-half in the Western Province Grand Challenge and Town Challenge competitions.

After displaying good form in the provincial club competitions, Nimb was selected for Western Province in the 1959 season. In addition to playing in the Currie Cup, he represented his union in friendly provincial matches. In the team were notable players such as Colin Greenwood, Rudi Hasse, Aubrey Luck and Hennie Van Zyl, who together with Nimb became pioneers in establishing rugby league in South Africa. As a good tactical and place-kicker, he made a significant contribution to the WP campaign and assisted them in winning the Challenge Trophy and the Currie Cup against a determined Transvaal team with Dawie Ackerman, a former Cape Town hero, in its ranks. To crown a solid season, Nimb played for a South African Invitation XV for a charity game at Newlands which further brought him to the attention of the national selectors.

Nimb's second season coincided with the arrival of the New Zealand All Blacks for the first time since 1949. Playing for WP, he kicked a conversion in a match which the locals lost 20–8. Following a season of consistent performances in inter-provincial friendlies, Nimb was selected for the 1960–61 tour of Great Britain and France. Competing against more experienced fly-halves such as Dave Stewart and Keith Oxlee, he did not play in any of the test matches. However, he did play in five tour matches.

Having had a first taste of Springbok rugby, the 1961 season saw Nimb become test Springbok number 369 in a short tour by Ireland, although WP did not have a good season. He represented WP in the first-ever South African knock-out competition, the Southern Cross Shield, which they won after beating Free State. On 13 May 1961, Nimb – together with Colin Greenwood – made his test debut against Ireland at Newlands before an appreciative crowd of 32,445. South Africa won 24–8. Greenwood scored two tries and Nimb added three conversions and kicked a penalty for a personal tally of nine points. This was their only rugby union test match.

With his move to rugby league, his rugby union career formally came to an end. In rugby league, Nimb joined Johannesburg City in the Rugby League of South Africa (RLSA). On 11 July, the *Johannesburg Star* reported that he was seen as "the most improved player among

RLSA's former Springboks since he turned professional about three months ago..." He kicked a couple of goals in a 12–9 defeat by Eastern Transvaal. In August, the paper reported under the headline 'Rugby League makes good progress' that "Repeated claims that rugby league players are fitter, tougher and faster than those in rugby union are being borne out by matches in South Africa, and there is has been a marked improvement by several players who have turned professional. The most notable examples are Willem Vermaas ... and the former Springbok fly-half Charlie Nimb." On 20 September, Nimb's influence was shown in a preview of City's match against Southern Suburbs: "Following their victory over Eastern Transvaal last week, City have an excellent chance of turning the tables. They have sharpened up their forward play to the extent that they can expect a liberal supply of the ball, and with Charlie Nimb at fly-half to control the attacks, they will give Suburbs' defence a trying time."

At the end of August 1962, the Great Britain team on their way home from Australia and New Zealand, played three matches against a Rugby League South Africa side. Nimb played in all three, at full-back in the first, stand-off in the second and centre in the third. This exposure clearly helped bring him to English rugby league scouts' attention, and he signed for Hull FC. Ironically, the Great Britain coach was Hull KR's Colin Hutton, who played as a substitute in one of the matches.

Nimb made his debut for Hull on 13 October 1962. Bill Dalton, the Hull FC historian, recalls that the match was a 25–25 draw, and an error by Nimb enabled Workington to score the equalising try. This was Hull's highest scoring draw until 2008. He says that Nimb joined a Hull side who were in decline following two Wembley Challenge Cup Final appearances at the start of the decade. He also had to face the worst winter since 1947 in the first three months of 1963. Nimb played 26 first team games in the two-and-a-bit seasons he played for Hull, scoring a try – the week after his debut – and kicking 20 goals. He also scored around 20 tries for the Hull 'A' team. As with the other backs, he faced the problem of playing behind a weak pack, which led to some 'un-memorable' performances.

In November 1962, Fred Griffiths's stay at Wigan would come to an end, and he was planning to continue his career in Australia. To replace him, Wigan signed another South African, a young full-back called John Winton.

John Winton

In 1957 the Rhodesian national team won five matches in the South African Currie Cup competition. They were, however, unfortunate to lose narrowly against the Boland and Transvaal sides in tough home and away encounters. Leading the Rhodesian charge were Tom Van Vollenhoven, Poensie Griffiths and Ted Brophy. Van Vollenhoven together with fellow Springbok Jack van der Schyff as well Junior Springboks Francois Roux, Lance Nel and Des Van Jaarsveldt also assisted Northern Rhodesia in capturing the Clark Cup, Rhodesian rugby's premier trophy. The presence of experienced international players in domestic rugby was an important stimulant for young upcoming players such as John Winton who played for

Salisbury RFC, who were affiliated to the Mashonaland Rugby Union, the home of Southern Rhodesian rugby.

Given the military situation in Rhodesia, the young Winton, like all other Rhodesian men after school, enlisted for training in the regional territorial forces, the Royal Rhodesian Regiment, Number 6 Platoon of B Company. After training, he enlisted for active service and stayed in the Army reserve ranks for at least four years. In this capacity, he was eligible for selection – and soon became a regular member of – the Rhodesian Combined Forces rugby team. At the tender age of 19, in 1958, Winton was selected to represent Southern Rhodesia in their season opener against Northern Rhodesia, defender of the Clark Cup, in a Black & White Trophy Competition encounter.

From that point on there was no looking back. Over the next five seasons, Winton honed his craft in the hurly-burly of Rhodesian Clark Cup regional rugby and was on the winning side eight times in 13 matches. 1958 was a non-Currie Cup season, so there was limited opportunity to measure himself against South Africa's Currie Cup veterans and to fast-track his development. This, however, was fortunate for him because the Rhodesian national team, in comparison to the previous season, had a nightmare campaign with six successive losses. This situation was aggravated by the departure of several experienced players such as van Vollenhoven, Brophy, Griffiths, Athol Brown and Ernie and Ossie Deysel to rugby league in England. The only option for Winton was to use the domestic regional contests and club competitions to try to make a breakthrough to the national team.

With the resumption of the Currie Cup Competition in 1959, Winton – who was relatively new to representative rugby – still had to prove his worth for national selection. The national team's losing streak continued because the number of South Africans playing in Rhodesia decreased rapidly. Although this created new opportunities for local players, it also weakened a team which had depended on South African residents for many years. In the midst of a season of discontent, however, players such as Percy Landsberg continued to give a good account of themselves. As new playing opportunities became more readily available, Winton continued to compete at club level and in the Clark Cup despite problems with distance, selection and other factors. Right at the end of his second season, with a scheduled match between Southern Rhodesia and Northern Transvaal, he played at a higher than regional level. The visitors, fielding Springboks Frik Du Preez, Mof Myburgh and Oupa Du Pisanie, however, totally dominated the game and won 32–3. This opportunity was repeated the following season when the Southern Rhodesia XV met the Northern Transvaal Country Districts at Pietersburg and won 14–11.

In 1961, Salisbury RFC undertook a tour to South Africa and played against some of the country's foremost clubs in Cape Town. They also, during a visit to the Transvaal, defeated Diggers RFC. The team also captured the Globe & Phoenix League Trophy and defeated a Rest of Rhodesia XV. All of this further refined Winton's skills and those of the new Rhodesian players in preparation for the new Currie Cup and international season.

After four years of apprenticeship, Winton finally made it into the Rhodesian national side in 1962. Winton's season started off with games for the Federal Combined Services and Southern Rhodesia against the British Combined Services tourists. He was then finally selected to represent his country and played in four Currie Cup matches.

1966 Oldham team – John Winton is in the back row on the far right.
(Photo courtesy Oldham Rugby League Heritage Trust)

He also showed his mettle against the South African Universities and Northern Transvaal teams which toured Rhodesia. Despite credible personal performances, the team's fortunes were faltering with three successive Currie Cup defeats in South Africa. As the season draw to a close, so did Winton's career as a rugby union player. He then signed for Wigan, but found the going tough at Central Park.

Members of the Oldham Rugby League Heritage Trust reflect on the career of one of the few South Africans to appear for the club: "Oldham's Ben Andrew, a Lancashire County forward, left the club in 1895 to seek fame and fortune in South Africa surely unable to contemplate that in less than a year's time he would represent his new country against the touring rugby union British Lions.

In those days, Oldham progressed quickly too, building one of the strongest teams in the league recruiting top class union players from the four corners of the UK, importing star names from Australia and New Zealand and signing the best of the local talent. Losing players of Andrew's status was no longer in the plan. It would be 70 years though before there would be any further connection with Southern Africa.

When it did eventually happen it was because midway through the 1964–65 season Oldham's player-coach Frank Dyson, the former Huddersfield and Great Britain international full-back, wanted to coach more and play less.

96

The Oldham committee turned its attention towards Wigan, having had the nod that their Rhodesian international goalkicking full-back John Winton might be available. Signed by Wigan following trials, the former Salisbury Sporting Club star made his first team debut in a league match against Bramley in 1962. Former Springbok star full-back Fred Griffiths had left the club to go and play in Australia for North Sydney at the end of his contract. Jack Winstanley outlined in his club history that Winton was signed to replace Griffiths, but that "The handsome Rhodesian made a good start with a try and three goals in his debut against Bramley, but he never enjoyed the confidence of the Wigan selectors in big games." He only made 33 first team appearances and missed out on the Challenge Cup Final in 1963, Dave Bolton playing at full-back. For the first team, he kicked 86 goals and scored four tries.

Negotiations between Oldham, the Central Park club and the player himself weren't straightforward. The 24 year old had built up a second-hand car business in the town with his fellow Rhodesian and Wigan's star winger Trevor Lake. Also, his existing contract would make him a free agent in two years. Eventually, on 18 March 1965 he signed – the deal was believed to include Oldham in due course paying the cost of the Rhodesian's return home.

Having committed himself to life at Watersheddings towards the business end of the 1964–65 campaign, Winton was quickly slotted into the Oldham side. He made his debut at Keighley just two days after leaving Wigan. He made nine first team appearances that season and kicked 26 goals. Oldham finished ninth at a time when there was just one division in the Rugby League made up of 30 clubs. It was a mark of the strength of the Watersheddings side that during that season six of the club's players were selected to the county sides and 13,800 turned up to watch the home league match against Swinton.

In the following season – 1965–66 – Winton topped the club's appearance chart. He played in 40 out of a possible 43 first team matches, kicked 117 goals and scored two tries. This put him fourth in the seasons' points scoring chart topped by St Helens' South African goalkicker Len Killeen who clocked up 336 points. Runner-up was Huddersfield's full-back Brian Curry who scored 256 points and who would soon replace Winton at Watersheddings. Killeen also became the season's top goalkicker with 120, just three ahead of Winton who was joint third alongside Hull KR's Cyril Kellett. The pair kicked 117 goals apiece.

Oldham again finished ninth in a 30 club division. Winton had played a star roll in the club's 28–13 home win against Wigan in the Lancashire Cup, kicking eight goals before putting over a further four against his old club when Oldham won 22–8 in a league match at Central Park. The Roughyeds were eventually knocked out of the Lancashire Cup in the semi-final, losing 21–10 at Warrington despite the Rhodesian being in good form. He scored all Oldham's points from five goals. The Watersheddings side were awarded a match against the touring New Zealanders that season, and lost 5–2 with Winton scoring Oldham's points.

It is understood that John Winton returned home to Rhodesia at the end of the 1965–66 season, but details of his life since then are limited, although it is believed that at the time of writing he is alive and well living in Durban in South Africa after enjoying a successful career in advertising.

Left: Rudi Hasse with Bradford Northern chairman Jackie Barritt. (Photo courtesy Trevor Delaney)

Below: The historic occasion when for the first time players from the African, Coloured, Afrikaner and English South African racial groups (as defined under Apartheid) were all on the same rugby pitch.
The line up in the match programme shows Goolam Abed (number 3), Enslin Dlambulo (number 11) and Rudi Hasse (at number 12) playing for Bradford Northern and Colin Greenwood for Wakefield Trinity. Wakefield Trinity won 15–3.
(Programme courtesy John Pitchford)

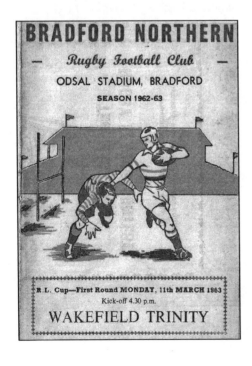

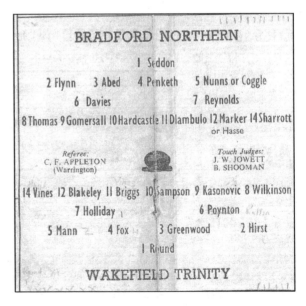

12. Bradford Northern's South Africans

By the early 1960s, Bradford Northern were in sharp decline. From being one of the sport's leading clubs in the pot-war period, they were now in the bottom half of the league, and when the league split in 1962, were in the Second Division. Desperate to strengthen their side, but with very little money, they looked to South Africa for new recruits. Goolam Abed joined the club from Leeds, and in 1962, three more recruits arrived.

On Friday 10 August, the *Johannesburg Star* reported that "Rudolf Hasse, the rugby union forward signed by Jack Barritt, an official of the Bradford Northern club on a recent holiday in South Africa, will see his first rugby league match tomorrow. He will watch Northern play Keighley in a pre-season game. Goeli Abed, the non-white South African, will be one of the Northern centres." In fact, Barritt was the club chairman, and was – apparently – genuinely on holiday rather than a desperate scouting mission to try to improve his struggling team. Hasse was recommended to the club by the ubiquitous Ronnie Colin.

Rudi Hasse

Rudi Hasse, one of the hard men of Western Province (WP) rugby cut his teeth in the Grand and Town Challenge competition playing for Northerns RFC in Cape Town. In an era when representative games were few and far between, players had to make their mark in provincial friendlies and playing for select combinations against international touring teams.

As a reward for solid performances at club level, Hasse made his provincial debut at lock in 1955, a non-Currie Cup year. His debut coincided with the arrival of the British Lions. He did not make it into the Western Province side which played the Lions on 9 July at Newlands. He was, however, in a group of 28 players that played inter-provincial friendlies. Among his team mates were Dawie Ackerman, Ivor Dorrington, Alan Skene, Tommy Gentles and Gert Rheeder, all of whom became pioneers of rugby league in South Africa.

In the next season, a Currie Cup year, WP provided 11 players to the Springbok team that toured Australia and New Zealand. Although their absence created opportunities for players such as Hasse, it denied the less experienced players a chance to learn from their more experienced counterparts. The renowned rugby writer A.C. Parker described the 1956 season as "not a vintage year". Western Province lost the Currie Cup semi-final against Natal and thus relinquished the title that they won in 1954. But Hasse was a winner in 1957 when his team captured the Board Trophy after defeating Transvaal.

During Western Province's Diamond Jubilee in 1958, Hasse got his first taste of international competition when he was selected for his province in a game against the touring British Barbarians at Newlands. He was, however, unlucky not to be chosen for the select combination XV of WP, Boland and South Western Districts which played the French tourists. He continued be part of the group of players that represented WP in friendlies. The results of the season were best described as 'moderate'. Also, Hasse had to wait for two years before his next taste of international rugby.

In his fifth season of provincial rugby, 1959, Hasse kept his place in the squad. He played in most matches, including the Currie Cup clash with Griquas prior to the final, but missed out on the final against Transvaal.

Hasse played against the 1960 New Zealand All Blacks in South Africa in a hard-fought match which WP lost 20–8. He also played six friendlies for WP. Although the team provided 13 players to Springboks on their way to Europe, their season's results were poor and neither did things improve much in the 1961 season. In his last season, Hasse represented WP in eight friendlies and the Southern Cross knock-out competition. His performances were not good enough to warrant a national call-up. When Colin Greenwood quit rugby union for league after his debut test against the Irish and departed for the north of England, it became a matter of time for others, such as Hasse, to follow suit. At the end of a mediocre WP season, Hasse left rugby union and set sail for a career with Bradford Northern RLFC.

Hasse soon established himself with Bradford Northern, after watching a few games to become familiar with his new code. In his first season he played 27 matches, mainly in the second row, scoring two tries in a Northern team that finished bottom of the Second Division with just five points, from two wins and a draw. Given he had missed four games at the start of the season, he was close to being ever-present. He only played four games in the 1963–64 season, as Northern's fortunes continued to sink. He had injured a finger at work in the close season, and only returned to action in October. He played in Northern's last game, at home to Leigh on 7 December, after which the club withdrew from the league.

In January 1964, he signed for Wakefield Trinity. However, he found it difficult to win a regular first team place in one of the sport's top sides, and only made four first team appearances before the end of the season. The following season he made just two appearances in the first team, and at the end of the season returned to South Africa with his family. His wife had become homesick and with two young daughters they returned home. He died in Cape Town in 2011.

Bradford Northern also recruited two more South Africans in 1962, Vernon Peterson and Enslin Dlambulo. Goolam Abed had suggested to Northern that they sign Dlambulo, who he had played against in the Coloured versus Bantu matches in South Africa. Dlambulo arrived in the middle of the dreadful winter of 1963, and made his debut in February at Whitehaven. Parts of the pitch were rock hard, and it is hard to imagine more alien conditions for a South African player. Trevor Delaney says that "the mobile, slightly-built South African showed impressive ball skills and defended better than most of the team. Northern lost 34–8. Dlambulo finished the season with 12 first team appearances, and made another 12 the following season before the club collapsed. He then joined Keighley, but only made nine first team appearances, including one off the bench, scoring one try, until the end of the 1966–67 season. At the time of writing he is believed to be living in Spain.

Another recruit for Northern was Vernon Petersen. Like Abed, he had played for South African Rugby Football Board team, and was a winger, although he played at stand-off for Bradford. He played six times for Northern in the 1962–63 season before returning to South Africa. Apparently the climate – the worst winter for years – was a factor in him returning home, although the matches he played were at the end of the season in May, when it had stopped snowing.

These players presence at Bradford Northern did result in a then unique event in the history of South African rugby of either code. On 11 March, Bradford Northern played Wakefield Trinity in the Challenge Cup at Odsal. Northern put up a good display against their much-stronger local rivals, who went on to win the Cup that season, before losing 15–3. Goolam Abed scored Northern's try. However, it was the first time that players from the four main South African racial groups: Afrikaner, English, Coloured and African had been on the same rugby pitch together in a formal match in either code. Rudi Hasse, Colin Greenwood, Goolam Abed and Enslin Dlambulo were probably not aware of this at the time, trying to keep warm was probably more of a priority for them.

It is likely, but would require a huge amount of research to prove, that this was the first time this happened in any sport.

Left: Gert Coetzer and Colin Greenwood celebrate winning the Challenge Cup in 1963.
(Photo: Courtesy Robert Gate)

13. 1963: Gert 'Oupa' Coetzer

While there were still prominent South African players in English rugby league, and a few in Australia, from 1963 for the rest of the decade there were very few new arrivals. The nascent rugby league competitions in South Africa had merged in 1963, and although a tour of Australia and New Zealand was organised in August 1963, the competition collapsed. The reasons for that are beyond the scope of this book. Also, from the mid–1960s, a handful of Australians started to appear in English rugby league. Sometimes they could claim British ancestry, others came on short-term contracts in the Australian close season. The chance to have an established Australian player for a few months had many advantages over the signing of a South African rugby union player who may not succeed in switching codes.

In 1960, Ken Thornett had come to Leeds from Australian rugby union. He played with Leeds until 1963, when he returned to Australia to join Parramatta. From December 1960 there was discussion between the RFL and the Australian Rugby League about international movements of players. In March 1963, it was agreed that Derek Hallas could move to Australia, on the basis of a transfer between clubs. By October 1964, although each move had to be ratified, this was the system that was used to regulate player movements, although there was still concern about 'working holidays' in the close season, and players playing all year round.

Bob Hagan, who had been capped by Australia, joined Huddersfield in 1965, where he stayed for two years. Garth Budge and Errol Stock joined the resurrected Bradford Northern for the 1964–65 season. Later in the decade, Australians such as Bobby Fulton and Artie Beetson came over on short-term contracts; people in Hull still talk about Beetson's spell with Hull KR.

The last South African to come to England in this period who made a major impact on the sport was Gert 'Oupa' Coetzer. He came to Wakefield Trinity for a trial early in 1963, having played league in South Africa for the Bloemfontein Aquilas and Johannesburg Celtic. He had also played against Wakefield on their 1962 tour.

Gert 'Oupa' Coetzer

Gert 'Oupa' Coetzer had considerable success in rugby union, with 44 appearances for the Orange Free State team, and a Springbok trial game in 1959 before he switched to rugby league. He was also a high jumper in athletics and a sprint cyclist.

His arrival in Great Britain was also different to most league recruits from union at this time. His interest in British rugby league did not involve a player's agent. Instead, he paid his own way to West Yorkshire, and asked Trinity for a trial. They immediately recognised his talent, and signed him before the trial period had finished.

He was joining a Trinity side who were at the top of the sport. However, he was soon playing for the first team on a regular basis, and, despite his relative inexperience of top class rugby league, was selected for Wakefield's team in the 1963 Challenge Cup Final against Wigan. He had played 14 first team matches, including four in the Challenge Cup, and had had to contend with the worst British winter for a generation.

He missed out on the team's first round at Odsal, but played five days later in the second round, was selected for his first team debut on the left wing, with Neil Fox inside him, and scored a try as Trinity narrowly beat Liverpool City 14–12. He kept his place for a 9–9 draw at York, and notched two more tries as Trinity won the replay 25–11 at Belle Vue. 10 days later, Wakefield narrowly beat Warrington in the semi-final to face Wigan at Wembley.

Wakefield were the cup holders, and were making their third Wembley appearance in four years. They took the lead just before half-time. Wigan's hopes were hit when their full-back Dave Bolton was concussed and missed the first 20 minutes of the second half. Ten minutes after half-time, Coetzer's first try gave Trinity a clear lead. According to Les Hoole, he "sped half the length of the field for a glorious try in the corner." He scored again just before the final hooter; Trinity won comfortably 25–10.

He went on to be selected for the South African touring party to visit Australia and New Zealand. But a shoulder injury against Canberra in the first match meant he did not play again for the tourists. An operation followed, and later a further one to reset the shoulder. The 1963–4 campaign saw Trinity have a transitional season, with no trophies or finals. However, Coetzer scored 29 tries to finish sixth in the national try scorers list and top scorer for Wakefield. In 1964–65 he only managed 17 tries, but won his second medal in rugby league, being part of the Wakefield team that beat Leeds 18–2 at Fartown to win the Yorkshire Cup.

An unusual international appearance came at the start of the 1965–66 season. He played as a substitute for a Commonwealth XIII against the New Zealand tourists at the Crystal Palace National Sports Centre. Fellow South African Trevor Lake also played; the Kiwis won 15–7 in front of 1,200 fans.

Trinity won the Yorkshire League, with Coetzer scoring 19 tries, which made him joint top try scorer at Belle Vue with former international sprinter Berwyn Jones. He finished joint 10th in the national try scorers list. There were five South Africans in the top 21, with Len Killeen and Trevor Lake heading the list.

Remarkably, for a club of their stature, Trinity had never won the Championship. They finished third in the league table in 1966–67, but the title was decided through a 16-team play-off at the end of the season. Comfortable wins over Salford and Workington Town saw Trinity into the semi-final, and an 18–6 win at Craven Park over Hull KR. In the final they faced St Helens who had finished a place behind them in the table. A 7–7 draw at Headingley on 6 May was followed by a replay on 10 May at Swinton, and a comfortable 21–9 win. Coetzer played in both games, but did not score. He had, however, finished as Trinity's top try scorer with 22, which put him in 9th place in the national list. Just before the final he had become the fifth player in the post-war period to score 100 tries for Trinity, and, according to John Lindley, had "once again displayed his remarkable consistency and determination." [71]

The 1967–68 season saw some changes at Trinity, and the team took some time to settle down. However, the end of the season brought a dramatic climax that saw them finish within one point of a Championship and Challenge Cup double.

Trinity finished runners-up in the league table, beat Wigan in the Championship play-off semi-final 26–9 and faced Hull KR in the Final at Headingley. Trinity won 17–5, with Coetzer on the right wing.

In the Challenge Cup semi-final, Trinity had drawn 0–0 with Huddersfield before winning the replay 15–10, with Coetzer contributing two tries. A week after the Championship Final, on 11 May 1968, they faced Leeds in the Challenge Cup Final at Wembley. The game was played in monsoon conditions and decided by Don Fox's missed conversion in the last minute, Leeds winning 11–10. Coetzer switched to centre, in place of Neil Fox who was injured, and was the team's regular goalkicker. He finished with 21 tries in the season.

At the start of the following season, the shoulder trouble that had plagued him since 1963 forced him to retire. 'Dreadnought', writing in the *Rugby League Magazine*, said that "The loss to Trinity is a considerable one for not only has this player succeeded in rugby league football (only four players have scored more tries for Wakefield since the war), but his dedication and sheer professionalism made him a firm favourite amongst colleagues and supporters, and an opponent to be feared both on attack and defence.

For this was no ordinary winger. His determination brought him as many tries as speed did, and his tigerish tackling was an object lesson in the art of courageous defence. He never knew what it meant to be beaten – in the quest for tries, in defending, or even in his moments of troublesome injury."

Overall, he scored 122 tries in 191 matches for Trinity. He was the last of the group of South Africans recruited in the late 1950s and early 1960s to play for Trinity, and arguably the most consistent. It is believed he returned to South Africa, but little is known of what he did when he returned there and his whereabouts now.

In September 1966, John Southey played one match for Wigan, and scored a try against Barrow. He is believed to have been a Rhodesian, but never played for the first team again. Apart from him, as far as can be ascertained, St Helens were the only club to sign any South Africans for the rest of the decade. In the autumn of 1967, Garth Robertson joined St Helens. He was Rhodesian, and had played for the national team. Apparently he had 'plenty of pace', and made his first team debut in December 1967 against Oldham. He played 11 first team matches, including one off the bench, and scored a try, three goals and two drop-goals. The St Helens Heritage Society website says that he returned to rugby union. This seems unlikely, but a match programme for a Rhodesia versus Italy match in 1971 does include a Garth Robertson. It is unclear if it is the same player.

The story of Errol van Niekerk's brief time with Saints is equally confusing. He wrote to the club in the spring of 1965, asking for a trial, and enclosing three press reports of matches he had played for Uitenhage Swifts. Presumably he was invited to England, and the third letter says that news of his venture has leaked out, and there is no longer any need for secrecy! He was offered a trial, and arrived at the end of July 1965. He was initially given permission to stay for a month, and St Helens found him board and lodging, and paid him £5 a week until he found a job. However, it was reported to the club's board on 13 September that van Niekerk felt that he was not suitable for the game. The club had paid his fare from South Africa, and funded his return home.

In January 1969, it was reported to the board that van Niekerk was back in England and had asked for a trial. He played for the 'A' team, and then played two matches for the first team in March 1969. He scored both times, but never played again. Apparently he was then not satisfied with the terms offered, and wanted a signing-on fee of £4,000. Given that he was now aged 27 the club felt this was not worthwhile and he returned to South Africa.

It does seem unlikely that St Helens would have needed a winger in 1965, with van Vollenhoven on one wing and Killeen on the other. After his appearances in 1969, the St Helens Heritage Society website says he returned to rugby union. He may have played under an assumed name, which was not unknown, but could not have played first class union again if it was known he had played rugby league, let alone professional rugby league.

```
21
26th July 1965.

Depart   Port Elizabeth    13.45.
Arrive   Johannesburg      17.45.
Depart   Johannesburg      18.45.
Arrive   London            09.00.  27 July.
Depart   London            11.50.  28
ARRIVE   MANCHESTER        12.40.



Flight from London 4082.

    S.A. 516.    B.O.A.C.,
```

Errol van Niekerk's flight schedule for his visit to St Helens in 1965.
(Courtesy Alex Service)

14. Playing at home

In 1957, Louis Japhet had promoted three matches between Great Britain and France to test the water for rugby league in South Africa. He subsequently died, but in 1961, two rival organisations started developing plans to launch rugby league in South Africa. On 3 January 1962, Rugby League South Africa announced its formation. It claimed official recognition from the RFL, which it did not have, and said that it would launch its new club competition in August. A British Lions rugby union tour was scheduled for June, so presumably they planned to avoid a head-to-head clash with one of the other code's biggest events.

Three days later, the National Rugby League was launched, but said that it planned to start a club competition in 1963, aiming to establish clubs in all the main urban centres except Cape Town. But by February, the NRL had brought forward its plans, and announced that it would run in 1962 as well.

Both competitions proceeded to recruit rugby union players, start to form clubs and identify stadiums. Of course, the rugby union stadiums were strictly off-limits to them. The full story of these competitions will be told in our forthcoming history of rugby league in South Africa. Both organisations were clearly commercial initiatives. The RFL was in contact with both, and did offer coaching support. National coach Laurie Gant visited the country, and Australian Dave Brown came to provide coaching for the RLSA players. Later in 1962 Bill Fallowfield, the RFL Secretary, visited on his way to Australia.

For the code to have a chance of surviving, a united competition was necessary. As it was, for the crucial first year, the NRL and RLSA ran separately. Rival teams were created in areas such as Johannesburg and Pretoria. Former union stars did provide a draw, as did the tours by Wakefield Trinity, under the auspices of the NRL, and at the end of August the British Lions, who played three matches against an RLSA side.

Between them, the two competitions established nine sides in 1962, but they were based in only six cities, all in the Johannesburg – Pretoria – Bloemfontein regions. The RLSA had five teams, the NRL only four. As well as having to recruit players, they also had to find stadiums to play in, and the inevitable hostility of the rugby union journalists, although some newspapers did give the sport fair coverage.

Needless to say, rugby league was only based in the white community, although both English and Afrikaner players were recruited. Apartheid absolutely forbad mixed race sport at this time, and neither competition had any interest in any activity in the Coloured or African populations, where rugby union had a base. At a time internationally when some sports were starting to not play with South Africa, rugby league, which had a proud record of including players from ethnic minority backgrounds in England, Australia and New Zealand, was becoming involved with apartheid sport.

In an article in *Windsors 1962–63 Rugby League Annual*, the *Yorkshire Evening Post's* Leslie Tremlett welcomed the establishment of rugby league in South Africa, but pointed out that a united competition was essential, as was junior development. The two competitions did unite in 1963, but some players became disillusioned and tried to return to rugby union. The tour of Australia and New Zealand by a South African rugby league Springboks team in

July and August 1963 was the code's last stand. The RLSA collapsed at the end of 1963, and rugby league was not played in South Africa again until the late 1980s.

Rugby league at this time was concentrated in three counties in the north of England, two states in Australia, New Zealand and parts of France. There was some activity in Italy and Yugoslavia, although by the mid–1960s the sport had collapsed there. The sport had no international development strategy and even if it had, it faced enormous hostility from rugby union. Even to play a trial game as an amateur for a rugby league club could attract a life ban from rugby union. In some cases, even talking to a rugby league scout was enough to jeopardise a player's future in union. Almost 20 years on from 1995, when union went open and all players could move between the codes without hindrance, it is difficult to appreciate the absolute hostility union had towards rugby league in the 1960s.

The players

From 1957 to 1963, at least 40 players went from South Africa to play rugby league in England. Of them, six were Coloured or African. Three white players, Mike Brown, Charlie Nimb and Gert 'Oupa' Coetzer, had switched codes in South Africa. So, overall 31 players were lost by white South African rugby union directly to English rugby league.

Records for both competitions in South Africa are non-existent as far as we are aware, so calculation of how many players switched from rugby union to play rugby league can only be done from newspaper reports of players switching codes, team line ups etc. There may also be some errors through misspelling of names, the use of nicknames etc. Our research shows that in the NRL, 64 players have been identified who switched codes, of whom five had previously played in England. In the RLSA, there were 70 players, of whom two had played in England.

In total, from 1957 to 1962, white South African rugby union lost 165 players to rugby league. Those who joined the new competition were mainly, but not exclusively, from the areas where their clubs were based. From the information available, there seems to have been a mix of experienced and younger players who came to rugby league. Six players had played for the Springboks, five of whom were with the RLSA. Many of the players had won provincial honours in rugby union.

Certain clubs seem to have lost players to rugby league more than others. This is understandable as players would follow their team-mates into the new code. A similar pattern was seen in the migration from union to league in South Wales. In the early 1970s, for example, Aberavon lost five players in just over two years, mainly to Warrington RLFC. Diggers and Simmer & Jack seem to have been particularly hard hit. At Diggers Annual General Meeting, the chairman praised the English-speaking players who had stayed loyal to the club.

At this time, white rugby union was gradually being taken over by Afrikaners, as part of their general grip on society. The movement of Afrikaners to rugby league was particularly sensitive. Gardens RFC in Cape Town lost Rudi Hasse to Bradford Northern. Their chairman, George van Reenen, said that Afrikaner players taking the lead in moving to rugby league was particularly painful and hurtful. Interestingly, Western Province administrators said that players should not be seen as enemies if they switched codes – maybe they had hopes of them returning to rugby union in the future. On the other hand, Ben-Piet van Zyl, a former Springbok, said 'good riddance' to the players who had left rugby union. Flappie Lochner, another former Springbok and chairman of Wellington RFC, said that some of issues raised by the players should be addressed, such as loss of income on long tours.

The occupations of the players are difficult to assess. Of the 20 tourists who went to Australia and New Zealand, which included four players who had settled in England or Australia, 14 had white collar occupations, one was a farmer and the other five had skilled manual jobs. However, of those in white collar jobs, six were clerks. Most probably reflected Afrikaner society as a whole, with skilled or supervisory blue collar jobs in areas such as the South African railways or worked as tradesmen. Those with clerical jobs could have been working for the state as well.

Jan 'Das' Prinsloo, who was selected for the 1963 tour, but missed out through injury.
He is shown here in his tour blazer, which he was awarded.
(Photo: Hendrik Snyders)

Southern Suburbs RLFC 1962 – winners of the RLSA and arguably the best club team in South Africa in 1962 and 1963. Inserts: P.G. Booysen, P. Coetzee, V.H. Jacobs, P.C. Oberholzer, W.S. Roelofse; back: J. Spies, J.J. Verwey, J.J. Baartman, G. van Zyl, H.J. van Zyl, S.J. Geel, P. Boshof, S.E. Louw; middle: J.H. Buys, I.J. Rens, E. Singer, D.S.P. Ackermann, W.R. Aab, J.G. Rheeders, P.J. Woest; front: F.W. Gericke, L.P.A. van Os, P.A. Erasmus. (Photo: Courtesy J.H. (Johnny) Buys.

SOUVENIR PROGRAMME	SOEWENIER PROGRAM
20 Cents	20 Sents
Wakefield Trinity	*Wakefield Trinity*
Rugby League Tour of	Beroepsrugby toer van
South Africa	*Suid - Afrika*
Under the Auspices of	Onder die beskerming van
NATIONAL RUGBY LEAGUE	NATIONAL RUGBY LEAGUE
(PTY.) LTD.	(EDMS.) BPK.
Organised by Terresmarine Sport and Tour Organisers	Gereël deur Terresmarine Sport en Toer Organiseerders

The programme from Wakefield Trinity's tour in 1962, organised by the National Rugby League.
Left: The front cover in English. Right: The back cover in Afrikaans. (Courtesy Peter Lush)

15. The union stars who switched codes

Limited information is available about the rugby league records of the players who stayed in South Africa. The players covered in this chapter are mainly ones who made their names in rugby union, and were seen as particularly significant recruits to rugby league. Undoubtedly the most significant signing for rugby league was former Springbok Dawie Ackerman.

Dawid Schalk Pienaar (Dawie) Ackerman

The responsibility of leading a national sports team is an honour awarded to only the best of the best. Leading a 'rebel team' of professional rugby players that claimed for themselves both the right to be called the Springboks and to represent South Africa (in rugby league) during rugby's amateur era in defiance of vehement opposition from the establishment, was an even more daunting task. This was the responsibility that Dawie Ackerman, former University of Stellenbosch, Western Province and South African rugby union lock- and flank forward assumed in 1963. He was the captain of the first national South Africa rugby league team which toured Australia and New Zealand. Given his string of representative honours in union for both province (Western Province, 1955 to 1958 and Transvaal, 1959 to 1961) and country (1955 to 1958); a relatively well paid career as a teacher and then a Personnel Officer with SABC, Ackerman really had no reason to embark on a professional career in rugby league.[72] At least, that is what Danie Craven thought. Craven had a decade-long association with the player since his arrival as a physical education student at the university in 1948. Craven was probably more bitter about Ackerman's 'defection' to league than any other player.

Ackerman, according to Craven a loner, was born on 3 June 1930 in Aliwal-North in the rural Eastern Cape, where he also received most of his schooling. In 1948 he enrolled at Stellenbosch to study to become a teacher. He attracted attention for his rugby skills and a reputation as a spoiled brat rather than for his academic abilities.[73]

Under Craven's tutelage, he switched to a specialised physical education course run by Craven. Benefitting from the personal attention of one of South Africa's foremost former players and rugby administrators, he was soon in the University's First XV; first as a lock-forward, and later as a flanker. He represented the University from 1948 to 1955 in the Grand Challenge, Knock-out Cup and Town Challenge Western Province competitions and in annual tours and intervarsity matches. He won his first honours when Stellenbosch won the Grand Challenge Championship in 1951, 1955 and 1956.

In 1950, after a win against the University of Cape Town, Ackerman made his debut for Western Province in both friendly matches and the Currie Cup.[74] However, he missed selection for the team to face Transvaal in the Final. He won full honorary colours from the university, and kept his place in the provincial side until 1957. As a result of the preparations for the 1951–52 tour to the United Kingdom and the 1953 Wallabies tour, no Currie Cup competition was played in 1951. Ackerman played in club rugby and for select provincial combinations against visiting touring sides.

He also played in five intervarsity matches and against the touring Oxford-Cambridge combination which Stellenbosch beat 11–8. He was chosen for the Southern Universities XV (Stellenbosch and Cape Town) against the British tourists as well as Western Province. In the 1952 season, his team defeated UCT, Cambridge and various rural clubs in the North Eastern districts of the Cape Province. [75] His consistent performances saw him selected for a Universities XV for a tour of Rhodesia and a match against the Australian Wallabies.

When the Currie Cup competition resumed in 1954, Ackerman was playing with at least four future rugby league players in Rudi Hasse, Gert Rheeder, Alan Skene and Ivor Dorrington. As one of only 24 players selected for Western Province that season, Ackerman played in his first Currie Cup Final against Northern Transvaal – with Tom van Vollenhoven in their ranks – on 18 September. After intercepting a pass, he scored a critical try to help to cement a WP 11–8 victory. [76] He was chosen for a South African Invitation XV against Eastern Province. This put him on the threshold of full national recognition.

In 1955 season, Ackerman remained part of the WP team. In July 1955, prior to the arrival of the British Lions, Ackerman, along with Wilf Rosenberg and Tommy Gentles, was chosen for the Junior Springboks coached and managed by Danie Craven for a short tour of South Africa and Rhodesia. The idea was to use the junior team (later known as the Gazelles) to develop future Springboks. The team played and won three matches. This was a good opportunity for players such as Ackerman, with aspirations to play for the national side, to prepare for international competition.

Finally, Ackerman received his national call-up to the Springbok side for the remainder of the test series against the British Lions. He made his debut on 20 August 1955 in the second test at Newlands. His task was: "check the irrepressible Cliff Morgan". [77] Before 46,000 supporters, Ackerman crowned his debut with his first test try in a 25–9 South Africa victory. Future rugby league stars Tom van Vollenhoven scored three tries and Wilf Rosenberg one. After South Africa lost the third test in Pretoria, Ackerman helped his team to avert a series defeat when he sent Daan Retief away for a critical try, converted by Roy Dryburgh, in the deciding fourth test in Port Elizabeth. This was the start of a successful international career and won him a place in the 1956 team to tour Australia and New Zealand.

On tour, Ackerman scored eight tries against provincial sides and the New Zealand Maori, including two tries in a match on at least three occasions. He played in four of the six test matches on a tour that had a long list of injuries, what the South Africans considered the brawling and violent tactics of All Black forward Kevin Skinner and a test series defeat. It was on this tour that Ackerman first saw a rugby league match, when the tourists watched New South Wales play Queensland. Apparently Craven instructed them not to comment on the match.

After qualifying as a teacher, Ackerman moved to Paarl and played for the local team from 1957 to 1958. He also continued to play for WP in the Currie Cup and SA Rugby Board Challenge Trophy competitions. WP won the Board Trophy that year. He was part of a group of 28 players that represented the Union in local competitions during WP's diamond jubilee celebrations the next year. The only consolation for an otherwise very 'moderate year of friendlies' [78] was the arrival of the British Barbarians and French tourists. Ackerman, however, did not make it into the national side and had to be content with selection for a combined side of the WP, South Western Districts and Boland on 30 July at Wellington. His team won 38–8 with tries by Giepie Wentzel, Hugh Gillespie, Alan Skene, Jan Pickard, BGV Lynn and Ackerman. Eight members of this team, including Ackerman, were selected for the second test at Ellis Park on 16 August 1958. They were, however, not up to the challenge and South Africa lost the series 1–0 against the first French team to visit the Republic.

This was Ackerman's swansong in rugby union test matches because he made way for Martin Pelser and Hugo van Zyl. Pelser also later switched to rugby league. Ackerman then moved to Johannesburg where he played for Wanderers RFC in 1959, Diggers in 1960 and Pirates in 1961. This came at a time that the Transvaal RU Annual General Meeting was warned against rugby league agents' recruitment activities. He also represented Transvaal in 18 games between 1959 and 1961 to conclude a very productive union career.

Dawie Ackerman was one of the most high profile Springboks to switch codes. Many of the players who moved to rugby league in the late 1950s and early 1960s were at the start of their careers, often with one or two caps. Ackerman was aged 31 when he took up rugby league, and stayed in South Africa, where he had a good job. It is unlikely at that age that he would have been able to play at the top level in England, given the period of adjustment needed for a forward. However, the profile of him in the match programme for the first rugby league test in Australia said that "It has been said of this player that had he converted to the league code at an early age, he would have been one of the all-time greats.

Ackerman signed for the Southern Suburbs club, part of the RLSA competition. In July 1962, the *Johannesburg Star* reported that the club's "progress has been largely through the efforts of Rens and Ackerman". Natie Rens captained the side. A report of their 32–21 win over Johannesburg City said that "Martin Pelser and Dawie Ackerman showed up well at forward."

On their way home from the 1962 tour of Australia and New Zealand, the British Lions stopped off in South Africa to play three matches against a Rugby League South Africa team. The two rival organisations could not agree to field a united team. Ackerman played at loose-forward in all three matches, and scored a try in the second match in Durban, which the Lions won by six points. In the report of the first match in the *Johannesburg Star*, he was said to be "always prominent" but was facing top class opponents vastly more experienced in the game.

The high point of the two years of rugby league in South Africa in the early 1960s was the tour of Australia and New Zealand in 1963. Much of the limited press coverage the sport got was about the build up to the tour. The *Star* commented on who should captain the tourists: "If he is to be one of the local players, then Dawie Ackerman would seem a certainty..." Ackerman's previous touring experience in union played a part in him being given this honour; there were other players with far more rugby league experience in the squad. He was also involved in the coaching and selection of the party. Fred Griffiths took over the captaincy when Ackerman was injured in the last match in Australia.

Of all the players who switched to rugby league, Dawie Ackerman came in for particular criticism from Danie Craven, possibly because their time together at Stellenbosch; and that Craven saw Ackerman as one of his protégées. Paul Dobson's biography of Craven, *Doc*, says that Craven was on the same flight to Australia as the rugby league Springboks, and when the plane stopped in Mauritius, "Ackerman... went to speak to Craven who, amongst other things, told him he was a pig and a disgrace to himself and Stellenbosch. The handsome Springbok's reaction was one of sorrow. 'Please don't rub it in, Doc,' he said." On the next page, Dobson outlines how Craven called rugby league players 'prostitutes' to a newspaper reporter, but then asked the man not to use the word, so he replaced it with 'traitors'. It should be noted that Dobson is very much the establishment historian of South African rugby union and would be hostile to rugby league. His *Rugby in South Africa* book, published in 1989 by the South African Rugby Board, while it covers African and Coloured rugby, does not mention the 1962 development of rugby league and the 165 players who switched codes. There is some coverage of this in his biography of Craven, but the three pages include several errors which try to belittle rugby league.

In fact, there was considerable worry in South African rugby union about rugby league at this time. There was concern that the union game had become uninteresting to watch, partly because of the loss of a series of promising backs to rugby league, and also because of the rules. Craven was on his way to Australia to discuss with the union authorities there changes to the rules to make the game more interesting. A report from Australia in the *Johannesburg Star* said that he was on a "secret trip" to Australia, and on 2 July the correspondent reported: "As one wrote yesterday, rugby league in South Africa seems to be worrying the union administrations, and possibly even more so with the first overseas tour being undertaken here. South Africa has not been prominent for wanting any laws change in other years..." But the British unions had an iron grip on the International Rugby Board at this time, and – reflecting their inherent conservatism – no changes were made.

So why did Ackerman switch codes? He had a financially secure job, and was clearly a part of the Afrikaner establishment – he was head of personnel at the South African Broadcasting Corporation when he died of a heart attack in January 1970 aged only 39. Maybe he did want a new challenge to reinvigorate his rugby career. When the 1963 tourists arrived in New Zealand, he was very positive about the game, saying "We came on this tour to learn and that we've done. We found the game in Australia more open and constructive than we had expected." He said that they had learnt from not just "playing among ourselves" and said that he preferred rugby league to union: "Undoubtedly. The forward has much more of a chance to play constructive football." [79] And maybe that is what Danie Craven couldn't accept.

Sadly, the game in South Africa collapsed after the 1963 tour, and Ackerman retired from rugby football, because he was now banned from any participation in rugby union.

After Ackerman, the next most prominent Springbok to switch codes was Hennie van Zyl.

Hendrik Jacobus (Hennie) van Zyl

Diggers RFC in Johannesburg is one of South Africa's oldest and most well-known rugby union clubs and continues to be a prolific producer of provincial and national players. It is the home of former greats like Alf Larard and Natie Rens and has been a major presence in Transvaal rugby for many decades. From the mid–1950s to the early 1960s, it was also the home of Hennie Van Zyl. This speedy winger was born on 31 January 1936 in the Ventersdorp district in the North West Province of South Africa, and made his entry into senior club rugby in 1954 in the Diggers under-19 'A' side which won the Central Division Trophy. Within two seasons, he graduated to the senior side in 1956, when they yet again were Pirates Grand Challenge Champions. Van Zyl's club and provincial career saw Diggers win the Pirates Grand Challenge nine times.

Making his provincial debut for Transvaal was only a matter of time, and came in the 1959 Currie Cup. He scored three tries against South West Africa on his debut, which set him on course for a first-class rugby union career of 29 games for Transvaal. He scored nine tries in his debut season.

This mercurial rise continued in 1960 with the arrival of 13 touring teams in the country. Van Zyl made his debut for the Springboks on 30 April at Port Elizabeth against Scotland and in the Springbok victory twice sent namesake Hugo Van Zyl away to score after taking a tactically-well-executed inside pass. On 25 June in the first test against the New Zealand All Blacks, "the elongated left-wing" scored two tries. Danie Craven described the second try thus: "The left wing was the best part of 40 yards out and had to take the ball virtually standing. He was quickly into his stride, however, and running on to Clarke, beat and outpaced the full-back on the outside. There was still the cover defence to cope with, but the amazing Van Zyl brushed off two or three tackles and a final desperate effort by the number eight, Conway, to hurl himself over the line. It was a great individual try." [80] Although he also played for Transvaal against the All Blacks at Ellis Park in August, Van Zyl did not score in a 19–3 defeat.

Van Zyl kept his place in the series against Ireland in 1961. He also played against the Australian Wallabies. Van Zyl scored three brilliant tries against the Wallabies in the first test and followed this up with a further try in the second. He played 10 provincial friendlies to cap a provincial career of 24 tries and Springbok one of 10 tries.

With the launch of rugby league in South Africa, Diggers lost 17 first team players. One was Hennie van Zyl who joined Southern Suburbs Rugby League Club in Johannesburg. While players such as Ackerman, Natie Rens and Mannetjies Gericke may have had more experience, van Zyl was the player the crowds wanted to see. On 12 July, previewing the first rugby league matches in the RLSA, the *Johannesburg Star* commented: "The league game offers plenty of scope for runners like Hennie van Zyl and Johan Pieterse. Van Zyl promises to become the code's best draw card." The paper also reported that Bradford Northern had offered a R16,000 (£8,000) transfer fee for van Zyl, which Southern Suburbs refused. Mr A. Porteous, the club chairman commented: "We have declined it because we feel that the public deserve to see van Zyl in action as he is today." Mr Jack Barrett, the Bradford Northern chairman who was visiting South Africa, had said that van Zyl is the greatest prospect he has ever seen – much better, in fact, than Tom van Vollenhoven was at a comparable stage.

In the match against Johannesburg City, van Zyl, scored three tries "which revealed all his brilliance" according to the report in the *Star* and was the outstanding player. Wakefield Trinity coach Ken Traill was watching the game, and reported to be ecstatic about the winger. The next week, the *Star* said about the match against Eastern Transvaal: "Hennie van Zyl will be on the left wing and this alone should ensure a good gate. Eastern Transvaal have given former provincial player Mike Lubbe the task of holding him. If van Zyl shows the form he displayed last Friday Lubbe will have the most difficult job on the field." Van Zyl scored a try, but his team surprisingly lost 11–10. Against Vaal a couple of weeks later, he scored two tries early on and added a third later for a hat-trick.

On 23 August, van Zyl scored two tries for an RLSA side against the British Lions. Refreshingly, *The Star's* reporter did not make tedious comparisons with rugby union, which was common in reports in this type of match, but just reflected on the game as he saw it and the crowd's reaction. He said that "Playing with a strength and speed not often seen in South Africa, the British rugby league team struck a decisive blow for their code...they thrilled a crowd of about 9,000...Yet despite the power-house play of the touring team, who demonstrated all that is good in the game, the determined opposition provided by the local team, and particularly the brilliance of the left winger, Hennie van Zyl, were the most pleasing features from the spectator's point of view." [81]

Hennie van Zyl stood out for the South African side. His second try "late in the game must rank with the best he has scored. In a movement started by Willem Vermaas near the South African goal-line, van Zyl beat five men down the touchline with subtle change of pace."

Van Zyl missed the rest of the series through injury. The crowd for the third match were particularly disappointed because there had been press coverage that he was going to play. There was some speculation that the extent of his injury was kept quiet so as not to affect the attendance. Certainly, at the end of the season the RLSA acknowledged that he was the only player who could attract fans to matches in his own right.

Van Zyl played in the domestic competition in South Africa in 1963, and in the trial matches for the tour party. There was some newspaper speculation that he would not go on tour unless he was offered more money. In the end, he withdrew from the party "for domestic reasons" and Johnny Gaydon replaced him. This was a pity, playing against the Australians would have been a good test for him, and could have led to further offers to play in England or Australia.

At the time of writing, Hennie van Zyl is believed to be living in South Africa.

Ignatius Johannes (Natie) Rens

Born on 19 July 1929 in Potchefstroom in South Africa's North West Province, Natie Rens grew up during the Second World War. During this time, the Currie Cup, was suspended and representative provincial rugby was confined to friendlies. Rens joined Diggers RFC in 1945. He played for the under–19 'A' team in his debut season. They won the Transvaal Knock-out Trophy, his first trophy in a successful union career. By 1949, when international rugby returned to South Africa, he graduated into the senior Diggers side that claimed the Pirates Grand Challenge Trophy.

As a member of a successful club, it was only a matter of time before Rens played for Transvaal. In 1949, he made his debut in a series of provincial friendlies. This launched his 81 game career for his province. He also won a place in the Transvaal Urban XV against the touring All Blacks. Although they lost 6–3, Rens, one of seven Diggers players in the side, learned valuable lessons that benefitted him later on.

Rens was ready for the 1950 Currie Cup campaign and played in nine friendlies. Although he did not play in the Currie Cup Final, as a member of the victorious squad, he sampled national glory at the age of 21. Still relatively inexperienced, he missed out on the Springbok tour of the United Kingdom at the end of the season. Diggers won the Transvaal Union Lilienfeld and Divisional Trophies.

Rens kept his place in the Transvaal side. The provincial team also contributed eight players to the national side, which gave younger players like him more opportunities. At club level Diggers claimed both the Divisional and Pirates Grand Challenge Trophies.

1952 was another good Currie Cup season for Transvaal with Rens in the side. When Transvaal played Boland in the Currie Cup Final at Wellington in October, he scored the crucial drop-goal to seal an 11–9 win. He also kicked a penalty and conversion for a total of eight points. During the season he scored 34 points in the Currie Cup and 33 more in friendlies for a total of 67 points in 14 matches. He also contributed to Diggers' success.

Rens made his way into the national side. Although he was not in the Springbok side against the Wallabies in 1953, he kicked eight points in Transvaal's 20–14 victory against them in front of 45,000 supporters at Ellis Park in June. This won him a Springbok jersey for the third and fourth tests. In the latter match, he contributed 13 of his team's points in their 22–9 win over the Wallabies.

He scored 35 points in six provincial matches and assisting Diggers in winning the Pirates Grand Challenge Cup. However, the two tests that he played were the last of his rugby union career. Following his successes in 1953, Rens was part of a disappointed Transvaal season the next year with only one Currie Cup victory. But he still scored 42 points in the season and contributed to a successful Diggers Championship defence.

With the arrival of the British Lions in 1955, Rens, despite being a seasoned Currie Cup and international campaigner, was not chosen for the test series against the tourists. He was not chosen for the Springbok party that toured Australia and New Zealand.

Now aged 27, and after seven years of competition at the highest level, Rens concentrated his efforts on his province and club. Together with Mannetjies Gericke, Jan Prinsloo and Piet Botha, he helped maintain Transvaal's competitiveness at provincial level. As vice-captain of Diggers, with Hennie van Zyl in the team, they yet again captured the Pirates Grand Challenge.

The new season saw a rejuvenated Rens captaining both Transvaal – after an injury to regular captain Ben de Meillon – and his club. He led the team to four victories with only a loss against Natal en route to a place in the SA Board Trophy Final against Western Province. They lost 12–5 at Newlands against a team that was equally brimming with talent.

With the arrival of the French tourists in 1958, Rens was not chosen for the Transvaal, Natal and Eastern Transvaal Select XV that played the tourists in July. He also missed on playing international opposition in 1960 and 1961. This left him to play out the rest of his career at provincial and club level. Although he continued to captain Diggers to Grand Challenge victories in 1958 and 1959 and made a contribution in Transvaal's campaigns as shown by his 64 points in 1959, very few incentives beyond Currie Cup rugby remained. With his omission from the match against the All Blacks, the writing was on the wall. By the end of the 1960 season, after 12 provincial seasons, 291 points and 14 tries, his career beyond club rugby was practically over. With the launch of rugby league in South Africa in 1962, Rens became one of the pioneers of the 13-man code locally.

Rens became captain of the successful Southern Suburbs side in the RLSA in 1962, along with various former Transvaal and Diggers team-mates. He played in the first match against the British Lions in August 1962 at stand-off, and toured Australia and New Zealand with the Rugby League Springboks in 1963. The pen picture of him in the programme for the first test said that he was a "shrewd tactician, safe hands and capable defender." His occupation is given as 'farmer' and maybe that was the reason he never played overseas. Had he switched to rugby league in the late 1950s or early 1960s, in his late 20s or early 30s, all the indications are that he could have been successful.

Natie Rens died on 19 December 1989 in Johannesburg, at the age of 60.

Chris de Nysschen never played a test match for the Springboks, but did play 10 matches on tour.

Christiaan Johannes (Chris) de Nysschen

Chris de Nysschen was born on 31 January 1936. He was educated at Ladysmith High School in KwaZulu Natal, and worked as a clerk on the South African Railways.

After school de Nysschen initially joined Natal University RFC and later Wasp-Wanderers. The club played in the Natal Union's Moor Cup, Murray Challenge Cup, Dewar Shield, and Frank Norris Cup competitions. Being a member of a strong club put de Nysschen in a good position to develop his game and rugby union career.

De Nysschen played 25 games for Natal from 1955 to 1960. A solid and fast player who could run 100 yards in 10.2 seconds, the 'tall, promising and stripling young lock with interesting prospects' was particularly prominent in line-outs.[82] In his first season with Natal he played against the British Lions before 20,000 excited spectators at Kingsmead in Durban. The team played well and made the Lions work extremely hard for their 11–8 victory.

He was invited – 'literally out of nowhere' – to the 1956 Springbok trials aged just 19. At 6 feet 5½ inches he was the tallest player there and initially started the trials in the lowest team. He was immediately promoted in the subsequent selections, staking a progressively stronger claim for inclusion into a future national team. He displayed a remarkable agility and 'manoeuvrability' for someone of his size. He finally made the 'Possibles' side to meet the 'Probables' in the final trial on the Thursday afternoon at Newlands. It was the 'Possibles' last chance to win selection. They put everything into the match; had "better ideas and more ball possession" and outclassed their more fancied opponents. Leading the way was the young Natal lock forward. The party announced to tour New Zealand and Australia in

1956, included two Natal players and de Nysschen, "a quietly spoken, even-tempered and studious young man" was one of them.[83] As the youngest in a very experienced group of forwards, he did not make the test side. Overall, he made 10 appearances on tour and scored a try against Queensland.

In 1958 he played for the Combined South African Universities against the French tourists, who won 32–16. However, de Nysschen was not always an automatic choice at provincial level, and did not play for the national side.

In 1960, he missed out on selection for Natal when they played the All Blacks, the Springboks when they played Scotland and Natal again when they played the South African Barbarians. So de Nysschen packed his bags and headed for Bloemfontein and a new rugby union career with Collegians RFC, the Free State's second-oldest club.

De Nysschen made his Free State debut on 13 May in a friendly against Griqualand-West. In July, having played four matches, de Nysschen captained the team against Natal. His team lost 9–6, but beat North Eastern Districts a week later 23–6. On 19 August De Nysschen played his last match against Transvaal in Kroonstad and concluded his union career on a high after a 20–8 win.[84]

De Nysschen was the only former Springbok to play in the National Rugby League. This meant that he did not play against the British Lions in 1962, because the team they faced was selected from the RLSA clubs. However, he did play against Wakefield Trinity on their tour in June, and is featured in the tour souvenir programme as one of the NRL's 'outstanding players'. He played for Bloemfontein Aquilas, and captained a South Africa Invitation XIII that played Trinity twice at the end of the tour. He also played against the tourists as a guest for Johannesburg Celtic. The Trinity side was reinforced by some South African players as an additional attraction for the fans, but were missing some players who were with the British Lions in Australia. Trinity won the matches comfortably, but de Nysschen features in the match reports prominently. Although his height was an advantage in rugby union, in rugby league, with no line-outs, it was probably a disadvantage, and top level players in league of that height have been comparatively rare.

De Nysschen did not tour Australia and New Zealand in 1963, and never played rugby league overseas.

Another Springbok who switched to rugby league was Mannetjies Gericke. He was a half-back, and the pen picture of him in the Australia versus South Africa first test programme described him as a "Brainy all round player with prolific pass. Excellent place kicker and forceful runner."

Frederick Wilhelm (Mannetjies) Gericke

Mannetjies Gericke was born in Kimberley on 8 June 1933. He was the first student from his school, Hoërskool Diamantveld to become a Springbok. He was a scrum-half, and faced competition from future rugby league convert Tommy Gentles among others. He worked on the railways after leaving school and played for Griqualand West including against the 1953 Wallabies. Later he moved to the Transvaal and worked for South African Breweries as a sales representative. At provincial level, he played for Western Transvaal and 34 times for Transvaal. He scored two tries on debut against Orange Free State. He played for the Junior Springboks against the 1955 Lions and was vice-captain of the Junior Springboks on their South American tour in 1959. In 1960 he played his only test match, against Scotland in Port Elizabeth. The Springboks won 18–10.

Gericke joined the RLSA and played for Southern Suburbs, along with Dawie Ackerman and Natie Rens. He played in all three matches against the British Lions in August 1962 at scrum-half. He kicked four goals in the first game, and in the third match scored a try and kicked four goals. Willem Vermaas was the goalkicker for the second game.

Gericke also played baseball and cricket. He later returned to rugby union and coached the Transvaal Rooibokke and Roodepoort. He died on 22 October 2010, aged 77.

Another significant Springbok recruit by the RLSA was Martin Pelser, who in 1960 was rated as the best loose-forward in South Africa, and was known as the 'Iron Man of Rugby'. His cousin Ken, who switched from association football to rugby union aged 24, played in the NRL. Both players were on the 1963 tour. Another family member, Sarel Pelser, also played rugby league.

Martin and Ken Pelser

Hendrik Jacobus Martin Pelser
The role of mining companies and mine workers in South African rugby is a largely unresearched subject although the industry directly contributed to the establishment of some famous clubs and provided a platform for some of the country's iconic players. Rand Leases Roodepoort RFC, a mining club was established in 1943 on the West Rand of Johannesburg and was part of the Transvaal Union. It competed in the Pirates Grand Challenge, President's Knock-out, Rademeyer Cup and the Boet Michau Trophy; won their share of honours and produced a significant number of Springboks. One was Martin Pelser who made his national debut in 1958 against France. Pelser was born on 23 March 1934 in Johannesburg. After a poor 1954 season, Transvaal embarked on a search for new blood. Martin Pelser, one of the hard men of Roodepoort rugby, made his debut in this rebuilding phase. After facing Western Province that season, Pelser represented his province for six consecutive seasons.

With the Springboks tour of Australia and New Zealand in 1956, there were opportunities for young players such as Pelser. From the season-opener against Rhodesia Pelser played in seven provincial friendlies. Although he kept his place into the 1957 season and the return of the Currie Cup, Pelser was omitted from the side that faced Western Province in the Board Trophy Final at Newlands. The 1958 season saw the arrival of the British Barbarians and France. Pelser played twice against the Barbarians, for Transvaal and Transvaal XV – combination of the best of Transvaal, Western Transvaal, Eastern Transvaal and Northern Transvaal.

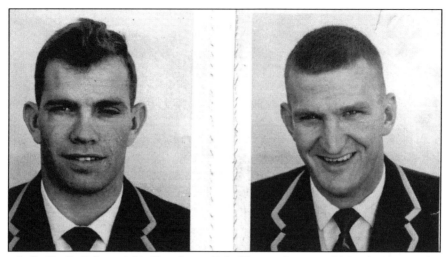
Left: Martin Pelser; right: Hennie van Zyl. (Photos: Courtesy SA Rugby Museum)

He also played for the Transvaal XV against the French, and lost 16–14. He was then selected to represent South Africa against the French in the second test at Ellis Park on 16 August 1958. The Springboks lost 9–5 and the series 1–0.

The 1959 and 1960 seasons were extremely busy ones for South African rugby players. In addition to the Currie Cup in 1959, there were 13 tours including New Zealand (twice), British Lions (twice), Australia (thrice), France (twice), Scotland, Ireland, Wales and Argentina in 1960. Pelser represented South Africa against New Zealand, Ireland and Australia. In the latter series he also scored his debut test try. He also represented Transvaal against the All Blacks and captained the Transvaal side in 10 provincial friendlies in 1960. He continued as captain in 1961 until he switched codes to play rugby league.

Martin Pelser played for the Johannesburg City club in the RLSA. He played in the second row in all three matches against the British Lions in August 1962, and was on the 1963 tour to Australia and New Zealand, when he scored three tries. He worked as a fitter and turner. According to the Australia versus South Africa match programme, he turned down a substantial offer from Workington Town to join them. Remarkably, he only had one eye when he played rugby in both codes. At the time of writing he still lives in Johannesburg.

Ken Pelser

Ken Pelser, a hard second-row forward came into rugby union in the late 1950s at the age of 24, after focusing his energies on association football. Part of a rugby playing family, he eventually switched codes and joined the Johannesburg Municipals RFC, part of the Johannesburg Municipal Sports Club, since he worked as a tradesman for the local authority. It was seen as a Cinderella club, and produced only three Transvaal provincial players in the first century of the province's existence. Among this handful of players, four in over a century, was his cousin, Martin Pelser, the club's only Springbok, and Schalk Geel who like the Pelsers also joined rugby league in the 1960s, when he played for Johannesburg Celtic in the National Rugby League. His entry into rugby union coincided with Johannesburg Municipality RFC entering the Transvaal senior competition, along with powerhouses such as Diggers and Pirates. His late start meant that Pelser still had a lot to learn about the game before he could challenge for a place in any representative team. Pelser settled down in the Municipals team over the next four years.

With the launch of rugby league in South Africa and after four years of extremely hard competition in one of South Africa's premier rugby union competitions, Pelser at the age of 29 years was finally ready to challenge for more honours. Coming from a soccer background where professionalism had long been established, the introduction of rugby league immediately attracted him. Unsurprisingly, he became one of the first recruits of the NRL.

With the launch of the NRL Cup, Pelser was an enthusiastic participant in the pre-competition series of friendly games against fellow founding members, Boksburg Vikings, played at the Old Maristonians Fields in Johannesburg. Newspaper reports described these first rugby league matches as 'keenly contested' with Celtic emerging triumphant. Over the course of a four club official league competition, Celtic were outplayed by both the Boksburg Vikings and Bloemfontein Aquilas and therefore missed the one and only NRL Cup final.

Despite his club's average performances, Pelser still got an opportunity to impress against international competition when he represented Celtics against the touring Wakefield Trinity side in 1962. Although they lost 52–6, critical lessons were learned for the development of the code. This was the first time that most of the players had faced established rugby league players and had to adapt their game and move away from their rugby union roots. This was, however, not enough to earn him a place in the South African Invitation XIII that twice played the visitors. Over the course of the regular season, however, he did enough to win a place in the first South African national league team to go overseas in 1963 when he opened the tour as prop together with his cousin, Martin. He scored two tries on the 1963 tour.

According to one source, Pelser, who was noted for robust play, played rugby union until the age of 53 and only retired when he was selected for the second team, not the first. It is interesting to note that as a well-known player, having played rugby league, he would have been officially banned from union. But presumably his presence was 'tolerated' at the game's lower levels providing that it did not attract attention from the game's higher authorities.

One player who was originally selected for the 1963 tour, and still has his tour blazer to prove it, was Jan 'Das' Prinsloo. He played in the NRL for Pretoria, and is not to be confused with the player of a similar name who played for Wakefield Trinity and St Helens in England.

Jan 'Das' Prinsloo

Eleven days after the birth of Jan 'Das' Prinsloo in the Free State town of Bethlehem, on 30 May 1937, the Springboks kicked off the first match of the Australian leg of their tour down under. Twenty years later, at Prinsloo's matriculation in 1957 at the Warmbad (now Bela-Bela) High School, the Springbok team, which the New Zealanders described the team as "the best ever to leave New Zealand" with reference to their clean sweep of the series, was a shadow of its former self. In addition, it was still smarting after suffering a crushing series defeat against their traditional rivals. These years, when the mercurial Tom van Vollenhoven showed his finesse as a world-class winger, turned the impressionable Prinsloo into a life-long fan of the 'Van'. Van Vollenhoven's departure into rugby league left a lasting impression on the young man and he followed his hero's overseas progress through the local media.

Coming from a working-class family, Prinsloo, not yet 20 years old and unable to register for university study, joined the South African Army Gymnasium in 1958, with the aim of becoming a soldier. After several noteworthy performances at full-back for the Gymnasium's First XV, Prinsloo was selected to represent Northern Transvaal (now the Blue Bulls Rugby Union) at under–19 level. He was potentially on track for senior provincial and eventually national colours.

In pursuance of his dream of studying theology, Prinsloo resigned from the Army and applied for admission to the University of Stellenbosch. There he naturally caught the attention of Danie Craven. But shortly after his admission to Stellenbosch, misfortune struck. After a bad fall, his mother was left in need of long-term care. Studies became a privilege and the young Prinsloo therefore dropped out of university to become a breadwinner for his family.

Finding a job, however, was not easy. He received a telephone call from an acquaintance at the South African Broadcasting Corporation (SABC), imploring him to return to Johannesburg, with the possibility of employment at SABC. He was appointed as a journalist and assigned to the crime reporting desk in which capacity he reported on the famous Rivonia Trial of Nelson Mandela and other ANC leaders. This started a career of 21 years in broadcast journalism.

After a short stint at the Johannesburg headquarters, he was deployed to the broadcaster's regional offices in Bloemfontein. A chance meeting with a former school and rugby friend in the Rose City, did not only offer accommodation, but also membership the Free State's most famous club, Old Grey RFC for the 1959 season. Prinsloo left this club in 1959 and joined Collegians RFC, another of Bloemfontein's well-known clubs who played in the province's premier competition. This stay was equally short because the SABC transferred Prinsloo back to Johannesburg and Pretoria. Back in his home area, he joined Pretoria RFC, who played in the Carlton Cup. His arrival in Pretoria coincided with the last leg of the 1957–59 Currie Cup. This was the last Currie Cup rugby until 1964. Ambitious young players like Prinsloo had little opportunity for top-flight competition. Consistent performances at club level helped him stake a claim for provincial selection in 1961. Some of his peers included future league players such as Ontie Odendaal, Chris Geyer and Willem Vermaas.

Soon after the start of his provincial career, Prinsloo received offers from rugby league clubs in Australia and England, including Wigan. Mindful of the success of van Vollenhoven, his life-long role-model, he approached the secretary of the Pretoria RFC in the hope of getting sound advice about the offers. Beyers Hoek, the club secretary, told him that his consideration of the offers meant that he forfeited his amateur status and had become a professional. So his playing career with Pretoria RFC was over. Prinsloo said farewell to rugby union and joined the fledgling rugby league game initiated by Rugby League South Africa and the National Rugby League. He joined Pretoria Koedoes Rugby League Club in

1962. In this context he played with former Northern Transvaal rugby union team mates and friends such as Corrie Vermaak, Albie Kruger, Tony van Zylichgem, Johan Mitchell, Dawid van der Merwe and Ryan Lombaard who provided the backbone for league in the capital.

Pretoria Koedoes joined Johannesburg Celtic, Boksburg/East Rand Vikings, and Bloemfontein Aquilas, the other foundation clubs in the NRL Cup, the official club competition of the Norman Lacey grouping. Most of the players also came from an Afrikaans background. John Mitchell was coach of Pretoria RLFC, formerly of Transvaal, Free State and Natal rugby union.

Based on a series of solid performances, including 40 tries as a winger and full-back, Prinsloo was included in the first South African Rugby League national side scheduled to tour Australia and New Zealand in 1963. Misfortune, however, struck one week before the team's departure when he seriously injured his ankle during a social match. Bitterly disappointed, Prinsloo was forced to withdraw. Although the national body decided to award him national colours retrospectively given the historic nature of the tour, this incident continued to haunt him. Post-tour problems such as inaccessibility of training and match venues, however, put paid to his national ambitions. In addition, the South African Rugby Football Board initiated a new strategy to finally break the code by extending an offer for readmission to the amateur ranks provided former players' commitment to destroy the code themselves. Frustrated by their existing circumstances and a campaign of social isolation within their communities, a large number of players accepted the offer. Prinsloo, in particular, played a central role in these negotiations. The strategy of divide-and-rule effectively sabotaged the efforts of Rugby League South Africa to launch the 1964 season. By keeping players on a string through both subtle and direct encouragement and promises for the full year they dealt the code a mortal blow. As a result by the end of 1963, rugby league in South Africa was effectively killed. Efforts in late 1963 and early 1964 to play the code firstly in modified form and thereafter on an amateur basis also failed.

Prinsloo for many years continued to wear his honorary national rugby league blazer as a sign of his continued commitment to the cause. When the code was revived during the late 1980s, he served as Vice-President of the new body, South African Rugby League Association. He continued to serve in this role at the present time. Away from rugby in his senior years, he continued to be involved in Masters Athletics and recently participated in both the South African and Africa Masters Championships in the age group 75 to 79 years where he gained a bronze medal in the 100 meters.

16. International matches and the tour

The first international matches in this period were organised by the National Rugby League. They invited Wakefield Trinity, one of the top English clubs at the time, to tour South Africa at the end of June 1962, and play five matches in two weeks. Wakefield were missing five players who were with the British Lions in Australia and New Zealand, but augmented their squad by including South African 'guests' such as Tom van Vollenhoven, Fred Griffiths, Wilf Rosenberg and Ted Brophy who would be an attraction for the local rugby union fans. Trinity also had South Africans Alan Skene, Jan Prinsloo and Colin Greenwood with them

Wakefield's arrival in Johannesburg was front page news in *The Johannesburg Star*, the main local English-language paper. The matches were promoted on the basis of a chance to see former Springbok stars. Trinity's captain for the tour was South African centre Alan Skene. He said that Wakefield would take the matches seriously: "I can promise that we will not be playing touch rugby. Tom van Vollenhoven is thrilled at [his first] chance to play in South Africa since turning professional. *The Star* said that "The visit of the Wakefield Trinity team could entrench the game as a popular new spectator sport in South Africa. Just as surely, a failure of the tour would be a critical setback to its sponsors. Trinity's first opponents on 30 June, the day after their arrival, were Johannesburg Celtic. *The Star* added that the "team is a good one by rugby union standards, but many of its players are inexperienced at rugby league. Chris de Nysschen and seven others have represented their provinces. Piet Botha will take his place at fly-half despite Leigh's statement that he is still on their books." The NRL said that Botha would play as a guest, and they were trying to resolve his position with Leigh.

Johannesburg Celtic 6 Wakefield Trinity 52

Despite Trinity's tour clashing with the rugby union British Lions being in South Africa, the match report made *The Star's* front page with a photo. "Wakefield win rough game 52–6" ran the headline. Around 5,000 attended the match, despite ticket prices being expensive, partly to cover the cost of hiring stadiums. The kick-off was delayed for 15 minutes due to the size of the crowd.

The Star wrote that "The game was hard and rough, with the referee frequently warning players for over-robust tactics. This did not lessen the crowd's enjoyment however, and they seemed pleased with the entertainment." Wakefield's handling was shaky early on, which was not surprising as they had been in the country for less than 24 hours. Trinity scored after 15 minutes play through Briggs. Trinity continued to control the game, and were 23–0 ahead at the break.

After the interval, Chris de Nysschen broke through and was tackled by Fred Griffiths. *The Star* commented that "Play was becoming over robust."

Wakefield were 28–0 ahead when Celtic scored the best try of the match at that stage. Greyling cut through from full-back, de Nysschen and several players handled before scrum-half Kruger scored near the posts for an unconverted try.

Wakefield were 42–3 ahead when the Johannesburg side scored again. Centre Ivan de Jongh broke through before passing to left winger Coetzer, who scored in the corner. Firth and Prinsloo scored further tries for Trinity, both converted by Griffiths.

A couple of days later, *The Star* confirmed that "Wakefield Trinity kept their promise... [and] did not play touch rugby. The touring team pulled out all the stops in their 52–6 victory... and in the process demonstrated many of the good points of rugby league.

They also showed that South African teams have a long way to go before they will be able to match the fast and rugged play of top league forwards. The speed and handling of the Wakefield pack were the most impressive features of the match.

It would be unwise to judge the chances of rugby league becoming established in South Africa on the evidence of Saturday's rough, one sided match, but one had the impression that the crowd would be well prepared to watch the game again. The need to gain possession causes a lot of high tackling in league. The high tackling and general looseness of play are aspects of the game which do not appeal to the rugby union follower. Yet there is no denying the appeal of the brilliant running of players like Jan Prinsloo, Wilf Rosenberg (who is out of the tour with a broken jaw) and Albert Firth, the 202 pounds forward who scored four tries on Saturday.

Alan Skene said after the match that his team would play all their games in the same way: 'We see no point in trying to make the local teams look good. The game would be a farce'."

Boksburg Vikings 15 Wakefield Trinity 42

Trinity's next match was on Tuesday 3 July under floodlights at Rand Stadium against Boksburg Vikings, who included former rugby union stars Chris Geyer, Stoffel Landsberg, Sarel Pelser and Hans Lourens.

The headline of *The Star's* report was "Local players learn quickly," and the paper reported: "There were more lessons from Wakefield Trinity last night, but the local rugby league players are good students and Boksburg Vikings did well... in their 42–15 defeat... Vikings were much quicker to play the ball after a tackle than Johannesburg Celtic had been, but were completely out-hooked in the scrums, bunched too much behind the scrum-half, surrendered possession too easily, passed haphazardly for much of the game and often missed their tackles."

Wakefield coach Ken Traill said "They made plenty of mistakes, but the South Africans were much better than they were on Saturday." He added that he had been impressed by the play of Nols Greyling and Sarel Pelser.

Trinity were clearly settling down in South Africa, and *The Star* said they were "more impressive... than in their opening match. They switched play continually, gained possession for three-quarters of the match and seldom missed a pass. Tom van Vollenhoven scored two fine tries before being hurt in a heavy tackle (the injury is not serious) and Fred Griffiths played an outstanding game at full-back. He also kicked five conversions.

Vikings were overwhelmed in the forwards and in the first half they did nothing but tackle. But when they saw more of the ball in the second period they used it well. Peter

Draper and Hans Pretorius ran strongly at centre. Draper made a try by the hardworking forwards Chris Liebenberg. Pretorius and scrum half Stoffel Landsberg scored the other tries and Sarel Pelser converted all three."

The report concluded that if the South African teams continued to improve, Trinity could be tested on the tour. For the next encounter, Trinity headed south to Bloemfontein.

The local team, the Bloemfontein Aquilas, were no match for the tourists, who won 48–9. Two days later, on Monday 9 July, in Durban, Trinity demolished a South African Invitation XIII 59–3, with Tom van Vollenhoven scoring five tries.

The South African team included one former Springbok, Chris de Nysschen, and three former Free State provincial players: R. Pothas, Gert 'Oupa' Coetzer and P. Botha. The full team was:

R. Pothas (Bloemfontein Aquilas), G. Coetzer (Aquilas), M. Brown (Johannesburg Celtic), I. De Jong (Celtic), N. Greyling (Celtic), P. Botha (Aquilas), P. Kruger (Celtic), P. Pieterse (Aquilas), N. van Rooyen (Boksburg Vikings), P. Peacock (Pretoria Koedoes), R. Botha (Celtic), C. de Nysschen (Aquilas, capt.), J. Bowles (Koedoes).

The match was covered by the *Durban Daily News*, who sent one of their rugby union writers to cover it. He clearly did not enjoy the match, compared it with the recent union encounter between Natal and the British Lions, and was not impressed.

The writer argued that "the National Rugby League has attempted to rush its fences. Its players were palpably outclassed; it had no programme to offer and no explanatory comment. In fact, it forgot to invite this newspaper to attend its match, which is by the way."

He said that many of the 2,000 crowd left before the end, and thought that the referee had blown for time before the 80 minutes were up. To be fair, the writer did say that he had seen league played 'overseas' and "at its best it is a far, far better game than this. It was easy to imagine the likes of van Vollenhoven, Prinsloo, Skene and company longing for the good old days of a full-blooded cut through the defence, the full-length tackle (hardly ever seen), the fast heel from the loose and the launching of a new attack, in one fast and fluid movement."

As so often with rugby union writers when watching league, he questioned 'play-the-ball' which he said "seemed to serve no better purpose than punctuate the flow of the game." He also felt that a feature of the game was to be to 'die' with the ball, and did not see the constant movement that league claimed. He did not see any "good tactical fly-half play". However, he did recognise that the game had been one-sided, unlike his Natal side's recent match against the rugby union British Lions.

Trinity's next encounter was back in the Transvaal, in Benoni, again against a South African Invitation XIII. It proved to be the closest match of the tour.

SA Invitation XIII 25 Wakefield Trinity 38

It is interesting to note that in previewing the game, *The Star* said: "Rugby union on the East Rand has been particularly hard it by the start of rugby league in South Africa", showing that the loss of players to league was having some impact, despite the massive resources union had. The preview also said that Trinity were "probably the world's best professional club side."

Around 2,500 fans saw a tough game "marked by sporadic bouts of punching". *The Star* said that although Trinity "were never in danger of defeat, they had to fight hard all the way." The Wakefield pack was again far superior to the South Africans. The Invitation XIII took the lead through Hannes Heyberg, with Sarel Pelser converting. Tries by Albert Firth and Ken Hirst and a conversion by Griffiths made the score 8–5 to the tourists. However, a thrilling 75-yard try by the left winger Daan van der Walt, converted by Pelser, put the Invitation side ahead again.

Hirst scored from the kick off. Griffiths converted to restore Trinity's lead. Hirst then completed his hat-trick, with Griffiths' conversion making the score 18–10.

The South Africans were providing real opposition for the first time on the tour. *The Star* said that "Their tackling was more determined than in the past and their forwards gained a good share of the ball." From a scrum, their forwards kicked through and Gert Venter scored; Pelser converted.

Another try by Hirst, again converted by Griffiths, made the half-time score 23–15. Stoffel Landsberg was injured just before the break and he was replaced by Piet Kruger.

Dennis Williamson scored by the posts and Griffiths' conversion meant Wakefield led 28–15. Alan Skene and Jan Prinsloo scored tries for Trinity. Van der Walt and Venter replied for the South Africans, and the final score was 38–25.

The final match was in Pretoria, which Trinity again dominated to beat an Invitation team 46–8.

South African Invitation XIII 8 Wakefield Trinity 46

Once again, the South African side was outclassed, particularly in the pack. Geoff Oakes, Don Vines and Brian Briggs all played well for Wakefield. Vines and C. de Beer were sent off in the second half. De Beer had replaced Lourens, who broke his leg in the first half. Trinity's tries came from a hat-trick by Prinsloo, two each for Briggs, Holliday and van Vollenhoven, and one each for Brophy, Williamson and Skene. Griffiths contributed five goals. Venter scored twice for the Invitation XII, with Sarel Pelser adding a goal.

Ken Traill commented when Wakefield returned home: "I am confident there is a future for rugby league in South Africa provided that the NRL and RLSA get together and amalgamate. If they don't they'll find themselves fighting a losing battle." He said that the players were enthusiastic and "did very well... but they have a tremendous lot to learn and it is unfortunate they could not have had the benefit of coaching by someone well versed in rugby league football before we went out there."

Traill and Eddie Thomas, the Wakefield secretary had been particularly impressed by the first game staged by RLSA under floodlights. "The football was quite good rugby league" commented Traill, "and I would say the standard was higher than anything we met. I was greatly impressed by Hennie van Zyl, the former Springbok." Mr Thomas was also impressed by van Zyl, and said he thought he was among the top 10 rugby league wingers.

The NRL lost money on tour, but they felt that it did a "tremendous amount of good" for their players. Trinity clearly played the matches seriously, and gave the South Africans a standard to work towards.

At the end of August 1962, the British Lions played three matches in eight days against a Rugby League South Africa team. The Lions were on their way home from a long tour of Australia and New Zealand. All three games were very high scoring for the time, but the home side was generally competitive.

"The British rugby league team has a duty to the game and the public when their three match tour opens in Pretoria tomorrow night. The future of rugby league in South Africa will depends heavily on their performances. The farcical matches played by British and French teams a few years ago are all too fresh in the memory. It will be the touring team's task to present a new image of the game".[85]

The Johannesburg Star's reporter had a point. The three matches in 1957 had produced little for the game in South Africa except maybe prompting some players to seek their fortune in rugby league overseas. The two rival organisations were both running competitions, but, despite the presence of some former Springboks and other prominent union players, their club matches were relatively low key.

This was a strong British side. They were the reigning World Champions, having won the title in 1960 in England. They had been on tour since 15 May, and had played 30 matches, 21 in Australia and nine in New Zealand. In Australia they had retained the Ashes, winning the test series 2–1, and only lost two other matches. However, in New Zealand, despite winning six of their nine matches, they had lost the test series 2–0. Arthur Walker, the assistant tour manager who was the manager on the South Africa visit as the tour manager Stuart Hadfield did not make the trip, said that this had been because of injuries and having to play players out of position.

Seventeen players made the trip to South Africa, out of 26 who had been to Australia and New Zealand. The black Wigan star Billy Boston had been injured and returned home, although he had already made it clear that he would not visit South Africa. Tour captain Eric Ashton also missed out, as did star scrum-half Alex Murphy. However, the party did include Eric Fraser at full-back, Neil Fox in the centre, Mick Sullivan and Ike Southward on the wing, Dave Bolton and Harold Poynton in the half-back positions, and among the forwards were Jack Wilkinson, John Shaw, Laurie Gilfedder, Dick Huddart and Derek Turner. The team for the opening match in Pretoria only had two players who had not played against Australia in the test matches.

On arrival in Johannesburg, Arthur Walker reassured the press that "The team is determined to show the public the game at its best... We are in a new country to rugby league and we hope to do the game a service. We do not regard our visit as a holiday and will pull out all the stops in our matches. We certainly will not regard the games as an exhibition. You can't play friendly matches in rugby league." He said that Fox and Huddart had been the outstanding players on the tour so far.[86]

There was another incentive for the South Africans. A week before the tourists arrived, the Rugby League International Board had met in New Zealand. Seemingly oblivious to the political situation in South Africa, they had declared that "provided the game makes suitable development, South Africa will be recognised as a rugby league nation for the purposes of the World Cup tournament to be jointly staged in Australia and New Zealand in 1963. They were also going to be allowed to nominate a referee.[87]

The RLSA had been preparing to face the Lions, and had announced a training squad of 21 players, including six former union Springboks. Ronnie Colin had been working with the backs, and Jan Pansegrouw trained the forwards. The Lions were in South Africa for just under two weeks. All three fixtures were against a Rugby League South Africa XIII, which at least gave them the appearance of 'test' matches. Unfortunately the rugby union British Lions were on tour at the same time, which inevitably overshadowed the rugby league team, although they received reasonable coverage in the press. Stuart Hadfield had written to RFL secretary Bill Fallowfield from New Zealand, saying that the players were exhausted, but Fallowfield had insisted that the tour go ahead, saying that "If we fail to send our touring team then we can say goodbye to rugby league football in South Africa."

In his biography by Robert Gate, published in 2005, Neil Fox recalled Gary Cooper getting into difficulties in the sea and having to be rescued by team-mate Peter Small, but does not comment on the matches. He was also shocked by some of the conditions he saw: "...after we flew in we travelled through some of the townships to Johannesburg. We couldn't believe the conditions people were living in – tumbledown shacks and tin huts." [88] He also says that the crowds at the games were multi-racial, but if there were African or Coloured people present, they must have been in segregated areas. He also says that the players were so tired of travelling that they turned down the offer of a trip to a national park. He concludes: "The experience in South Africa was a good one, but by then we really did want to get back home. We had been away for more than three months..." [89]

The first match was scheduled for the Pilditch Stadium in Pretoria, to be played under floodlights on a Thursday evening. The preview in *The Star* said that "The British side includes some of the world's great players and if they are unable to entertain the discriminating South African rugby follower, there will be little hope of local players gaining support for their competitions... on paper they should whip the RLSA's side... the task of gaining possession will be the South African side's main problem, for although they have good forwards by local standards, including former Springboks Martin Pelser and Dawie Ackerman, they oppose six experts... The South African backs face the match with reasonable confidence. All had good reputations in rugby union and four are former Springboks. They have adapted themselves well to the new code, and given opportunities they will certainly test the British defences to the full." [90]

A crowd of between 9,000 and 10,000 came to watch the match, bigger than any of those which had seen the Wakefield Trinity matches. The teams lined up:

RLSA: C. Nimb, H. van Zyl, R. Lombard, G. Lubbe, K. Boonzaier, N. Rens, M. Gericke, F. Holthauzen, J. Veriuty, H. Bennett, W. Vermaas, M. Pelser, D. Ackerman.
Great Britain: G. Cooper, F. Carlton, P. Small, N. Fox, M. Sullivan. D. Bolton, H. Poynton, J. Wilkinson, J. Shaw, J. Taylor, L. Gilfedder, R. Huddart, D. Turner.
Substitute: E. Fraser for Carlton
Referee: D. Coetzee

The Lions won fairly comfortably, 49–30, with Peter Small, Neil Fox and Dick Huddart contributing two tries apiece, Cooper, Carlton, Taylor, Gilfedder and Fraser each scoring once, and Neil Fox kicking eight goals. For the RLSA side, Willem Vermaas and Hennie van Zyl each scored twice, Gericke kicked four goals and Vermaas five. Although the scoring was high for a rugby league match at this time, possibly reflecting the Lions' tiredness at the end of a long tour, the supporters seem to have enjoyed the match.

The report noted that some of the British forwards, Huddart, Gilfedder and Turner, were similar to the threequarters in their runs. Naturally, the "huge centre" Neil Fox stood out. As predicted, the greater experience of the British pack meant that the tourists dominated possessions, but the South African defence was "outstanding", in particular Charlie Nimb.

Hennie van Zyl stood out for the South African side. Vermaas "also had an excellent game", although some of the former Springboks found the going harder. Ackerman "was always prominent, but it was not until late in the game that Martin Pelser got to grips with the match. Natie Rens was badly out of touch and he looked quite frail as he faced up to his bullocking opponents."

Arthur Walker commented after the match that "Hennie van Zyl is wonderful" and said that he could get a place in any team in Britain. He said that he had been impressed by the South Africans and "All they need is experience. After one more season they will be a match for anyone", although this comment proved to be over-optimistic. [91]

The Star's sports diary reflected on the game the next day. In a piece headed "Rugby league makes good progress", it said that "repeated claims that rugby league players are fitter, tougher and faster than those in rugby union are being borne out by matches in South Africa, and there has been a marked improvement by several players who have turned professional. The most notable examples are Willem Vermaas and Charlie Nimb. There are some that feel that even Hennie van Zyl is a better player today than he was against the All Blacks." The article also named four NRL players who had improved. It is interesting that all the players were backs or half-backs, as it is generally recognised that rugby union forwards had far more difficulty in adapting to the league code.

Two days later the teams met again, this time on the Indian Ocean coast in Durban. Great Britain won again, but this time by the narrow margin of six points, 39–33. The report in *The Star* said that this was "rugby league at its best" [92] and that the match had "erased much of the harm done to the code by the two earlier exhibition matches here." The matches referred to were one of the 1957 series, and a 59–3 win by Wakefield Trinity over a South African XIII.

Great Britain dominated the first half of the match, and the home team was "engaged in constant last ditch defence against a merciless battering by bigger, heavier and more experienced opposition." The report said that the "British team did turn in an exhilarating and heady display of swift-running rugby, backed by superb handling and bewildering switches in direction on attack." Once again Dick Huddart, Derek Turner, Neil Fox and Colin Hutton (the team's coach who came on as a substitute for Ike Southward) standing out.

For the RLSA side, Hennie van Zyl was missing through injury, but his replacement, Mike Lubbe, was "outstanding". Gert Smit had a great game at full-back, and without their resolute defence the tourists' 20–10 half-time lead would have been even greater. The reporter felt that the "gem" of the evening was not one of the 16 tries, but a cover tackle by Lubbe on Peter Smith by the corner flag after a 60 yard chase.

Martin Pelser, Charlie Nimb and Willem Vermaas also stood out for the South Africans. The report commented that "It would be difficult to conclude after Saturday night's spectacle that rugby league has gained a solid foothold in Natal. But one thing is certain, it would be well worth RLSA's while to try again at a more opportune time."

For the Lions, Eric Fraser scored four tries from full-back, Mick Sullivan got a couple, and Dick Huddart and Peter Small notched one each. Neil Fox also scored a try and added six goals. For the RLSA, Holthauzen scored two tries, Smit, Lubbe, Lombard, Boonzaier and Ackerman got one each and Vermaas kicked six goals. The teams were:

RLSA: G. Smit, G. Lubbe, R. Lombard, A. Du Plessis, K. Boonzaier, C. Nimb, M. Gericke, F. Holthauzen, J. Veriuty, O. Oostuizen, W. Vermaas, M. Pelser, D. Ackerman.

Great Britain: E. Fraser, I. Southward, P. Small, N. Fox, M. Sullivan, D. Bolton, H. Poynton, J. Wilkinson, J. Shaw, K. Noble, L. Gilfedder, R. Huddart, D. Turner.

Substitute: C. Hutton (for Southward)

Referee: D. Coetzee.

The teams returned to Johannesburg, and had a six day break before the final match of the series, on Friday 31 August at the Rand Stadium. Sadly, the quality and close fought nature of the match in Durban was not repeated. Arthur Walker commented afterwards that "We played test match rugby league... There is no need for South Africa to feel depressed about the game... [we decided to] pull out all the stops in an effort to gain an accurate impression of the state of the game in South Africa". [93] Wanting to avoid ending a long tour with an embarrassing defeat was probably also an incentive for the Lions.

Mr Walker pointed out that the South Africans still had much to learn. Asked whether British hooker John Shaw's ball-winning ploys had been legal, he replied that Harold Poynton would do a 'dummy' throw to allow Shaw to get his legs across in the scrum, and thus ensure possession. "Your hooker did not know what to do about it ... but he does now. We have told him" he added. [94]

The 7,000 crowd were disappointed when it was announced that Hennie van Zyl had failed a fitness test, despite assurances a couple of days earlier in the press that he was fit for the game. *The Star's* reporter was clearly disappointed with the home team's performance, saying that they "looked like they had never played the game before." Although Nimb, Pelser and Smit played well, "most of the players seem to have forgotten everything the Australian coach, Dave Brown, had taught them. They left gaps everywhere, tackled poorly and surrendered the ball with little resistance." [95]

Once again, the Lions had most of the possession, and "they made so few mistakes in open play that they were nearly always on the attack... The speed and strength of all the British players must have been a revelation to the spectators."

There was some consolation for the South Africans. Their centre, Fanie Naude, scored a good try after a solo run, and the move that lead to Gericke's try was one of the best in the match. For the Lions, Cooper and Small both scored hat-tricks of tries, Gilfedder added two more and kicked a goal, Bolton and Poynton both scored a try, while Neil Fox kicked five goals and scored a try to notch up 50 points in the series. For the South African side,

Boonzaier, Naude and Gericke all scored tries, Gericke also kicked four goals and Vermaas added another three.

RLSA: G. Smit, K. Boonzaier, C. Nimb, F. Naude, G. Lubbe, A. Du Plessis, M. Gericke, S. Steenkamp, H. Bennett, O. Oostuizen, W. Vermaas, M. Pelser, D. Ackerman.

Great Britain: E. Fraser, P. Small, G. Cooper, N. Fox, M. Sullivan, D. Bolton, H. Poynton, J. Wilkinson, J. Shaw, J. Taylor, L. Gilfedder, R. Huddart, D. Turner.

The match report concluded that "it was all too clear that there is a lot of work and practice ahead before officials can again take seriously of sending teams on overseas tours." However, Arthur Walker commented when the squad arrived back in London that the "South Africans will be ready for the next World Cup in 1964".[96]

In fact, the World Cup did not take place until 1968, by which time the game in South Africa had collapsed, and most of the players who had gone to Great Britain in the late 1950s and early 1960s had retired or were coming to the end of their careers. Was Arthur Walker's assessment correct? It is difficult to judge the South African strength from this tour, as their team was composed of players only from one of the domestic competitions, although arguably the stronger one. Of the RLSA players, only Ken Boonzaier had played in Great Britain at this time, although Charlie Nimb was soon to leave to join Hull FC.

Had the South Africans been able to select from all their players, they could have fielded a far stronger team. There were the NRL players to consider, but more importantly those playing overseas. On 12 October 1961, a Rugby League XIII played a French XIII in Paris. The match was in the same week as Lancashire played Yorkshire in the County Championship, and Cumberland played New Zealand, so a lot of the leading Great Britain players were presumably unavailable. All the backs were South African: Fred Griffiths at full-back, then a threequarter line-up of Tom van Vollenhoven, Alan Skene, Colin Greenwood and Jan Prinsloo. Ted Brophy played in the front row. While Brophy was probably not of true international class, the other five players were. However, this shows the weakness in the South African set up. Based exclusively on former union players, albeit some of the highest calibre, the forwards found it far more difficult adapt to rugby league than the backs.

Putting any political considerations aside, never easy to do when discussing South African sport at this time, on paper South Africa could have fielded a competitive team in a World Cup in 1964, and this may have given the game a higher profile in the country. The French side was not particularly strong by the mid–1960s, but, ironically, that was the reason for the Australian Rugby League unilaterally postponing the World Cup from 1965 to 1968. The French had been uncompetitive on their 1964 tour to Australia and it had been a financial disaster. Never entirely convinced about the value of international tournaments, the ARL postponed the tournament for three years, fearing that the French side would not be an attraction. Ironically, the South Africans could have given the tournament a boost, and some much needed fresh blood.

In 1963, there was only one rugby league competition in South Africa. To help develop the sport, a tour was arranged to Australia and New Zealand. The tour was in July and August, and some players from English clubs, including Tom van Vollenhoven and Wilf Rosenberg, did not take part. Hennie van Zyl also missed the tour.

The 1963 South African tourists. Back: G. Coetzer, A. Skene, H. Bennett, B. Oberholzer, G. Jacobs, J. de Waal, G. Smit, J. Gaydon; second row: W. Moore (trainer), R. Peacock, B. Erasmus, K. Pelser, W. Vermaas, G. van Zyl, P. Oosthuizen, J. Verwey, D. Brown (coach); front row: M. Gericke, F. Griffiths, I. Benson (co-manager), D. Ackermann (captain), H. Kelley (co-manager), N. Rens, M. Pelser; front : C. Greenwood, J. Pieterse, O. Odendaal.

After winning their opening two matches in Australia, the tourists suffered some heavy defeats, but in New Zealand beat Wellington, and then New Zealand

The tourists originally chose a party of 23 players. Trial matches had been held in South Africa, and the following players were selected, led by Dawie Ackerman:

Fred Griffiths, Gert Smit, Johnny Gaydon, Jan de Waal, Johan Pieterse, Bart Erasmus, Alan Skene, Natie Rens, Colin Greenwood, Mannetjies Gericke, Ontie Odendaal, Roelof Peacock, Ockert Oosthuizen, Bunny Oberholzer, Ken Pelser, Jan Verwey, Harry Bennet, Gerhardus van Zyl, Martin Pelser, Willem Vermaas, Victor Jacobs and Ackerman.

Alan Whiticker and Ian Collis in their *Rugby League test matches in Australia* book say that Australia won 34–6 in Brisbane "in second gear" after being 15–4 up at half-time, and 20–4 ahead when the tourists lost Martin Pelser with torn shoulder ligaments. South Africa's points came from three goals by full-back Gert Smit.

Australia: L. Johns, K. Irvine, G. Langlands, R. Gasnier, E. Lumsden, E. Harrison, A. Summons, J. Raper, K. Day, R. Thornett, P. Gallagher, I. Walsh, N. Kelly.

Scorers: Tries: Langlands 2, Irvine, Gasnier, Lumsden, Harrison, Raper, Day; Goals: Johns 5.

South Africa: G. Smit, J. Gaydon, A. Skene, J. Pieterse, B. Erasmus, C. Greenwood, M. Gericke, V. Jacobs, D. Ackerman, W. Vermaas, J. Verwey, B. Oberholzer, M. Pelser.

Scorer: Goals: Smit 3.

A week later in Sydney, Australia won comfortably 54–21, although it is interesting to note that in 1960 they had beaten France 56–6; a bigger score and winning margin. Johan Pieterse scored South Africa's first try after a couple of minutes, but Australia were ahead 28–3 at half-time. South Africa had lost hooker Jan Verwey with a broken leg after 18 minutes, he was replaced by Harry Bennett. The second half was more even, but Whiticker and Collis say that South Africa's tries were scored against some "half-hearted" defence. Greenwood scored twice, along with Oberholzer and Gericke. Griffiths kicked three goals.

Australia: L. Johns, K. Irvine, R. Gasnier, K. Thornett, G. Langlands, E. Harrison, B. Muir, J. Raper, K. Day, R. Thornett, P. Quinn, N. Kelly, P. Gallagher.
Scorers: Tries: Langlands 2, K. Thornett 2, Irvine 2, Harrison, Gasnier, Johns, Muir, Raper, Gallagher; Goals: Johns 9.
South Africa: G. Smit, J. Gaydon, A. Skene, J. Pieterse, B. Erasmus, C. Greenwood, M. Gericke, V. Jacobs, D. Ackerman, W. Vermaas, J. Verwey, B. Oberholzer, M. Pelser.
Scorers: Tries: Greenwood 2, Oberholzer, Gericke, Pieterse; Goals: Griffiths 3.

At the end of the Australia leg of the tour, the South Africans only had 18 fit players. Skipper Dawie Ackerman had aggravated a finger injury in the last match in Australia. Then Fred Griffiths said that he could not go to New Zealand, although he did actually play in the end. The South Africans asked the Australian Control Board for some help, because there was no chance of bringing over replacements from home.

So two Australian forwards, Fred Anderson and Graham Wilson played as guests for the tourists in the test match, so it is not seen as an official test. But it was still a remarkable result. On a very heavy Carlaw Park pitch, two penalties from Griffiths saw South Africa home 4–3. The Kiwis' try came from Gary Blackler. Griffiths played at stand-off and skippered the side. On a very heavy pitch, his touch kicking proved to be crucial, often gaining 40 to 50 yards in the mud. Playing at full-back, Smit handled New Zealand's kicks immaculately. Some critics said that the conditions allowed South Africa to play a rugby union type game, but the conditions were the same for both sides, and Carlaw Park was notorious for heavy pitches.

It is interesting to consider how the tour might have gone if South Africa had been able to field their strongest team. The backs were quite strong, although Tom van Vollenhoven, Wilf Rosenberg and Hennie van Zyl would have added even more pace and experience. At half-back, Charlie Nimb now had played for a year at Hull. In the forwards, although Ted Brophy had left English rugby league in 1962, his experience could have been useful. Rudi Hasse had played for a year in England, albeit with a struggling Bradford Northern. And of course, Louis Neumann and Goolam Abed could have added to the team, but apartheid meant that they were not considered.

David Barends in action for Bradford Northern at Keighley in 1982.
(Photo courtesy Robert Gate)

17. The 1970s: Three wingers

For most of the 1970s, it was relatively straightforward for English rugby league clubs to sign Australians and New Zealanders. Some British players also went to Australia, in search of better weather, a new lifestyle and a good contract. The transfer ban was eventually reimposed in 1977, until it was removed for the final time after the 1982 Kangaroos tour.

Only three players came to England from South Africa in this time. Toby du Toit joined Warrington, and found some success before losing his place. Rather than try to find another club, he returned home.

The other two players were from the Coloured community in South Africa. David Barends played for the non-racial South African Rugby Union and Green Vigo for the South African Rugby Football Federation, two of the three national federations at the time for non-white rugby, before coming to England to play rugby league. Although they were both wingers, they were very different players.

Tobias (Toby) du Toit

Toby du Toit must surely rank as one of Johannesburg Police RFC's most talented rugby players ever. In the run-up to his provincial debut in 1967, du Toit, a winger, successfully represented his club in both the Bailey and Pirates Grand Challenge Cup competitions organized by the Transvaal Rugby Union.

Although Transvaal played against two touring teams in his debut season, du Toit, who lacked experience at provincial level, was not selected either against the French or the Scottish Borders teams that visited South Africa in 1967. He did, however, play in all eight representative matches, including six wins. This adequately prepared him for the first taste of international rugby that awaited him over the coming seasons.

With the arrival of the 1968 British Lions, du Toit was selected for the senior Transvaal side to face the tourists on 18 June at Ellis Park. He scored his first international points through a penalty kick and a conversion in a famous victory. It was the only match that the tourists lost on the tour. Building on this, he continued to excel and played in all eight Currie Cup matches in 1968. With seven victories, du Toit's team qualified for the final against Northern Transvaal in Pretoria. They were, however, not up to the task and were soundly defeated. Their earlier 17–8 victory over Western Province in the Southern Cross Shield competition in May in Cape Town provided some consolation. This concluded a most satisfying season for du Toit who was also the top scorer of the year with 63 points, including eight tries.

Continuing his good form, du Toit also played for Transvaal against the Australians at Ellis Park in 1969. Although they lost 23–14, they were still good enough to reach the SA Board Trophy final against Western Province. They were, however, defeated and finished the season with no silverware. Du Toit, in particular, was en route to a possible place in the Springbok team.

With the arrival of the New Zealand All Blacks the following year, du Toit took the first step towards Springbok honours with his inclusion in the Gazelles – the South African under–24 representative side. This was preceded by a notable performance for Transvaal against the tourists. Following consistent performances, he was also included in the Gazelle teams that faced the French and the Argentinean Pumas who toured the country in 1971. Equally satisfying was Transvaal ending the season with a draw against Northern Transvaal in the final of the Currie Cup. Despite consistent performances, du Toit never received the long-anticipated call-up to the national team, which prompted him to end his representative rugby union career after 41 provincial games and 18 tries.

Warrington rugby league historian Gary Slater reflects on du Toit's time at the club: "Toby du Toit was the first – and remains – the only South African to play for Warrington. He was recommended to the club by Tom van Vollenhoven and, for a winger, there could be no higher recommendation.

He flew into London's Heathrow Airport on Sunday 5 December, 1971, where he was met by Warrington's charismatic player-coach, Alex Murphy, who had played with van Vollenhoven at St Helens. Du Toit signed a three-year contact that week.

Du Toit threw himself into training and the business of learning the rules of this alien game. Murphy vowed not to rush him into the first-team, but his hand was forced by a spate of injuries to his outside backs and du Toit made his debut at Hunslet on Sunday 19 December. Warrington won 13–6, with du Toit kicking two goals.

He then played in every game until the end of the season – 24 in all – and scored points in his first nine appearances with eight tries and 15 goals. This resulted in premature comparisons with the club's two greatest wingers: Brian Bevan and Jack Fish.

The bronzed and powerful South African became a big favourite with Warrington fans and delivered the performances to match, including a hat-trick of tries at Doncaster in March 1972. On the way home from this match, three Warrington players – Mick Henighan, Conrad Barton and Derek Whitehead – were injured in a car crash.

Henighan and Barton suffered minor cuts and bruises, but Whitehead, the club's brilliant Great Britain full-back and first-choice goalkicker, was so badly cut about the hands and face that he was ruled out for a month. In his absence, du Toit became the number one goalkicker.

Warrington had embarked on a thrilling Challenge Cup run with victories over Batley, Castleford (after a replay) and Bramley to earn a semi-final against St Helens, Murphy's old club, at Wigan's Central Park on Saturday 15 April 1972. The match, which was televised on BBC1 with commentary by Eddie Waring, finished in a 10–10 draw with du Toit scoring a try and kicking a goal. The replay was at the same venue the following Wednesday night. It captured the fans' imagination, and attracted a crowd of more than 32,000. Du Toit kicked two goals and Murphy added a drop-goal, but they were powerless to stop St Helens from winning 10–6. The Saints went on to lift the cup, beating Leeds 16–13 at Wembley, while Murphy continued his job of rebuilding and revitalising the Warrington team. Despite an impressive first season in rugby league featuring 24 appearances, 14 tries, 26 goals and 94 points, du Toit had not fully convinced Murphy that he was good enough to be part of a trophy-winning side.

1972 Warrington team with Toby du Toit in the front row far right. (Photo: Courtesy Gary Slater)

The South African made only six more appearances for the first team in the 1972–73 season (including three as a substitute) and signed off with a try in a 34–16 victory over York at Wilderspool in November 1972. He was later put on the transfer list, but there were no takers and he eventually returned home.

His replacement on the left wing was John Bevan, the former Cardiff, Wales and Barbarians player, who had been a big success with the British Lions on their 1971 tour of New Zealand.

Welsh forward Mike Nicholas, who played in du Toit's last match for Warrington, recalls: "He scored a wonderful try for Warrington in the 1972 Challenge Cup semi-final against St Helens, but Murph didn't rate him and he was out of favour when I signed. He had the South African mentality. He was very much a loner and had his own lifestyle. He didn't mix with the other players. He lived in Lymm and played golf when a lot of the other guys didn't. I got quite friendly with him and liked him. I identified more with him than some of the others because he was an all-round sportsman. He was obviously talented, but Murph didn't rate him."

Murphy, of course, was vindicated as Warrington won four cups in the 1973–74 season with Bevan leading the way with 22 tries in 35 appearances, but du Toit had played his part in the Wire revolution. His exotic signing had helped to rejuvenate the club after a period in the doldrums when it flirted with going out of business."

In international rugby league today, the qualification rules are far looser than they were years ago. Residence can qualify a player to play for a particular country, let alone having one grandparent who was born there. But when David Barends was selected for the Great Britain squad to tour Australia and New Zealand in 1979, it was quite controversial within the game. David remains the only player of South African heritage to play for Great Britain at full international level.

David Barends

In October 2000, the South African Rugby Union honoured players who had achieved high levels of performance in rugby, but due to the laws and selection practice in the apartheid era in South Africa, had been unable to play for the Springboks. Until the early 1990s, only 'white' players were eligible for Springbok selection.

Only one rugby league player was involved in the ceremony – David Barends, although he points out that Green Vigo, who played for Wigan in the 1970s, was equally eligible for the honour "and should have been there". Also uniquely, David is the only South African born player to play for Great Britain. David was very pleased to be made an 'Honorary Springbok', and to be presented with a Springbok blazer and tie, which he regards as the ultimate honour for a South African rugby player. He also recalls that "some white players who refused to play for the Springboks because of their beliefs received the award, and I look up to them. They are the people who worked with Mandela for a better South Africa for all." David met Nelson Mandela in Johannesburg, and recalled it as a "most amazing day… meeting Mandela was just very, very special." He was also presented with an award by the Western Province Rugby Union.

Rugby Union in South Africa on the national, provincial and professional franchise level continued to be dominated by white players, while the grassroots game at club level is dominated by black players. At the time of the 1995 Rugby World Cup, the black rugby tradition was particularly strong in the Western and Eastern Cape. David's achievements in Britain did register with the coloured and black rugby players in South Africa, In 2002, Chester Williams, a black player who played for the Springboks in their 1995 Rugby Union World Cup victory, said in an interview with Jim White: "What I regret is that in my younger days I was just so ignorant about the apartheid system. Even in rugby I knew nothing of the struggle of our rugby players, guys like David Barends who couldn't get a game at home and had to come over to England to play rugby league and played for Great Britain." In a feature on rising black rugby star Conrad Jantjes in 2001, Andy Colquhoun wrote about "Black South African sportsmen such as Basil D'Oliveira – who played cricket for England – and David Barends who played rugby league for Great Britain."

David comes from Elim, a small village in the Bredasdorp District, near Cape Agulhas in the Western Cape. Rugby union has a strong following there. He first played rugby at school when he was eight years old. He continued to play at secondary school, and remembers going with his grandfather to watch matches in Elim. He moved to Cape Town after finishing at school and established himself as a winger in the coloured rugby union set up there. He played for the Roslyn club. After playing for Western Province, he was selected for the SACRFB XV to play the national Bantu (African) XV when he was just 21. But he recalls that "I had gone as far as I could in sport in South Africa at that time" by playing for the SACRFB XV. He could have stayed in South Africa, and developed his career in the finance industry, but was spotted by former Springbok and Wakefield Trinity forward Ivor Dorrington. Dorrington arranged for him to play for Wakefield, and after a few weeks delay while he got a passport, he arrived at Heathrow in December 1970. Jim Windsor had also been involved in bringing the 21-year-old to Great Britain. His attempts to get a passport were supported by the MP for Wakefield.

David was one of only a handful of non-white South Africans to play rugby league in Britain. Unsure about what language he spoke, the Wakefield officials who met him at Heathrow said slowly "Are you David Barends?" before establishing that he spoke perfect English. He made his debut a few days later at home to Blackpool Borough in a 44–8 victory. He was given "enthusiastic support" by the crowd and managed to score two tries from the wing.

He settled in Wakefield, living in the same house as Michael Hunte, Trinity's other black player, and established himself in rugby league and in Britain. He says that "rugby league taught me the discipline to be successful" and recalls the helpful advice that Tommy Smales gave him. He got married to a local girl and moved to Hemsworth, where he was the first black person in the village.

After a couple of seasons at Wakefield, where arguably the team was just starting to decline from their triumphs in the 1960s, he felt the need to move on to a new challenge and joined York.

David has fond memories of York, despite the club moving between the First and Second Divisions during his time there. He says: "York will always be in my heart. The people there loved their rugby and were very generous to me. It is also a beautiful city. I was also captain for a time" During this period, David played five times for the Other Nationalities team created to enliven the County Championship, scoring four tries. He remembers playing with Green Vigo, who although also from the Cape Province, did not have the same education as David and had more problems with the language in England, although David says he was a "brilliant player". He enjoyed meeting players from different backgrounds in that team.

It was a visit to his family in South Africa that inspired him to look for a bigger club. "My family wanted me to win trophies. I had not realised the importance for the people at home and my community for me to achieve things in rugby league. It would show that it was not only white people who could play rugby."

In 1977, Peter Fox was appointed coach of Bradford Northern, and built a side that over the next six seasons became a major force in the game. David was one of his first recruits. He found that Peter Fox "had good technical knowledge and could get the best from his team. He promised me that we would win trophies, and we did."

Peter Fox kept his word. In six seasons at Odsal, David played 202 games, scoring 70 tries. In 1979–80, Northern won the First Division title, and repeated the honour the following season. In the cup competitions, David got winners' medals in the John Player Trophy, Yorkshire Cup and the Premiership, as well as two runners' up medals in the Yorkshire Cup.

It was during this time that he was selected for Great Britain, although David says that he was considered for a cap in 1972. His qualification came through a rule that a player who had first played rugby league in a country could play for them. For David, his selection was very important: "It meant so much to the people who had helped me at home in South Africa – my family, my village, my church, the teachers at my school. And it meant that I felt

I was a real citizen of Great Britain." Although there was controversy over his selection – he was the first player not of British origin to play for the Lions – he was accepted by the players and tour management: "the coach Eric Ashton was a real gentleman," and has many fond memories of his time down under. He played 16 times, including the first two tests against Australia, and scored 10 tries. Although the Lions were successful outside the test matches, Australia won the test series 3–0. David's debut was in a 35–0 defeat in the first test in Brisbane, although he did have a try disallowed. He also played in the second test in Sydney, which Great Britain lost 24–16.

Ironically, David had played – with Green Vigo – for the Other Nationalities team that had been introduced into the County Championship in the mid–1970s, to try to revive interest in that competition. He scored four tries in five appearances.

David compared the "how integrated the Aboriginal people were in rugby league in Australia" with his experience in South Africa. He also recalls in New Zealand "meeting the Maori Queen and their settlements; I found their culture fascinating."

David's rugby league career finished in 1984. He played for Featherstone in 1983–84, and had a couple of matches for Batley as a finale. Looking back, in an interview with Mike Rylance for the book *The Glory of their Times*, he reflected on how tough rugby league was compared to union back home: "Rugby league shows you about real life. When you've got the ball, you have to take responsibilities. It's also about decision-making. If you put your team mate under stress, if you pass the ball and he gets taken out, it may mean you've made the wrong decision. The decisions you make have to be achievable, so they have to be simple. I think it took me several years to get to grips with the game…"

In 1979, following a discussion with his priest, he felt that he should take up a career that was more beneficial to the community, and became a probation officer. He has now retired, but his achievement of being made an 'honorary Springbok' were supported and publicised by the Probation Service. While working for the Service, he served on a national committee dealing with work with ethnic minority communities. He was also active in his trade union, UNISON.

He still lives in Hemsworth, and has strong links with his family in South Africa. His Great Britain caps and shirts are with his family there. In 1994, he visited South Africa for the first time with his wife Janet. She is white and such a trip would have been impossible prior to 1994 and the abolition of apartheid.

David coached in the amateur game for a period after he retired from playing, but has little involvement with the game today, although he watches it on television. His nephew has played for the junior Springboks, and David arranged for him to play for Leicester for a time. When the South African rugby league team toured England in 2008, David was the guest of honour when they played against Yorkshire at Dewsbury. Earlier, he had been offered the chance to go to South Africa to help develop rugby league there, but had to turn the opportunity down because it would have meant leaving his job in the Probation Service.

Had his career started today, David probably would have been able to fulfil his sporting ambitions in South Africa. As it was, apartheid drove him overseas, and as with his compatriot Basil D'Oliveira, he won international honours in Great Britain. Rugby union's loss was rugby league's gain.

Green Vigo is regarded as one of the most naturally talented players to ever play rugby league. Former Wigan forward Bill Ashurst recalls him destroying Leeds and Great Britain winger John Atkinson at Headingley in a cup match that caused Atkinson to briefly retire from the game. Wigan fans also recall him scoring seven tries against St Helens in a Lancashire Cup match in August 1976.

Green Vigo

In 1971, during the first rugby tour of the United Kingdom by a Black South African team, a young and very talented centre took his first steps towards rugby fame and recognition on a bigger stage. Sadly, like most of his generation, he never got the opportunity to represent his country at any of rugby union's biggest stadiums around the world.

When the South African Rugby Union decided to give recognition to past players that represented their segregated national rugby bodies, but never had the chance to represent their country in official test matches through the 'Yesterday's Heroes" Programme' [97], a small but significant group of players never bothered to claim their symbolic Springbok colours. It seems that the South African Rugby Football Union also erred by expecting these players to apply for recognition and receipt of the official colours. A significant number of former players rejected this requirement as an insult. Others also refused to receive something that they continued to associate with apartheid. One of those players was Green Gregory Vigo, who represented the Proteas, the national team of the former South African Rugby Football Federation (SARFF) in the 1971 tour and against the visiting England side in a memorable match at the Goodwood Show Grounds in Cape Town in 1972. Following a successful career in representative rugby with the Swartland Union and Proteas, Vigo switched from rugby union to rugby league in 1973. The lack of opportunities for further progress in rugby union, combined with the discrimination he faced in sport and everyday life must have influenced his decision. He was spotted by a scout from Wigan and went on to make a name for himself playing for Wigan, Swinton and Oldham.

Green started his rugby career in the coastal village of Saldanha in the 1960s at Tigers Rugby Club, an affiliate of the Swartland Rugby Union which was affiliated to the SARFF, which served clubs from the Coloured community.

It is said that the young and talented Vigo and another friend had a run-in with the law, but thanks to the timely intervention of the club leadership, especially Abe Williams (the Springbok manager of the 1981 tour of New Zealand) the energies of the two young men were channelled into rugby. [98] This proved to be their saving grace. Soon Vigo proved to be an exceptionally talented player and was selected to represent his home union, Swartland in the Gold and Silver Cup competitions of the SARFF. Other honours soon followed.

By 1970 he was selected for the Proteas. He played inter-racial tests against the South African African Rugby Board, whose team by then was known as the African Springboks and later as the Leopards. These matches were bitterly fought and were important for players like Vigo to develop their skills.

Although he did not score a try on the 1971 tour of Great Britain, he was a valued member of the squad which won once, drew once and lost three games. The tour was particularly difficult because of increased anti-apartheid protests, following the campaigns against the South African rugby union and cricket teams the year before. The game against Hertfordshire, in particular, was seriously disrupted by on-field protests and demonstrations which undoubtedly had an impact on the tourists' performance.

Despite these difficulties, they completed the tour with a final game against the Netherlands national team which the Proteas won 28–23 at Hilversum.[99]

Following their first tour, 1972 and the England tour of South Africa brought new opportunities and further divisions for Black rugby. In response to the demonstrations and political problems associated with South African sport, the RFU indicated prior to the tour its willingness to play against Black teams. To prepare for this, the administrators from the various ethnic structures met to discuss a proposal for the selection of a unified Black team consisting of Green's Union, the SARFF and the South African Rugby Union (SARU) for the match. From the start, divisions between the two rival bodies dominated discussions.

The delegates from SARU argued that the timing of the tour was inappropriate and that participation in the match would amount to selling out and be tantamount to active participation in the oppression and segregation of their own people. It was also argued that such matches also contributed to the avoidance of serious discussion about the establishment of a non-racial society and sport. Given people's experiences of the damaging effects of apartheid since 1948, including forced removals, the pass laws, segregation and banning of political organisations and activists, divisions also occurred within the ranks of SARFF over the tour.

Despite SARU's objections, the leadership of the SARFF and SAARFB (African Springboks) decided to proceed with the match. This intensified the divisions within the various black rugby bodies and led to further splits. Against this background, Green Vigo played against the England team at the Athlone Stadium in Cape Town before 10,000 spectators. This historic match, described as 'ill-tempered', provided the players with their first quality opposition. Although England won 11–6, Green Vigo and Errol Tobias in particular, were singled out by the rugby media as the best players.[100] In his book *Rugby in South Africa*, Paul Dobson says that Green Vigo, among others, was 'outstanding'. This praise, however, was overshadowed by the match was being hit by a boycott by players and spectators and demonstrations outside the stadium.

Following the England tour and the dissatisfaction with the decision to proceed with this match, the SARFF split when a significant number of its clubs and unions joined the SARU. This significantly weakened the SARFF. Renewed attempts in 1973 to bring about the establishment of a united rugby controlling board, like so often before, again failed. For talented players like Vigo, there must have seemed little hope of progressing in rugby union. Vigo therefore decided in 1973 to accept the offer from Central Park to play professional rugby league.

The 1971 Proteas tour did not play a role in his decision to change codes. The match that brought him to the attention of Wigan was the 1972 match against England. He was approached to switch codes, but initially declined the offer and advised the scout to return a year later, in the hope of getting rid of him. The offer was renewed in 1973 [101] as Wigan were trying to rebuild. Vigo, aged 23, accepted a five year contract. With his background as a young fisherman and the limited opportunities for Coloured people in South Africa, the Wigan offer must have been hard to resist.

Apparently he left with the blessing of the South African Rugby Federation although some felt that he should have stayed until the 1974 British Lions tour in order to increase his monetary value. [102] Vigo himself hoped that he would be allowed to play local rugby upon his return. [103]

The British newspapers hailed Green as a second Billy Boston, one of Wigan's greatest players and a member of Rugby League's Hall of Fame. This was very flattering to a player who had yet to make his mark in rugby league. These early hopes was also frightening and caused some newspaper reporters to caution against unreasonable expectations. [104] His new coach was Vince Karalius. He changed Green Vigo from a rugby union player into a rugby league professional. Vigo himself regarded Karalius as the most important influence on his playing career in the hard world of rugby league.

After his arrival in Wigan, his new club still had to sort out his work permit [105] and provide appropriate accommodation. Having left South Africa in summer, the club also assisted him with acquiring clothes for the cold English climate. In addition, Vigo – as an Afrikaans-speaker from a rural background – had to settle down to life in a total new world with its bewildering range of English. To ease his integration, he stayed with an elderly couple, Mr and Mrs Halliday, who according to Vigo treated him "like their own child". Staying within such an intimate set up, helped him improve his English. This was supplemented, according to newspaper reports, with extra English classes. While he waited for his work permit to be sorted out, he worked as a club groundsman at R52 a week which far exceeded the equivalent rate for similar work in South Africa. [106] However, some players from that time say that far more could have been done by the club to help him settle into his new surroundings. Sometimes he even struggled to find his home. [107]

The process of finalising the paperwork, however did not prevent Wigan from immediately put to full use Green's "rippling mass of compact muscle" that seemed to have been "hewn from solid Cape oak" [108] at the TBA Sevens Tournament on 11 August 1973 at Central Park. Five tries later and after a "five star display of classy centre work", Green Vigo became "Super Green" for the Wigan fans after Colin Clarke, who captained the side, collected the Trophy. [109] In the aftermath of this tournament, the media headlines significantly read "Saldanha Tiger Roars" with a sub-head that said "Vigo, Gray shows class". [110] The reporter appeared quite stunned by what he had seen and used phrases such as "rugby renaissance", "some real class in the art of rugby", "dream debuts", "made two spectacular tries", "scored five beautiful tries himself," "being a magnificent effort" and "left the opposition standing."

After that dream debut, it was finally time to enter the real battlefield of rugby league with all its new rules, tactical plays and culture. At Whitehaven on 25 August, Vigo scored his first try in 17–12 defeat. He repeated this in a Lancashire Cup semi-final 20–4 win at Workington and against Oldham in an 18–0 triumph. Green's good form from the previous rugby union season had continued. He earned further nicknames, such as the 'Wizard of

Wigan'[111] and the 'Saldanha Iron Horse'.[112] Against Hull Kingston Rovers on 27 October, he scored a hat trick of tries in a comprehensive 38–3 victory.

His presence and potency on the field soon made him a target for opposing players. Unable to counter his blistering pace and physical approach to the game, an opposition forward was sent off for tripping him. As early as his full first professional game, he lost some teeth after a stiff-arm tackle.[113]

Underlining his continuing good form while still adapting to the 13-a-side man game, Green did more than enough to maintain his place in the first team and played 26 matches with 11 tries in his first full season. He won his first medal, in the Lancashire Cup Final against Salford on 13 October 1973. Wigan won 19–9. Wigan finished 11th in the First Division, just two points clear of the relegation places.

Despite a good start, the first three seasons of his new playing career was pretty ordinary without really setting the wider rugby league scene alight. He was consistent and established himself in the sport, playing on the wing. His second season, 1974–75 saw an improvement in his try tally. He played 27 out of 36 games and scored 13 tries. Wigan had a much improved league season and finished in second place in the table, 11 points behind the new league champion and traditional rivals, St Helens.

Vigo played 35 matches in the 1975–76 season. However, the campaign was dominated by St Helens, who won the Challenge Cup, Premiership Trophy and the BBC2 Floodlit Trophy. Vigo maintained his consistency in scoring tries and finished the season with 14. The club dropped from second to fifth place in the table, just six points behind champions Salford.

On 21 August 1976, at the start of the new season, Vigo entered Wigan's record books by scoring seven tries in a match against arch rivals St Helens in a Lancashire Cup match at Central Park. Saints had problems with a player-management pay dispute, and fielded a very weak team, but to score seven tries in a 37–5 win is still an achievement. This ensured a place for himself in the annals of Wigan rugby league history alongside some of their biggest heroes such as Billy Boston, Johnny Ring and Gordon Ratcliff. This record stood until 1992 when Shaun Edwards and Martin Offiah both scored 10 tries in a match.

Vigo ended the campaign with 18 tries and was Wigan's top try scorer. However, Wigan slipped to seventh place, 12 points behind the league champions, Featherstone Rovers and 10 clear of the relegation places.

The 1977–78 campaign was Vigo's most productive with 28 tries and a goal from 40 appearances. It also included one of the best performances of his career, a hat-trick in a 25–22 John Player Trophy win away to Leeds. Team mate Bill Ashurst recalls: "It was Green Vigo's game. Fans from both clubs, with the BBC television audience who watched the second half live, saw the best and full potential of Green. He made one of the best wingers of the previous decade for Leeds and Great Britain, John Atkinson, look out of place beside him. We were trailing by 10 points after 55 minutes and it looked as if we were going to be knocked out. Green then scored three of the best tries I have ever seen. John Atkinson, who was trying to mark him, briefly retired after that game."[114] Ashurst also says that Vigo was subject to racist abuse from someone in the crowd who threw bananas at him.

Green Vigo while at Wigan.
(Photo: Courtesy Robert Gate)

The 1978–79 season was disappointing. Vigo broke his arm and did not play in the first team. The 1979–80 season also started with his absence. The team was now struggling and Vigo only played four matches. Proud Wigan, one of the sport's greatest names, finished 13th and were relegated to the Second Division with Hunslet, York and Blackpool Borough.

Vigo played once in the 1980–81 season before being transferred to Swinton. During his stay at Wigan, he played 165+2 matches for the first team and scored 85 tries and one goal for a total of 257 points. Jack Winstanley in his *Illustrated History of Wigan RLFC* says that he "scored some brilliantly exciting tries" in his seven years with the club. [115] It was his misfortune to play for the club when they were a declining force in the game.

Winstanley says that Vigo was "a bit of a lad" and that his number of tries "could have been greatly increased by a more reliable and conscientious approach to the game".[116] Mike Rylance says in *The Glory of their Times*: "But although Vigo made his mark on the Wigan public, he found the transition from life as a fisherman in the Cape to that of a ...rugby league player in the north of England less straightforward. The segregation laws of his native country had not equipped him to deal with the freedoms of his new environment. Soon after arriving in Wigan, Vigo went into a pub not far from Central Park. As he stepped inside, he saw one door leading to the lounge and another leading to the vaults. Confused, he asked at the outsales window which room he was allowed to enter." Former team-mate Colin Clarke, interviewed by Rylance, says that "He was a great athlete who always wanted to do his best. He was a terrific trainer and scored some memorable tries. But he was brought over from the outback in South Africa, dropped in the middle of Wigan and just left there... He was a class winger and a great entertainer, but he couldn't get to grips with the culture." [117] Certainly the ready availability of alcohol, and the drinking culture in rugby league was not a good environment for him.

In his first season at Swinton, he scored a try against Wigan in the high-profile Boxing Day clash at Station Road. He stayed with Swinton for two seasons. He played 52 matches and scored 28 tries. But Swinton was also a club that had seen better times, although in his first season they finished sixth in the Second Division, just three points away from the promotion places.

Club historian Stephen Wild says that he was a major signing for the club, but had a "notorious bad boy image", although Vigo himself said that he was "settling down". In his second season with the club, they reached the semi-final of the John Player Trophy, a major achievement for a Second Division side. Vigo scored two tries against First Division York in the first round, and contributed to Swinton's 32–5 win with his defending: "In one incident he found himself as the last line of defence and faced by two opponents who had broken through alongside each other and looked certain to score. However, Vigo had other ideas and to make absolutely sure that he got the ball he literally threw both men virtually over the advertising boards in one mighty tackle."

After two seasons at Swinton, it was time for a third move and on to new challenges. Green then joined Oldham at the start of the 1982–83 season. During his three year stay with the club, he played 63 matches and scored 20 tries.

Bill Ashurst recalls how, when he left Wigan to join Wakefield Trinity, having fallen out with Vince Karalius, he tried to persuade Vigo to join him in Yorkshire. He convinced the club chairman to offer him a far better deal than he was on at Wigan. Vigo was interested in the move, but Ashurst believes that the Wigan directors told him that he would have to go back to South Africa if he did not sign the new deal they offered him.

Green Vigo retired from the game in 1985 and completely disappeared from the rugby league scene. His withdrawal was so complete that some people believed he was dead, and one newspaper mistakenly printed an obituary! He had some personal problems in the 1990s, but at the time of writing is living quietly in the north-west of England, far from the adulation of the supporters and the attention of the rugby league media.

Vigo says that he never planned an entry into coaching nor did he think that he would have made a good coach.[118] In his more senior years, he spends time with family and friends. In his home town, his example has not been forgotten and his career continues to serve as a source of pride and motivation for local youngsters. During a visit home in June 2008, he gave permission to the newly established West Coast Raiders Rugby League Province to attach his name to their provincial club competition. The organisation in turn forwarded his name for recognition to Rugby League South Africa and their Pioneers Programme.

Vigo played for the Other Nationalities side in the County Championship in the mid–1970s. It was his misfortune to play for Wigan when the club was in decline. Had he joined a club regularly challenging for honours, and been better managed in his early years, he could have made an even bigger impact on the sport.

18. The 1980s: Three South Africans at Wigan

Following the 1982 Kangaroo tour, British rugby league saw an influx of Australians and New Zealanders. South Africa was increasingly isolated in international sport, which by the mid–1980s was gravely restricting tours by international rugby union teams, but there was little interest in signing South African players who may have wanted a new challenge and the chance to cash in on their rugby skills.

The only exception was Wigan, who signed three players in this period. Nick du Toit came to Central Park in 1984 and asked for a trial. But the recruitment of two established Springboks in 1985 when Rob Louw and Ray Mordt were signed, was far more high profile.

Nick du Toit

In South Africa the Northern Free State gold mines rugby players are known as the 'Purple Man-eaters' from their deep purple and gold jersey and uncompromising style of play. They play a fearless and no-nonsense game, and have earned an enviable reputation for fancy-free and hard – at times brutal – rugby. On numerous occasions this has left some of South Africa's rugby powerhouses pondering the exact nature of the force that hit them. The Northern Free State Rugby Union (now the Griffons Rugby Union), a largely rural and Cinderella union was established in 1968. It played in the shadow of its more illustrious counterpart and big brother, the Bloemfontein-based Cheetahs. For a significant period it was the only rugby available to players on the Orange Free State's platteland. The arrival of professionalism saw the Griffons, like other rural unions such as Boland and the South Western Districts (SWD), become a feeder pool for senior provincial sides. This is the background from which Nick Du Toit, a product of Driehoek School in Vanderbijlpark and Welkom RFC emerged.

Du Toit was born in October 1955 in Welkom, and grew up there. The town was the headquarters of the current Northern Free State Griffons. Du Toit represented his union in 93 inter-provincial games in various competitions, including the Sport Pienaar Trophy, Lion Cup and Currie Cup, from 1978 to 1984. In this period the international sports boycott against apartheid meant that most South African rugby players were denied the opportunity to compete internationally. With tours few and far between and rebel tours even scarcer, domestic provincial rugby became inwardly focussed and fiercely competitive. The game became overtly robust; parochialism and playing the man instead of the ball frequently dominated.

Nick du Toit entered the field of provincial rivalry in 1978 in a 'friendly' between Northern Orange Free State (NOFS) and their Bloemfontein counterpart, the Orange Free State (today known as the Cheetahs). The Orange Free State outclassed and smashed their less-illustrious neighbours 50–3. This was a less-than-favourable start to du Toit's provincial rugby career. This heavy defeat did not augur well for the Goldfielders' forthcoming Sport Pienaar Trophy season. This competition was initially for South African rugby's mostly rural provinces. The NOFS was pooled with South West Africa (Namibia), Eastern Transvaal and

Northern Natal, all of whom lacked major rugby-playing universities and strong traditional rugby schools. Reaching the top echelons of South African rugby, the Currie Cup and eventually the Springbok national side, was an uphill battle. Du Toit's introduction to provincial rugby in 1978 was also significant because it was the season when the South African Rugby Board, a multi-racial body representing coloured, African and white rugby players came into being.

NOFS played 11 games in the normal season, but du Toit only played in four Cup matches and two inter-provincial friendlies – Orange Free State and Transvaal – because of breaking a leg. He missed an opportunity to compete for a place in the national trials for both the South African Country Districts and Gazelles fixtures against the touring American Cougars side in the second half of the season.

From 1979, as a result of changes to the competition structures of South Africa's premier rugby championship, the Currie Cup, and the creation of two divisions instead of one, Northern Free State and the other rural unions had to play a series of qualifying matches as part of the Sport Pienaar Competition. The winner of the series entered the Currie Cup B-Division. After topping Section 4 of the competition, Northern Free State beat South West Africa 12–3 in the play-offs to secure a place among the top unions.

Du Toit and his fellow players thus had a new incentive to work hard and aim for national honours. They had to face some big names as they worked their way through their own pool first and then against the top two teams of the A-Division. Relishing this opportunity, the Purple Jerseys set out to make an impression. After four victories, a draw and five losses, the NOFS finished fourth in their division. In the season, the team played 19 games, including against visiting overseas sides such as Surrey, Llanelli and Cardiff. Du Toit, who had fully recovered from his unfortunate injury the previous season, played in 18 matches.

The 1980 season brought new incentives since three incoming tours, the South American Jaguars, France and the British Lions, were expected. This was the first opportunity in four years for South Africa's top players to face international opposition. Despite consistent performances in the previous year, du Toit was overlooked for NOFS's match against the South Americans at Welkom in April. Given his relative youth and inexperience against established loose forwards such as Rob Louw, Morné Du Plessis, Theuns Stofberg and Thys Burger, he also missed selection for various select combination teams and matches involving the touring teams. Also, the Currie Cup campaign was a disaster for the men from Welkom. They lost eight of their 10 games and were relegated to the Sport Pienaar after defeat in the promotion-relegation contest against Eastern Transvaal. Fortunately, the withdrawal of Rhodesia from the Currie Cup upon becoming Zimbabwe gave Northern Free State a new lease on life and allowed them to stay in the top league. Overall, the team played 15 games, won one, drew two and lost the rest. Du Toit played nine times. Otherwise, he represented his club in the Rock Grout and Russell provincial competitions.

According to Reg Sweet, Chairman of the South African Rugby Writers Society, 1981 was a 'season of frustration' and 'part of the way it was a sheer disgrace' with the increased isolation of South African sport and high-profile protests against the country's continued involvement in international rugby. Things were, however, much better for the men from the Gold Fields after their disastrous 1980 campaign. The team played 16 representative games, including against teams as diverse as the South African Mines XV, and after winning seven out of 10 matches, qualified for the Currie Cup semi-final play-offs. This was their greatest achievement since their admission to the top flight. Du Toit played in 15 matches and was a proud and fiercely determined member of the semi-final team that lost 36–12 to the Blue Bulls. Also, he was among the season's top try-scorers in all first class rugby matches with eight tries.

As South Africa's international rugby woes continued in 1982, local players were treated to a menu of 'rebel' and exotic club tours as an antidote to full sporting isolation. In addition to a second visit by the South American Jaguars early in the season, a Five Nations Invitation Team toured. A cosmopolitan team called Tokkie's Dragons with players from Hong Kong, Singapore, Western Samoa, Tonga and Canada defied the international boycott to play five matches. For the rest, local players had to make do with visits by overseas club teams. Yet again du Toit was unfortunate to miss selection for various representative teams, including the South African Country Districts and the Currie Cup B-Division XV.

Continuing from the previous season, NOFS started their Currie Cup campaign successfully by beating Boland 18–10 at home. Despite two defeats and a draw in the first part of the competition, they maintained their momentum and completed the league stages of the series by topping the B-Division to qualify for their second successive semi-final. As a reward for their achievement, Northern Free State became the joint holders (with Natal) of the W.F. Simpkins Trophy. As before, Northern Transvaal blocked their way to premiership glory and the Purple Jerseys chased them all the way in a close defeat. Nick Du Toit played in all 14 games, including the semi-final and Northern Free State's game against the South American Jaguars. At the end of the season he had played in 60 representative games.

The 1983 season, lamented the South African rugby writers, was 'in many respects not a remarkable year'. For those making a living and playing rugby in the Northern Free State goldfields, the year was of huge historical importance. Not only did the provincial team top its division for the third year in succession after winning nine out of 10 matches to qualify for a Currie Cup semi-final against Northern Transvaal, but they also defeated Eastern Transvaal in a promotion-relegation match to gain a place among the top six provinces in the A-Division for the 1984 season. They were, however, unlucky to be knocked-out by the Orange Free State in the fourth round of the Lion Cup in its inaugural season. On the back of consistent performances in all 17 matches and 20 tries during the season, Du Toit, playing in his sixth season, received national recognition for the first time when the South African Rugby Writers Society placed him in the top 10 players of the year in his position. Also, his career details were in the *SA Rugby Annual* to signify his recognition as a player of note. To top it all, his club, Welkom RFC, recorded their 16th successive victory in the senior provincial league competition.

The 1984 season saw the arrival of England and the South American Jaguars for short tours of South Africa. Despite his noteworthy season the previous year, du Toit was yet again overlooked for the national trials. He also missed selection for the Gazelles and SA Country Districts teams. Also, his team found life in the Currie Cup A-Division extremely difficult and finished bottom of the table after nine successive defeats. They had to play a promotion-relegation match against Natal. Also, they lost in the Lion Cup third round to

Eastern Transvaal. Du Toit, after playing 16 out of the 17 games for the season therefore had to be satisfied with another Welkom RFC provincial league title as a consolation prize. Having established his rugby credentials beyond any doubt, except for failing to gain higher representative honours, the time arrived for Nick Du Toit, the small-town boy and outback rugby player to move on and search for his fortune elsewhere.

According to Paul Wilson in *The best years of our lives*, his book on the rise of Wigan from 1980 to 1995, "the enormous" du Toit made his own way to Central Park and asked for a trial. Nick du Toit joined Wigan at a time when the club was heading back towards the top of rugby league. The club's fortunes had reached an all-time low point with relegation to the Second Division in 1980. Promotion was won the following season, and in 1983 they won the John Player Trophy. In 1984 they reached the Challenge Cup Final, but lost to Widnes.

Maurice Lindsay was now the driving force behind Wigan's success, and he signed Nick du Toit to strengthen the team's pack. Australian winger John Ferguson had signed for the Central Park club in the summer, du Toit's signing in November 1984 was somewhat overshadowed by the arrival of Australian star international half-back Brett Kenny.

It took du Toit time to learn his new code. He made his debut on 11 November, from the bench at Workington in a comfortable win, replacing centre David Stephenson. His full debut came the next week on the right wing against Huddersfield in the John Player Special Trophy. After that he was used in his more natural place in the second-row. By the end of the season he had made 16 first team appearances, nine of which were off the bench. He did score five tries, a good return for a forward, and was an unused substitute in Wigan's memorable 28–24 Challenge Cup Final victory over Hull.

He found more success the following season. He played in the Charity Shield win over Hull KR that opened the season. In October, he played in his first Cup Final in rugby league, helping Wigan win the Lancashire Cup with a comfortable 34–8 triumph against Warrington. The Wire led 8–2 at one stage, and du Toit contributed to his team's win by knocking fearsome Australian forward Les Boyd "flat on his backside" according to Paul Wilson.

In December he was joined at Central Park by two more South Africans, when Springbok stars Ray Mordt and Rob Louw joined the club. In January 1986, he came off the bench at half-time to replace Ian Potter in Wigan's narrow 11–8 win over Hull KR in the John Player Trophy final. By now, Wigan had signed Andy Goodway from Oldham, increasing competition for places in the pack. However, by the end of the season he had played 42 first team matches, including 10 off the bench, and even kicked a goal in a comfortable Challenge Cup first round win at Workington.

However, changes in the regulations on the number of international players at a club, the arrival of Australian Ian Roberts, who had an English passport, the following season, along with Goodway's development, saw Nick lose his first team place. After four appearances, all off the bench, he joined Barrow on 1 November 1986. At Wigan he had made 62 first team appearances, but 23 of these were off the bench. His 15 tries was a good total for a second-rower, albeit one playing in a successful team. Another factor may have been the appointment of New Zealander Graham Lowe as coach. He was reputed to prefer his own countrymen to South Africans, although he always denied this, but by the end of his first season in charge, all three of Wigan's South Africans had left the club. Paul Wilson comments that Ray Mordt "like du Toit... put a lot of heart into his game".

At Barrow he scored two tries on his debut at Oldham in a 32–20 defeat. By the end of the season he had made 12 first team appearances, scoring four tries. In 1987–88, with Barrow now in the Second Division, he played 19 times, five off the bench, scoring one try. The 1988–89 campaign was his final one with the club. He played fairly regularly in the first half of the season and made his last appearance against Runcorn just before Christmas. *"Keeping the Dream Alive",* a comprehensive record of Barrow's players, says that "Nick will be remembered by Barrow fans as a strong running forward who, on his day, was as good a player of that type as you could wish to see."

He then took a break from rugby league, due to injuries, and Barrow released him. He played a game for Chorley in 1990, before joining Wakefield Trinity. He played 23 times for Wakefield in 1990–91 before retiring at the age of 35. Since then, he has worked as a publican in the Wigan area.

While the issue of playing South Africa was controversial during the apartheid era, signing individual South Africans usually was not. In 1990, when du Toit signed for Wakefield, the team were due to play Sheffield at Don Valley. In *When Push comes to Shove* (1993) the then Labour MP for Wakefield and life-long Trinity supporter, David Hinchliffe, before the match was discussing whether it was correct to sign a South African player with his fellow Trinity fan, trade union official Glynn Robinson. As the teams came out, they checked whether the new recruit was playing. "I wonder if that South African bastard is playing?" said Robinson. They were both somewhat taken aback when a large man sitting in front of them turned round and said "Nah, I'm not mate." Recalling the incident in 2014, Hinchliffe says that during du Toit's time at the club he "gave a good account of himself on the field".

A year after arriving at Central Park, du Toit was joined by two more South Africans, Rob Louw and Ray Mordt.

Rob Louw and Ray Mordt

In his book, published in 1987 while he was still at Wigan, Louw says that due to his commitments as a Springbok "I had reached the age of 30 without building any sort of permanent career outside rugby." He continues "When the idea of professional rugby came into the picture, it was inevitable that I would sit up and take notice. Talent scouts from Northern England gave notice that they were interested in South African players, particularly Ray Mordt, Danie Gerber and myself." Through various contacts, including Barney Esterhuysen of Pro-Sport, Roy Bailey, the father of Manchester United goalkeeper Gary Bailey, and David Smith, a visit to England was arranged, initially to meet Roy Waudby, chairman of Hull. By now Gerber had decided to stay in rugby union, so only Mordt and Louw flew to England. Although Hull did not pursue their interest, according to Louw, Waudby revealed to the press that discussions had taken place, and he felt that there was now no way back for them.

Ray Mordt, Rob Louw and Nick du Toit. (Photo: Courtesy *Rugby League Journal*)

He says that five clubs were interested in them, and after further negotiations, accepted Wigan's offer. They watched their new club easily beat Leigh in the John Player Special Trophy semi-final, at Knowsley Road, the home of Wigan's great rivals St Helens. Then they signed their contracts live on television. Wigan at this time were on the verge of becoming the sport's dominant club, although it would take two years and a change of coach that would be very significant for the South Africans, before that was achieved.

Paul Wilson believes that the signing was very significant for Maurice Lindsay. In *The best years of their lives* he comments: "The BBC *Grandstand* cameras, at Knowsley Road to cover the semi-final live, were hijacked after the final whistle by a Lindsay positively bursting with pride and self-importance. They were led to the St Helens boardroom, where ... Ray Mordt and Rob Louw were waiting to sign Wigan contracts with a suitably telegenic flourish. [Ellery] Hanley might have been Lindsay's best-ever signing, but this was surely the Wigan vice-chairman's finest hour. Mordt and Louw had in fact been touting for professional deals for a couple of months, and Hull and St Helens had expressed an interest in Mordt, a strong-running winger who Wigan had been tracking for several years. Like those clubs, Wigan quickly realised the pair wanted to stay together, but unlike their rivals, Wigan agreed to ... a double signing worth about £75,000. But that wasn't the point ... almost as if anticipating a less than thrilling match, Lindsay had a trick up his sleeve for the television audience. And although the twin signing was perhaps not as audacious a coup as club and television commentators made out, it was the very height of audacity to commandeer not only live television but the St Helens boardroom for five minutes of blatant Wigan self-promotion."

Both players had achieved much in rugby union in South Africa and internationally. By the time that Rob Louw, at the age of 30, decided to say farewell to rugby union and sign for Wigan in rugby league, he was an accomplished forward with little more – other than to make a little money from his rugby talents – to achieve. Over the space of 10 years, the player from Wynberg High in Cape Town and the University of Stellenbosch had played at all the different levels of South African rugby – from national age group level through provincial competition and up to the best international rugby.

After school, Louw went to Stellenbosch and the close attention of Danie Craven. This institution provided a nurturing home for the talented young man from Cape Town's southern suburbs. It was no surprise when Louw and four others from the University of Stellenbosch club, a few months after becoming students, were selected for the South African under–21 – Oribies – team to tour South America in June and July of 1975. Prior to their departure, they played a warm-up game against the senior Orange Free State provincial team. A member of the South African Rugby Writers Society noted in their review of the tour that already Louw displayed outstanding talent and ability and that he and Northern Transvaal lock Chris Faure outshone their fellow players in a 20–10 victory over their senior and more experienced provincial counterparts.

In the month long tour of South America, the South African side, which included at least eight future Springboks, played the national teams of Paraguay, Uruguay and Chile and a combined team of Valparaiso & Vina de Mar as part of South Africa's mission to support the development of rugby union in that part of the world. Louw played in six of the eight matches and scored a try against Chile. On their return, still too young to seriously challenge for representative honours and a place in the Gazelles (South Africa under–24s) or Western Province side, Louw honed his skills with the University club in the provincial Grand Challenge and Town Challenge Competition, intervarsity matches and the National Club Tournament in 1977. With two years of a rugby apprenticeship behind him, Louw finally made his debut for Western Province in 1978.

This season was an extremely busy one for Louw who played in five out of eight representative matches for Western Province in the Currie Cup. He also scored seven tries which placed him among the season's provincial top try scorers, despite playing far less games than his competitors. Western Province reached the final, but lost to Orange Free State. As well as playing Currie Cup rugby, Louw was also chosen for the Southern Universities and Gazelles sides which played the American Cougars on their South African tour. The latter game, billed as an unofficial test for only the second representative American team to visit South Africa, was a tough encounter and the South African future national side escaped with a narrow 20–16 victory. Louw contributed a try in his first international encounter.

With his second taste of international rugby and first stint of premier league provincial rugby behind him, Louw contributed to his club's success at the annual National Club Tournament in Durban. Representing Western Province at the tournament in their capacity as Town Challenge and the Grand Challenge Trophy Champions, Stellenbosch University beat their northern rivals, Pretoria University, 15–9 to become South African Club Champions. Louw scored the winning try after a fumble by Naas Botha. The SA Rugby Annual reported: "Two minutes before the end of the match, Tukkies won a line-out in their own 22 metres area. Louw shot through quickly to exert pressure on fly-half Naas Botha who fumbled. Louw snatched the ball to score at the death. Robbie Blair converted and Louw the hero was carried shoulder-high from the field."

Louw scored six tries in the tournament, a record. Given these achievements, the South African Rugby Writers Society voted Louw as one of the top 10 number eights in the country. This accolade put him with esteemed players such as Springbok captain Morné Du

155

Plessis, former New Zealand All Black and Rhodesian international, Allan Sutherland, and Oxford Blue and Springbok, Nick Mallett.

The 1979 season was a difficult one for South African rugby as the doors of international competition were rapidly closing. The incoming French tour was cancelled by the French government as part of the international boycott campaign and prospects for the new season looked bleak. The only highlight was a World XV tour as part of the celebrations of the opening of the revamped Loftus Versfeld Stadium in Pretoria. Also, several foreign club and county teams, such as North Western Counties, Cardiff, Middlesex, Llanelli, Newport and Surrey visited the Republic. This was an important opportunity for local players to face international opposition in the absence of official tours and tests. Louw was selected for the Craven XV against the World XV at Stellenbosch. Although he did not make the front of the sports pages, he was sufficiently impressive to be in contention for further representative honours.

In the Currie Cup, after another successful season, Western Province reached the Final against Northern Transvaal and drew 15–15. This concluded a very satisfying season for Louw. He was among the top Currie Cup try-scorers with six and managed a season's best of eight tries overall. He also played in 15 of his province's 17 matches.

Currie Cup glory, however, was not enough for a dynamic, energetic and fiercely committed Rob Louw. To crown this cracker of a season, Louw and his university team yet again clinched the National Club Championship after dominating the Easter Tournament. Louw scored five tries in a 97–9 demolition of Potchefstroom University and again was the tournament's top try-scorer. He also received the accolade for scoring the most tries in a match. With their final victory over Durban Collegians on the last day, Stellenbosch University captured the Toyota Trophy permanently by winning the tournament three times in succession. Louw also touched down in this match.

He finished the season by being selected for the SA Barbarians, a fully multi-racial team for their pioneering tour to the United Kingdom. This tour was part of the process of trying to 'normalise' South African rugby and make it more acceptable to the international rugby community. This team, the first-ever mixed race team to represent South Africa abroad had an equal number of White, Black and Coloured players and tour management. They played seven matches and were frequently the target of anti-apartheid protestors. Louw scored two tries; was rated as one of the players of the tour and held his own against top-class and experienced internationals.

Louw was now seen as a potential Springbok and was nominated as a candidate for South African Player-of-the-Year in competition with seasoned internationals such as Naas Botha, Morne Du Plessis, Louis Moolman and De Villiers Visser. The SA Rugby Writers Society also voted him the fifth best number Eight and the third best flanker in the country. Furthermore, 43 of the 51 writers voted for him as ready for immediate selection for the Springboks and questioned his omission from the first national training camps held during the year.

Louw was finally capped for the Springboks in 1980. He played in all nine tests and scored four tries on the Springbok tour of South America. He played 13 games for his province and ended the season as one of the top three flankers in the country. He also played in Italy in the South African off season from 1980 to 1985, and was probably the most eminent player in Italy at that time.

With his university days behind him, Louw started the 1981 season as a member of the Cape Town Defence Force RFC while on national service in the Army. He was soon selected for the SA Defence Force team to play Western Transvaal who they beat 30–28. He also played in the National Defence Force Rugby Week and reached the final against the Pretoria XV. Louw scored a vital try to help his team to capture the national title 13–12. His club finished second in the Western Province Grand Challenge Cup, although he only played four games for them.

In 1981, he represented Western Province in the Currie Cup and kept his place in the national side against Ireland, New Zealand and the United States. Louw played in four tests and scored eight tries in international contests.

Given the difficult New Zealand and American tour with anti-apartheid protests including pitch invasions, circumstances were problematic for the players. Louw, however, returned from these tours with an enhanced reputation. The SA Rugby Writers Society not only overwhelmingly voted him the second best flanker and the third best number Eight in the country but also put in the best international players for the season and a certainty should a South Africa / New Zealand XV be selected.

With ever diminishing international playing opportunities due to the international sports boycott, the 1982 season was bleak. When the South American Jaguars arrived for another tour, Louw played in both test matches. Otherwise, it was back to provincial rugby for him.

Matters improved in 1984 with the arrival of England and a South American & Spanish touring team. Louw scored two tries in both first tests against the visitors. In addition to this short venture into test rugby, the season was filled up with the provincial competitions, festival games and select combinations such as the Gold Festival XV and the Rest of South Africa XV. Louw gained further recognition with selection for a World XV for matches against Wales in Cardiff, Crawshays and England at Twickenham. He ended the season with a nomination as Player-of-the-Year and was rated as the top flanker in South Africa and among the top 10 in the world. His record stood at 73 games for his province with 18 tries.

The 1985 season saw the end of Rob Louw's rugby union career. The season started with the cancellation of the All Blacks tour. This effectively finished the official playing opportunities in the test arena for South African players. To mitigate this disappointment, the SA Rugby Board sent the national team, including Louw, on an internal tour to play various regional selections. This was not, however, universally popular. When the national team suffered a crushing defeat against the Cape Barbarians, they were booed by supporters. This shocked both players and administrators.

Louw, who had changed clubs at the start of the season and played for Gardens-Technicon RFC continued to play despite occasional injuries. After his eight Currie Cup games, including winning the Cup Final for the fourth successive year, and little success on club level, it was time for serious reflection. After 81 provincial games, 19 tests and 28 Springbok matches, Louw had nothing left to achieve in rugby union. Rugby league and the possibility of earning some money from rugby therefore became a viable and logical option for one of South Africa's foremost players.

The year 1957 was notable for a number of reasons. In addition to Tom van Vollenhoven quitting South African rugby union for rugby league, Raymond Herman ('Ray') Mordt, destined to become one of Springbok rugby's most iconic players, was born at Ceres in the Western Cape Province. Although South African born, Mordt received his formal and rugby education at David Livingstone and Church Hill High Schools in Salisbury (today Harare), the capital of Rhodesia. He was more interested in sports than in academic work.

He missed out on a place in the Rhodesian schools side although he was regarded as a 'great emerging talent'. After school he joined the Rhodesian Army for two years, but never played rugby. He joined the Police and by his own admission was asked to leave after three weeks because of his 'reputation as a troublemaker'. Fortunately, he befriended Springbok Ian Robertson who became his training partner and mentor, and succeeded in channelling his abundant talent and energy into competitive rugby. By 1977, aged 19, as a member of the Old Hararians club, he was selected on the wing for the Rhodesian national side coached by former New Zealand All Black Alan Sutherland. They played in the Currie Cup. He made his debut against Western Province at the Police Ground in Salisbury before 15,000 ecstatic fans. Mordt, 'thundering through the cover defence, shrugging off tackles and scoring the final try' helped his team to a famous 18–9 victory.[119] He scored further tries against Boland and Natal as well as for a Rhodesian XV against a South African XV at the end of the season. Although this was not enough to ensure an invitation to the 1977 Springbok trials and inclusion into the list of top players as selected by the South African Rugby Writers Society, his play was good enough to keep his place in the Rhodesia side the following season. Also, his club won the Inter City League Competition, participated in the Ford National Sevens Competition and won the C Division.[120]

Mordt started the 1978 season well, scoring tries at the National Club Championship in Durban, and with the start of the provincial season scored two tries in Rhodesia's 38–4 friendly win against the South African Rugby Football Federation's Proteas in Bulawayo. He was, however, criticised for being too tempestuous on occasions.[121] In the Currie Cup season, against top class opposition, Mordt scored eight tries to cap a super season; Rhodesia won eight, drew one and lost only three matches. He was regularly commended for his cover defence and try-saving tackles as well as his attacking play even when the odds were stacked against his team. His fine form was rewarded with selection for the South African Gazelles, the under–24s team. Due to injury, however, Mordt was not able to play and had to withdraw. Despite this disappointment, he still saw his team promoted to the A-section of the Currie Cup for the forthcoming season.

The 1979 season saw the end of Rhodesian rugby and the inauguration of Zimbabwe Rhodesia Rugby as the country moved towards a new political set up. Many players were on military duty throughout the country and therefore unable to attend training. From the outset Mordt scored tries, against Border in East London, the touring Surrey side in Salisbury and two against the South African Universities in Bulawayo. Mordt's star was shining even brighter while his team's campaign in the Currie Cup A-section faltered due to the impact of the political issues. Despite defeats in the uncompromising Currie Cup competition, the 'unstoppable' Mordt regularly touched down. His hat-trick on 22 September at Hatfield to in their 25–12 victory against Griquas made him only the second player in the history of Rhodesian rugby to achieve such a feat also. This also completed Mordt's rugby career north of the Orange River. He had scored 26 tries for his country.

In 1980 the Rhodesia Rugby Football Union became the Zimbabwe Rugby Union. Since they still participated in South Africa's rugby competitions their players were still eligible for the Springboks. Based on his consistent performances in the Currie Cup, Mordt was selected to play for South Africa, the country of his birth, against the South American Jaguars and the British Lions. Just eight days after Robert Mugabe was sworn in as the president of an independent Zimbabwe, Mordt made his debut on 26 April 1980 at the Wanderers in Johannesburg. He was one of the few players who became Springboks without having represented his province or union at Craven Week, South Africa's premier schools rugby tournament. He played well and capped his debut with his first international try. This was a solid foundation for an illustrious test career. Although he failed to score in the subsequent tests in Durban as well as in the British Lions tour, he established himself in the team.

As Zimbabwe settled down and moved into its political transition, severing its links with South African rugby and re-establishing new links with the international sporting fraternity was on the cards. As early as January 1980, newspapers reported on tentative plans for the new national team to tour Britain.[122] It became known that the British Lions were departing for South Africa despite appeals from the British government not to have further sporting contact with the country. They were due to play Zimbabwe in Salisbury in June and the Zimbabwean Deputy Minister of Sport, Cephas Msipa, objected on behalf of his government. Since the Lions tour was in direct contravention of the Commonwealth Gleneagles Agreement which banned sporting and other contact with the apartheid state, the Zimbabwean authorities saw the match as wholly inappropriate and an embarrassment to the country.[123] They denied permission for the Lions to play in Zimbabwe, much to the players' disappointment. Instead, the ZRFU sent its national side on a six match tour of the United Kingdom. Mordt was included in this team who played against Surrey, Gloucestershire and Lancashire. At the start of the tour, Nigel Starmer-Smith observed that: "Ray Mordt of the Old Hararians Club … is bound to impress with his fearsome running on the wing, especially on the counter attack, as he did against the Lions." [124]

At the end of 1980 season, Mordt, after having represented his adopted country with distinction, moved south and joined the Wanderers RFC, an affiliate of the Transvaal Rugby Union, in 1981. When Ireland toured the Republic, Ray joined three of his Transvaal team mates in the Springbok team for the Second test in Durban. He maintained his form throughout the season and was rewarded with inclusion in the Springbok team for the tour to New Zealand in 1981. In the last test of that tour, the so-called 'flour bomb test' at Eden Park in Auckland, Mordt scored three brilliant tries. During their return journey via the United States, the Springboks made a stopover to play the American Eagles in the first ever test between the two nations. Mordt scored three tries in this match to bring his tour total to nine, the most scored by any player on the tour. This secured his place in the test team to face the South American Jaguars. In the first test on 27 March 1982, at Loftus Versfeld, Mordt scored two tries in a 50–18 South African win. He played eight games that season,

159

including friendlies. In his two year stay, 1981 and 1982, he represented his adopted Union 10 times, but left as a result of differences with the coach.

After two eventful seasons, he moved further north in South Africa by joining the powerhouse team Northern Transvaal (now the Blue Bulls) as a member of Harlequins RFC under the coaching of Kitch Christie for the 1983 season. Christie not only saw Mordt as probably South Africa's first truly professional player, but also described him as "a catalyst for the whole club" and a "true gladiator".[125] Mordt on the other hand, said that the club had a "great team spirit" and hunger for victory. During his two-year stay until 1985, he also played for Pretoria University RFC and represented Northern Transvaal 44 times. He played in three Currie Cup Finals, a Lion Cup Final and Night Series Cup final and scored 23 tries for his last province in rugby union. Overall he scored 35 tries in the Currie Cup. At national level and in the absence of any international tours, he represented the South African XV (essentially a non-official Springbok team) against an Overseas XV at Newlands in the centenary celebration of Western Province in 1983 and in 1984 was selected for the Rest of South Africa XV.

The period from 1982 to 1985 is frequently described by South African rugby writers as 'the best of years, the worst of years'; in this period the country's gradual exclusion from international test rugby was concluded. As well as the termination of formal rugby links, the South African national team became a target for protestors the world over. This limited the possible achievements for most white South African rugby players and forced them to reconsider their options. Following the cancellation of the incoming New Zealand Tour, scheduled for 1985, the die was cast and motivated players such as Rob Louw and Mordt to consider rugby league as an option. Mordt commented: "Well I'd given my life to rugby and I had nothing to show for it. I never had any assets – I never had a house, or anything. And I was offered huge money."

The two Springboks were joining a Wigan club who were gradually returning to the top echelons of rugby league. They had won the Challenge Cup the previous spring, and were expected to compete for all the game's top honours. It was easier for Mordt, as a winger, to adapt to his new sport than Louw, whose flanker position did not exist in rugby league. In *For the love of rugby*, he comments that he learnt "as a raw beginner when I joined Wigan... Amongst the forwards, the difference between the two codes is quite daunting for a newcomer. For a start there are no lineouts. Scrums are nothing like those in rugby union." It was also their misfortune to switch codes in the middle of a very severe winter.

Ray Mordt made his first team debut against Swinton on 5 January 1986, and kept his place for a narrow 11–8 win over Hull KR in the John Player Special Trophy Final the following Saturday. Louw says that the match "was played in unbelievable conditions for a South African – freezing cold and rain turning to a blizzard." Paul Wilson says about Mordt's performance against Hull KR that he was "A direct and forceful runner with a surprising turn of speed, Mordt's unusual habit of running straight through defenders rather than trying to evade them was probably more effective in union than league... but the winger could obviously play and would certainly get better. Like du Toit, he put a lot of heart into his game, and his bristly, combative attitude instantly won the Wigan fans over."

Rob Louw played his first rugby league match for the 'A' team the next day, and says that he learnt his new code quickly: "Gradually I was eased into the first team squad and came onto the field as a second half replacement a few times. By the time I made my first full appearance for the first team I was ready. Everything went well and I managed to score two tries."

Ray Mordt's season was cut short by injury; he played five first team games and scored two tries. Rob Louw started one match, and played seven times off the bench. His two tries, at Castleford on 13 April, helped secure a 14–12 win for Wigan.

In the close season, New Zealander Graham Lowe replaced Alan McInnes and Colin Clarke, who had been joint coaches of the first team. While Louw is very positive about him in his book, saying he made the club more professional, his arrival saw the two players' rugby league careers terminate prematurely.

Ray Mordt missed the start of the 1986–87 season with an ankle injury, but went on to make 16 first team appearances, plus four off the bench, and scored a credible 15 tries. Wilson notes that he 'tormented' Hull KR at Craven Park and scored two tries in a 23–6 win. At Headingley on 11 March, Mordt and fellow winger Richard Russell both scored hat-tricks in a 30–0 win.

Rob Louw faced considerable competition to win a place in the Wigan pack. He played fairly regularly until the beginning of February, but did not feature in the first team after that. Overall, he started 15 matches, all in the second-row, and played seven times off the bench. He scored two tries. He won his first rugby league medal in the Lancashire Cup, when he came off the bench to replace Ian Roberts in Wigan's comfortable 27–6 win over Oldham.

Wigan won the league championship, John Player Special Trophy and the Premiership as well as the Lancashire Cup. But at the end of the season the two South Africans were on their way home, their contracts paid up. After an influx of overseas players following the lifting of the transfer ban, clubs were restricted to only five overseas players. One reason that Ian Roberts had been a valuable short-term signing for Wigan, apart from his playing ability, was that he had a British passport. Paul Wilson comments that "Lowe did not seem to rate the Springbok pair", and although he has always denied preferring New Zealand players over South Africans, they were replaced with Kiwis that Lowe knew, and presumably had more faith in. Wilson says that Rob Louw was "evidently an intelligent and skilful player, [but] had looked too old and inflexible to make an impact on rugby league, especially at the level at which Wigan were now operating." He does believe that Ray Mordt had been a success, and "was still young enough and certainly fit enough to get even better". He says that Mordt "never seemed to enjoy the coach's full confidence. He [Mordt] was, in fact, treated rather shabbily by Wigan, and only refrained from saying so because going quietly was a condition of his financial settlement."

In August 1987, Wigan needed Louw's place on the 'quota' as one of their overseas signings for Kiwi international Adrian Shelford and the Iro brothers, and made him an offer to leave. Mordt asked if he could go on the same terms. Wilson believes that Mordt's rugby league career could have lasted longer, but it was his "determination to stay with Louw which created difficulties." Wilson quotes their original coach, Colin Clarke, saying that

"Louw was not the awesome player I had been led to believe by some rugby union people", but that Mordt could have "been one of the all-time great rugby league wingers." He expressed surprise that Mordt was not persuaded to stay, but maybe being not used to the ruthlessness of the professional game, the pair became disillusioned. Even aged 32, Louw could have found another club, and Mordt certainly could.

An interview in *Open Rugby* (then Britain's leading rugby league magazine) in September 1993 said that "Both players believe it was a fundamental antipathy towards them on the part of ... Graham Lowe that sabotaged their careers with the club and led to them being released... 'Lowe made it clear that he wasn't interested in us; he just didn't want South Africans in the side', says Mordt. 'We could have made it in the game,' believes Louw. 'But we were never given a chance.'" Both, however, did say that they had good memories of their time at the club, including their team-mates and the supporters.

Interviewed by Timmy Hancox in *Southern Hemisphere News*, many years later. Mordt said that his first games were hard because he was targeted by opponents as a new rugby union signing with blond hair and a nice tan. Louw reflected that as a forward he needed to be a semi-backline player, which suited him and he played as a roaming loose-forward. However, he also said that they were both used as impact players, which was not a familiar role for them, and they both preferred to play the whole match. Mordt concluded that he won five medals with Wigan, had an incredible experience and enjoyed it, as well as earning some money. But, maybe not surprisingly, he prefers rugby union.

After his active playing career, Ray Mordt, who "didn't understand the politics – we just wanted to play", was reinstated in 1991 and joined the coaching staff of the Golden Lions (formerly Transvaal) together with Kitch Christie, the man destined to become the South African Rugby World Cup-winning coach in 1995. Attempts by Christie to involve him with the Springboks as a fitness instructor was, however, thwarted by the International Rugby Board under the rules that used to govern professionalism and pay-for-play: "'Mr. Mordt forfeited his amateur status when he became a rugby league player,' yesterday's IRB statement said. 'A fitness instructor acting as part of a management team is a person who is engaged in the organisation or administration of the game and, as a consequence, he is not eligible to act at national representative level.'" [126] Mordt also had some success as a coach at provincial level, and won the Currie Cup with Transvaal in 1994.

Rob Louw concentrated on a business career after retiring, but has had some involvement with rugby union as a coach and manager. He has also faced considerable health challenges, including serious injuries after a powerboat accident in 1990, and melanoma. He has been involved in campaigns to raise awareness of this disease.

At the time of writing, both players are living in South Africa. Rob Louw had experienced the difficulties many established rugby union forwards faced when switching to rugby league. However, had he wished to do so, he could have played at a high level in England for a couple more years. Ray Mordt, as a winger, adapted to his new game more quickly, and certainly could have extended his career in the north of England. Given Graham Lowe's success with Wigan, it is difficult to question his judgment, but if Alan McInnes and Colin Clarke had kept their jobs as first team coaches at the club, maybe the two Springboks could have fulfilled their potential at Central Park.

19. The 1990s: A new generation

In 1988, after an absence from the country of 25 years, rugby league was again alive in South Africa. Dave Southern, who was from Widnes and was working in South Africa, and Tony Barker, who was from Wigan, took the initiative to establish the sport. No support was forthcoming from the RFL because of the sports boycott, even though they said they wanted to establish the sport on a multi-racial basis.

Internationally, it was now accepted that players could play both rugby codes as amateurs. However, this was not always accepted in South Africa. Despite this, the sport did attract a layer of young rugby union players. Following the political change that started in 1990, it became much easier to build international support and links. Clubs started and the sport started to take shape.

On 13 November 1992, South Africa played their first full international since 1963, against the CIS (Russia), another country working to establish rugby league. The South African side won 30–26 in Johannesburg, and won again a week later when the teams met again in Pretoria, this time 22–19. Two players from that team, full-back Jamie Bloem and winger Mark Johnson, went on to have successful careers in British rugby league.

Jamie Bloem

Jamie Bloem played top class rugby league from 1992 to 2005. He played over 300 games, mainly for Halifax, including international appearances for South Africa and Scotland. In nearly 20 years in England, where he now lives with his wife and two children, he has also played and coached rugby union, been a radio commentator, and has one of few former professional players to become a referee in rugby league.

Jamie played rugby union at school, he recalls, "to quite a good level", and came close to playing for the provincial side in Northern Transvaal. In his youth he was also a good athlete, and did karate. He represented South Africa in athletics, and went on five kilometre training runs in the morning before going to school, and then running home after school.

After finishing school he went into the army and remembers: "I was stationed in Cape Town and played for my unit team. The Defence Force had their own team, it was a decent side. When I was discharged I joined Milnerton and played four games for their under–20 team before I was called up to the first team."

Jamie then played for the Western Province under–20 and under–21 teams, and was selected for the senior squad, but found that the "older heads" were chosen ahead of him. In 1992 he met Tony Lane, whose sister and brother-in-law lived in Castleford, who did some scouting for the Tigers in South Africa. He told Jamie that he thought his game was "well suited" to rugby league. Jamie played a few games for the Cape Town Coasters at Megawatt Park, and remembers winning an inter-club tournament with them. He was chosen to play for South Africa in the international matches against Russia, and was the highest profile modern day player to switch codes in South Africa. Suddenly he found he was "not welcome" at Western Province Rugby Union, so told Tony Lane he was ready to go to Castleford.

Jamie had never been to Great Britain before, and looking back thinks it was an impulsive move. He tested the water for other South African players looking to move to Great Britain at the time, and remembers speaking to Mark Johnson, who joined London Crusaders in March 1993. However, Castleford didn't really work out for him: "They offered me a contract to play in the Alliance – they had Graham Steadman and St John Ellis, and I would have struggled to get into the first team. However, Oldham wanted a utility back, so I went there and we got promoted."

Jamie did not stay at Oldham, but signed for Doncaster. After years in the doldrums, the South Yorkshire side were now potential promotion challengers in the Second Division. In a tight race for the top two spots, they won promotion on the last day of the season. Jamie made 34 appearances, and was undoubtedly one of the reasons behind their success.

But after a successful start in the First Division, including an early shock win at St Helens, he became the first professional rugby league player to be banned for using a performance enhancing drug, the anabolic steroid Nandrolone. He recalls: "The ban took me out of the game for two years. I had just met Louise, who later became my wife. I had trials for the London Monarchs American Football team, but it would have meant moving to London. I played American Football for six months, and set goals so that I could return to rugby league. I wanted to prove people wrong. I worked as a plumber, money was tight, but it brought Louise and me closer together. I didn't think of going back to South Africa."

When his ban was completed, he crossed the Pennines to join Widnes, who – not having got into Super League – were playing in the First Division. Jamie looks back at his time there fondly: "I signed for Widnes and suddenly things were going better. I had worked very hard to survive when I was banned. I was a full-time player and we bought a house there. Louise worked at the club and they really looked after us." Jamie played for one and half seasons at Widnes, and managed to fit in some rugby union in the league off season, including being selected for Cheshire. But in May 1998, Halifax, who were then in Super League, tempted him back to Yorkshire.

Apart from a short spell at Huddersfield, Jamie stayed at Halifax for the rest of his professional career, and still lives in the town. In his first season they finished third in Super League. He remembers: "Karl Harrison and Kelvin Skerrett were playing, people I had only watched before. They were really good, 'old school' players. Karl was the captain and our 'enforcer'. He was a real leader. Gary Mercer was also there and there was great camaraderie among the players. I really enjoyed that first season. I'm a robust character and the supporters took me to their hearts. It's the supporters who make a club, and that's why I stayed there. I've got a lot of friends at the club."

When he came to England, Jamie's best position was at full-back, but at Halifax he gradually became a second-row forward: "I would aim for 45 tackles a game and to handle the ball 15 times. I was always involved. At full-back my mind could wander."

His international career had come to a halt with the drugs ban, and he was clearly missed by a keen, but naive South Africa side in the 1995 World Cup. In 1997 he was selected for

South Africa who were touring France. He could not attend the tour preparations, but joined the team in France and played in two test matches and two games against club sides.

For the 2000 World Cup, he captained the side. It was on paper a stronger team than in 1995, but they were facing experienced opposition: "We knew it was unlikely we would win a match. Papua New Guinea was our best hope, but we lost 16–0. We did five weeks preparation in South Africa, including some development work in the townships. We played Wales and lost, but with a respectable scoreline. The match attracted 15,000 people in Loftus, a rugby union stronghold."

In 1999 Jamie made a short return to rugby union. In June he was given a 17 match ban from rugby league for biting Lee Briers. He is still bemused by this, because he was wearing a gumshield at the time. He was approached to play rugby union in France: "They wanted aggressive rugby league players. I played centre and Jon Scales came as well. We played for Racing Metro in Paris, in the Super Cup and the Heineken Cup." But he returned to Halifax and rugby league in time for the next season.

Jamie had signed a four year deal with Halifax that he hoped would see him through his rugby league career. But in 2002 Halifax had financial problems and asked him and some other players to take a 60 percent pay cut. He said 'no' and had lost faith in the people running the club at the time. He decided to cut his losses and moved to Huddersfield, along with Jim Gannon. He broke his leg in February 2003, but still made 22 appearances in Super League for the Giants. Huddersfield offered him a new deal, but coach Tony Smith was leaving the club, and his successor, Jon Sharp, told Jamie that he wouldn't select him. So he rejoined Halifax, who had by now been relegated from Super League, playing on a part-time basis: "I was beginning to look at life after rugby, and was starting my landscape gardening business. The club invited me back and it suited me to play part-time."

His international career took an unexpected switch. With the game in South Africa at a low ebb after the 2000 World Cup, he accepted an invitation to play for Scotland. He explains: "My mother was born in Edinburgh, so I was qualified to play for them. I played against Wales and Ireland, and my only international win was against Wales."

Jamie's final season as a professional rugby league player was in 2005. However, he had played union for Halifax in the league off-season, and had been selected for Yorkshire. He became player-coach for Old Brodleians RUFC, and says that "We lost our first five matches, but then won the next 17 and got promoted. It was their first promotion in 75 years. Then I had three years at Old Rishworthians and finished last year." Jamie broke a club record there in the 2007–08 season, scoring 375 points. He has also helped out with the coaching at Stainland Stags rugby league club, but does not have a position there, and has retired from playing.

Some media work as a rugby league co-commentator lead to his growing career as a rugby league referee: "I was doing some work for BBC Radio Leeds and was critical of the referee, who I thought was having a poor game. I am not always diplomatic and said 'I bet I could do better.' The next week Stuart Cummings [The RFL Controller of Referees] was on the phone, inviting me to come along and have a go. I never shy away from a challenge, and have started a long process. I'm now at Grade 2, and have done 'A' team and Super League under–20 matches." Other assignments have included Norway against Sweden for the Nordic Cup, and the 2011 Rugby League Championship Final at Warrington. There are players and coaches that Jamie played with and against, and he enjoys "a bit of banter" with them. He believes that his experience as a player helps him referee: "I know what's happening, it helps with my positioning and I can sort situations out. But I learn from the experienced referees." Jamie now referees regularly in the mainly semi-professional Championship, but has not refereed in Super League.

Jamie keeps in contact with rugby league in South Africa, and believes that the sport has potential there, although the distances involved are a major problem. He thinks that the game will never surpass rugby union, but that it could build a base. He still has family in South Africa, but his mother lives in Britain now, and he is clearly settled in West Yorkshire with Louise and their two children, Jordan and Isabelle. Jordan certainly takes after his dad as a talented sportsman, although he prefers cricket and football to rugby.

In the modern era, Jamie had the longest and most successful career of any South African in British rugby league. He still has much to offer the game, and is a role model for future former players to take up the whistle.

Mark Johnson

Mark Johnson was the most prominent South African Rugby League star of the Super League era until his retirement in 2000. He has a tremendous rugby pedigree with his older brother Gavin playing for the all-conquering rugby union Springboks and Leicester Tigers RUFC and two younger brothers who also play Union.

Mark, a South African English-speaker, was brought up in the Afrikaans-speaking town of Louis Trichardt in the Limpopo province. There were no English-speaking schools near there, so he went to school as a boarder in Pietersburg. He started playing rugby union at the age of seven, and at school played centre. After leaving school, he eventually gravitated to Pretoria where he played union for Harlequins and then on to Johannesburg to play for the Pirates, by now playing on the wing.

He started playing rugby league "in the union off season. We played touch rugby after work, but with rugby league rules. I met Dave Southern and Barry Haslam who were trying to get rugby league clubs started. There were five or six teams and I joined Dave's team, the Johannesburg Nomads. It was all union guys who were playing."

Mark had not made the regional Transvaal side in union and saw that league offered new openings for him. He was soon picked for two tests against the touring Commonwealth of Independent States (later to become Russia) team in November 1992, and scored a try in the second match. South Africa won both games and included Jamie Bloem. This led to the international Sydney Sevens in January 1993 which was the turning point in Mark's rugby career. *Open Rugby* reported that the South Africans had "played well" on their overseas debut.

In Sydney he was contacted by Glen Johnson of the Playmaker group which was involved with the tournament. They had links with London Crusaders and had helped recruit Kiwi scrum-half Mark Riley for the London club. Mark recalls: "He arranged for me to have trials with Australian Rugby League club Cronulla. I stayed for an extra two weeks after the

Sevens tournament, but I was very raw at the time, having just come to the game from rugby union. I made three sets of trials, but then the coach said I was too old at 24, so it was back on the plane to South Africa."

But Glen Johnson was soon back in touch and arranged with Mark to be offered a trial with London Crusaders. This coincided with the change of ownership at the club and the appointment of former New Zealand international coach Tony Gordon as the club's coach. Mark played a handful of games at the end of the 1992–93 season at Crystal Palace. "Glen said it was the last six weeks of the season. They would pay for my flight and accommodation, and give me some pocket money. It went really well. Two other players, 'Doc' Mulkerin and Chris Winstanley were also staying with me at The Swan Hotel [near Crystal Palace] and made me feel at home. But London was a great shock – I had grown up on a farm in South Africa and was very different to home."

Following that successful trial he was offered a full contract with the Crusaders who had just moved to Barnet Copthall in north London. Playing alongside such gifted backs as John Gallagher, Justin Walker, Scott Roskell and Logan Campbell (who followed him to Hull and Workington), Mark soon adjusted to the league game and smashed the club try-scoring record for a season at the first attempt with 43. His tremendous pace and ability to take tries fitted in very well with the team's attacking style.

Mark remembers: "I must have impressed Tony Gordon. I got offered a contract for just £3,500 plus accommodation and match fees. My mother had recently died suddenly and I felt it was the right time to make a change. It was so exciting to become a rugby league professional – something almost unheard of in recent times in South Africa."

Some credit must go to the attacking style of play of the coach Tony Gordon who seemed happy as long as the Crusaders scored more points than their opponents – never mind how many. Mark recalls: "That season was great. It was a good life – we celebrated our victories! Sam Stewart played a big part in helping my game develop – I owe him a lot. And Dave Rotheram was very hospitable and very knowledgeable. He always encouraged us at training. But I was still learning the game. In rugby union it does not matter if you are tackled over the side line, but giving the ball away like that in league is serious. In one game it happened to me twice in the first half. At half-time Tony Gordon threatened to put me on a plane back to South Africa if it happened again. I made up for it by scoring two tries."

Mark shared a house with three other Crusaders players "all single guys. It was a good life and a great season. I remember playing at York in the snow – a new experience. The Premiership Final at Old Trafford was the climax to the whole season. We had a well balanced team." Although the injury-hit Crusaders lost the Divisional Premiership Final to a strong Workington team, Mark scored a hat-trick in the match. Not only was Mark the top Crusaders try scorer, but also top in British rugby league that year. He followed in the tradition of great South African players such as Tom van Vollenhoven, Len Killeen, Fred Griffiths, Trevor Lake and others.

The popularity of a player is often shown by his nickname – if he has one he's usually popular, Mark Johnson had three: 'Johnno', 'Magic' and bizarrely the 'Cape Crusader', given that he was born nowhere near South Africa's Cape, still it was a good moniker.

Mark stayed with the club in 1994–95 after the Brisbane Broncos' takeover, but never seemed to quite fit in with new Australian coach Gary Greinke's plans. He remembers: "I don't feel I had a fair chance from him. At times I was playing in the 'A' team but felt I deserved a first team place." As Greinke broke up the 1993–94 team, Mark left in July 1995 to join Workington. "The club made me a free agent rather than pay me my outstanding contract money. Workington had been interested in me after the match against them at Old Trafford. Peter Walsh was the coach there and he was the main reason I went there. But as I arrived he left and Kurt Sorensen took over." Workington struggled in Super League. "But for me it was a step up. I got a better contract than at London. And another highlight was playing with Rowland Phillips. He is one of the best friends I have made in rugby league."

After Mark's contract finished with Workington, he returned to South Africa for four months. Disillusioned after a season of struggle in Super League which had ended in relegation, he tried to get back into rugby union. He played sevens in the Transvaal team, but decided that league did offer him a future after all. He was then approached to play for Hull. Two seasons there were followed by move for the 1999 and 2000 seasons to Salford. "For the first 10 games, with Andy Gregory as coach, I was in the 'A' team. But then he left and I got a first team spot and ended up scoring 15 tries." Mark was the club's top try scorer. In his final year at Salford, the 2000 season, he was joined by Martin Offiah from the London Broncos, who he says in training is fractionally faster over 40 yards. Mark spent much of his last season in professional rugby league starting on the bench. He started one game, made 11 further appearances as a substitute, and scored one try.

Another great memory for Mark is playing for South Africa in the 1995 Rugby League World Cup. "I had gone from playing touch rugby in 1992 to representing my country in a World Cup. We played Australia, the World Champions, England and Fiji. They were all a different class from us, but we gave Fiji a good game." Mark was the most experienced player in the team. "For the third game against England I played at stand-off and shouted at our players for 80 minutes telling them what to do. At least I can say I've played against the best teams in a World Cup competition."
He also played three matches in the World Cup in 2000, when South Africa lost all their group games, against France, Papua New Guinea and Tonga.

Mark believes that his main strength as a player was his finishing. "I can read the game quite well and see where the breaks will be. Timing is very important. I can't explain it – it happens so quickly. I try to look for work and not just stay on my wing. I'm not the fastest winger in the world but I am a good finisher. I'm trying to improve my weaknesses and I take it personally if opposing teams score on my wing."

After finishing at Salford, Mark returned to South Africa with his family. Mark scored 115 tries in 168 games in his British rugby league career. But he often played in struggling sides, limiting his scoring opportunities. Had one of the top clubs recognised his talent he could have regularly topped the try scoring charts. London fans will remember his contribution to the marvellous 1993–94 team and he remains the only London player ever to top the national try scoring list. In 2014 he was made an inaugural member of the London Broncos Hall of Fame.

Mark Johnson during his time with Salford.
(Photo: Peter Lush)

Jamie Bloem playing for Halifax.
(Photo: David Williams, RLphotos.com)

Right: Andre Stoop playing for Keighley Cougars.
(Photo: Courtesy *Rugby League Journal*)

Another player who came to British rugby league in the early 1990s, although this time coming to the end of his career was Andre Stoop. Initially recruited by Wigan, he found it difficult to win a first team place at Central Park, but enjoyed more success with London Crusaders, and then Keighley Cougars.

Andre Stoop

Andre came to rugby league relatively late in his rugby career. He was born on 8 October 1960 in Tsumeb, in South West Africa (SWA), now Namibia. He moved to Windhoek, the capital, when he was aged eight. He was "born a Boer" and spoke Afrikaans at home. He played 115 games for South West Africa and 11 for Namibia, scoring six tries. He toured Great Britain with the Namibia Rugby Union team in 1990, and played for Namibia against England 'B' at Leicester's Welford Road ground.

Ever since the founding of the Damaraland Rugby Union in 1916, players born and bred in the area known today as Namibia, plied their trade in South Africa's major rugby union competitions. Like their former Rhodesian counterparts, they could compete for Springbok caps. Given the vast distances between towns, the small number of players and scarcity of extra financial resources to invest in the general promotion of sport, only a small number of exceptional sportsmen and women had the honour of representing their country internationally. Often they were expat South Africans who were north of the Orange River for economic reasons.

Among those in rugby union who had to fight in order to gain recognition was André Stoop. He went to Windhoek High School, and on completing his secondary education, joined the SWA Territorial Defence Force for his national service and started training as an apprentice fitter. He played rugby for the Windhoek Defence Force RFC who competed in the Central Sub Union regional competition. He finally gained selection for the national team in the Sport Pienaar Trophy competition in 1982. He joined his older brother Leon in a side with many talented players.

As a largely rural-based competition, the Sport Pienaar Competition was not the same standard as the Currie Cup where the urban and city-based powerhouse teams played. SWA, like their resource-poor counterparts, was constantly engaged in tough battles to gain promotion to the top level of South African rugby.

Stoop, an agile and clever full-back, but still inexperienced at provincial level, played one representative game in his debut season. With no real opportunities to impress in the last 80 minutes of the season at his disposal, he made no great impression, and also failed to gain a review in the *SA Rugby Annual's* section on provincial players. This notwithstanding, he had sampled rugby on a level higher than the local sub-union fare that he was used to. His club won the Central Sub Union League title which was a source of great satisfaction. This situation was soon to change.

With more work to do to challenge for higher honours, Stoop committed himself well over the next two seasons. By the start of the 1983 season, he had emerged not only as a more mature individual, but also a well-rounded player with the necessary confidence to step up to a higher level.

In that season, SWA played in the Sport Pienaar Trophy's A-Division, and the knock-out Lion Cup. Admission to the latter depended on a series of qualifying matches and a series of cross-section matches against top Currie Cup sides. Despite their smaller player pool and lack of resources, SWA reached the third round of the knock-out series. SWA finally lost 15–9 to Transvaal. The team, however, learned from this experience and claimed the second place in their division and therefore qualified to play in a promotion-relegation match for a place in the Currie Cup. Although they stumbled at this final hurdle, their performances saw Stoop impress the national selectors enough to play for the South African Barbarians against the South African Defence Force XV in Johannesburg. He also played for the South African Country Districts XV against the Chilean national team. In both cases he played well and was a significant threat. His side won both times, which further enhanced his growing reputation. He went on a post-season tour of South America with SWA. At the end of the season, he had played in 14 out of 20 matches and scored seven tries.

Picking up from the previous season, the SWA team continued their good form in 1984. They won the Sport Pienaar Trophy again and the Paul Roos Trophy as Divisional winners. Their second year in the Lion Cup, however, was more challenging and again they were knocked out in the third round, this time by Northern Transvaal. Stoop was again recognised for his individual performances with 12 representative games and 11 tries. This put him among the top try-scorers in all first-class rugby that season. To crown it all he played for a Combined SWA/Griqualand West/North Western Cape XV against the British Lions. Although his team lost, Stoop scored a try to add to his growing reputation.

As the international sports boycott against South Africa intensified, Stoop entered the 1985 season as a recognised player on the local rugby scene. There was, however, no prospect of further building on his international experience because scheduled official tours to the Republic were cancelled. As compensation for the cancelled All Blacks tour, the SA Rugby Board sent the national team on an internal tour to play regional selections. Stoop, despite his growing reputation, did not make it into the national team. He was, however, recognised as a strong contender by being selected for the Cape Barbarians which was due to face the Boks at Newlands. The national team's surprise defeat shocked the rugby fans to their core. This result, however, benefitted Stoop who, after sterling performances in 15 matches including games for the SA Barbarians and a SWA XV against the Springboks and Matie Springboks respectively, was voted the second best full-back in the country by the SA Rugby Writers Society.

Over the last three years of his rugby union career, Stoop continued to hold his own among the full-backs playing in South Africa. In addition to Currie Cup and Lion Cup games, he played the odd festival game between regional or provincial and even national select combinations. The only international contact came in the form of a number of rebel tours such as the visit of the South Sea Barbarians consisting of players from various Pacific Islands in 1987. As one of the form full-backs, Stoop was selected for the SA Barbarians, a virtual national or Springbok XV, to play against the visitors in Durban and Johannesburg. He scored a try in these games to re-emphasise his quality and value as a player. He also represented the SA Barbarians in a match against a Crusaders XV in Port Elizabeth. This was balanced with outings for a variety of other sides such as for a SWA XV against a SA XV in

Windhoek. Although his side lost 25–21, Stoop had touched down against quality opposition. He also played for the Boksburg Centenary Festival XV against a Transvaal XV in Boksburg and the Currie Cup B Unions XV against the Sport Pienaar XV in Pretoria. His team again won the Sport Pienaar Trophy and was knocked out in the Lion Cup second round. Over the season he played 12 games for SWA and scored six tries. Overall, his career record for representative provincial games came to 71 games and 151 career points by the end of the season.

An incident that left a lasting impression on Stoop and his team mates that season was a players' protest and demand for financial compensation for displaying sponsor's logos on their jerseys. In June 1988, Stoop was selected as full-back for the Northern Regional XV which was to face a Southern XV in an ISM Shield Match at Newlands, Cape Town. The match sponsored by the local business ISM was arranged as a means of compensating the country's top players for their lack of international competition. Right from the outset, the run-up to the match saw many player issues, including coercion to participate despite other commitments. In response to the heavy-handedness of the national body, the players demanded payment for their participation. Unsurprisingly, this demand was ignored by officialdom, only for the players to take to the field with the sponsor's logo on their jersey covered by sticky plaster. This left the administrators both angry and severely embarrassed and South African rugby stripped of its commercial innocence. Stoop's contribution to this incident-ridden match was a penalty goal. In another long season, Stoop played 20 out of 24 provincial matches and scored 23 points for SWA. His club, Wanderers RFC, won the Senior League competition and he was rated among the top five players in his position in South Africa. He also pushed his first-class career for SWA to 91 representative matches.

The 1989 season witnessed the formal inauguration of an independent Namibia and the start of a process to officially detach itself from its links with South Africa. As well as working towards a fully inclusive and non-racial new national rugby controlling body, the season saw the national team's last year of participation in the Currie Cup and Lion Cup competition. But the team declined. They only won six out of 20 games to finish sixth in the Currie Cup. There were early exits from the Lion Cup and the new Yardley Gold Trophy. Despite all this, and injuries at critical times, Stoop reached a personal milestone of 102 representative matches for his country and a career record of 194 points. When the Namibia National Rugby Union finally announced its withdrawal from all South African competitions at the end of 1989, the curtain came down on André Stoop's South African rugby union career. For the next two seasons, he proudly wore the jersey of his newly independent and free country, Namibia, to start building a new rugby legacy which included playing 11 representative international matches between March 1990 and August 1991. He scored six tries before joining rugby league.

Andre recalled to Keighley rugby league historian John Pitchford in an interview for this book that he was contacted during the 1990 Namibia tour by a rugby league scout, but did not discuss a possible signing with him. Wigan then phoned him on his return to Namibia. He flew over to England and agreed a deal to play for Wigan, and joined the club on 24 September 1991. He thought that he adjusted to rugby league well, but felt wasted as a spectator as Wigan only played him when other players were injured and he returned to

Namibia. He did not play rugby league in Africa, but found it to be a much simpler game than union.

Despite his dissatisfaction at Wigan, who were by far the strongest team in British rugby league at that time, he still played 13 games, plus five as a substitute over two seasons, scoring a try and kicking three goals. The regular full-back was Great Britain international Steve Hampson. Andre did play in a World Club Challenge match, when Wigan were beaten 22–8 by the Brisbane Broncos at Central Park.

Andre may have had more opportunities had he not joined the strongest team in the northern hemisphere. In January 1994 he signed on loan from Wigan for London Crusaders. He joined a club who had survived a major crisis early in the season when their owners withdrew from the club and it was being funded by the RFL. Despite this, it was a season that all London fans will always remember. Inspirational Kiwi coach Tony Gordon had assembled a fantastic team playing great attacking rugby. Captained by New Zealand international Sam Stewart, and including former New Zealand international – and Londoner! – John Gallagher, and South African winger Mark Johnson, the team played exciting, attacking rugby. Andre thoroughly enjoyed his time at all his three rugby league clubs, particularly at London Crusaders. He shared a house with three Australians and built lasting friendships with them and the other international players at the club. The team missed promotion by one point, by which time the club had been purchased by the Brisbane Broncos. They also reached the Divisional Premiership Final at Old Trafford, and lost narrowly 30–22 to a very experienced Workington Town team. He had made 15 first team appearances and scored nine tries in his spell in London

The London club was keen to keep Andre, but he joined Keighley Cougars from Wigan in a £22,500 transfer in August 1994. He joined a club that was having a major impact in rugby league, using imaginative advertising and marketing linked to effective community work and a good team on the pitch. Attendances were climbing at Cougar Park, the new name for the club's Lawkholme Lane ground.

His Keighley debut was in the pre-season friendly at Cougar Park against Bradford Bulls on 14 August. He scored two tries in a 22–22 draw for the Joe Phillips Trophy. New Zealander Joe Phillips was a player and director at Bradford and was a leading light in reforming the Bradford club in 1964. He joined Keighley as player-coach in 1959 and was also a director at the club after his retirement as a player

Andre's full debut for Keighley was on 21 August 1994 in a 38–8 home win over Whitehaven in Rugby League's Second Division. He scored 14 tries in 32 games in his first season with Keighley Cougars, who won the Second Division Championship. They also triumphed in the Second Division Premiership Final at Old Trafford, beating Huddersfield 26–6. Andre added a winner's medal to go with the loser's one from the previous season with London Crusaders.

The end of the 1994–95 season was overshadowed by the heated debate on the proposals to introduce a Super League in 1996. For Keighley, the consequences were very severe. They did not fit the RFL's profile of clubs for the new competition, and were effectively refused the promotion to the sport's top flight which they merited on the pitch. This was to have serious consequences for the club.

The 1995–96 season a shortened one prior to the switch to summer rugby. The Challenge Cup was not competed for nor were there any play-off games at the end of the season. Keighley were badly hit by injuries and Andre only played 11 games out of 21, and scored five tries.

His injury problems worsened in the 1996 season. He only played in four games plus one as a substitute, scoring one try. A broken jaw in a 34–30 defeat at Hull on 8 April caused him to miss 11 games. He also missed out on a third consecutive appearance in the Divisional Premiership Final when Keighley lost 19–6 to Salford at Old Trafford. His last game for Keighley, on 21 July 1996, was ironically again against Whitehaven. This time it was in Cumbria and the result was a 14–14 draw.

Andre Stoop played all his games for Keighley at full-back and in total played 48 times, including his one appearance as a substitute, and scored 20 tries. Keighley were not able to offer him a new contract for 1997 owing to their financial situation and so he moved to Germany as player-coach to a rugby union team. Union going 'open' in 1995 meant that former union players who had switched to league could return to their former code, and Andre took advantage of this. His most treasured rugby league memory is Keighley's victory and the atmosphere in the Second Division Premiership Final in 1995 against Huddersfield at Old Trafford. He returned to live in Keighley after his time in Germany, and at the time of writing still lives in the town, working as a postman.

The programme from the South Africa versus CIS matches in 1992.
Jamie Bloem and Mark Johnson both played for South Africa.

20. Jaco Booysen and the 1995 World Cup

For the 1995 World Cup, the South African Rugby League invited Tony Fisher to coach the team, many of whom were recent rugby union converts. Fisher, who had been a tough hooker for Wales and Great Britain in his playing days, was also the coach at Dewsbury, and recruited some of the squad to play for the club. Sadly, the project did not last long, because the club could not fund it.

Rugby league in Great Britain at this time was in transition to becoming a summer sport, and Dewsbury were playing in the Centenary First Division, the second tier of the professional game, which lasted from the summer of 1995 until January 1996. They finished bottom of the table, with just two wins. In September, a couple of weeks before the start of the World Cup, Jaco Booysen, Guy Coombe, Tim Fourie, Kobus van Deventer and Gideon Watts all signed for the club. Fourie made the most appearances, with 11, Booysen played eight times, Coombe 7, van Deventer 6+1 and Watts did not play for the first team. In October, Pierre van Wyk also joined the club and played once that season. Coombe and van Wyk did stay on until the 1996 season, and played a handful of games.

In 1994–95, Fisher had been coaching at Doncaster, who were in the First Division for the first time. As well as Jamie Bloem, who played until he was suspended for using steroids, Fisher had recruited Pierre Grobbelaar in August 1994. He started two games and came off the bench once during his time at the club.

At the end of August 1995, almost 100 years to the day after the formation of the Northern Union, rugby union became an 'open' game, allowing professionalism for the first time. So the Dewsbury South Africans were able to return to rugby union if they wished.

Jaco Booysen

Jaco Booysen, who played most of his rugby at Springs RFC on the East Rand of Johannesburg, entered representative rugby at a time when South African sport was subject to an international sports boycott and had to make do with rebel tours. His provincial debut for Eastern Transvaal against Vaal Triangle in a Currie Cup game at Kempton Park in 1987 came two years after the cancellation of the New Zealand All Black tour to South Africa, an event that Paul Dobson, the noted South African rugby historian, called the "greatest man-made disaster" of international rugby. Furthermore, his debut season coincided with the inaugural Rugby World Cup for the William Webb Ellis trophy, organized by the International Rugby Board, the controlling body for international rugby union.

South Africa, who has voted for the launch of this significant event, was reduced to the status of spectator. In its stead the South African Rugby Board hosted a number of obscure teams such as the South Sea Barbarians, the Diaz XV, American Grizzlies and the SABRAS from Israel to try to compensate for its lack of international rugby and to offer local players an opportunity to play against overseas teams.

Playing for Eastern Transvaal, fondly known as 'The Red Devils' due to their reputation for uncompromising play, suited Booysen, a bone-hard and no-nonsense (but still untested on a wider stage) flanker, very well. As a provincial player in his first season, he was, however, not considered for selection for a combined Northern Free State & Transvaal XV that was scheduled to face the South Sea Barbarians at Welkom. Life in the Currie Cup B-Division, a league described by its critics as no more than a 'lucky-packet league', however, was tough enough. All the minnow unions on this level were intent on gaining qualification to the A-Division in order to join the elite and more lucrative arm of the local game. After playing a sole representative game for the Red Devils, he left at the end of the season to play for the Rand Afrikaans University (now the University of Johannesburg) in the Pirates Grand Challenge Cup under the auspices of the Transvaal RFU.

Despite his undoubted ability, having to compete against the likes of English international Peter Winterbottom as well as local Springboks Jannie Breedt and Wahl Bartmann, Booysen was not selected for the Transvaal senior provincial side. This prompted him to return to his playing roots on the East Rand and to rejoin his old club Springs in the ETVL President's League Competition in 1990. With three years of invaluable experience, gained in a tough and bruising league, behind him, he made an immediate impression in the local league. He soon returned to the provincial setup as a member of the Red Devils outfit in the Currie Cup B-Division playing for the Sport Pienaar Trophy.

After five successive victories over provincial opponents like WP League, Boland, South Eastern Transvaal, Eastern Free State, and Vaal Triangle, his team qualified to play in the final against Western Province League. Booysen was regarded as one of his union's match-winners and a key part of one of the most dominant loose-trios and forward packs in the competition. He gave his all in his team's efforts to secure the championship. As a result of over-robustness and aggression, he was yellow-carded and spent part of the final in the sin-bin. This, to a certain extent, contributed to his team's 22–16 defeat at the hands of the WPL. Overall, however, he could look back at a satisfactory season.

The 1991 season started on a poor footing for the men from the Eastern Transvaal. Not only did they struggle in early-season friendlies, but their loose-forwards were particularly disappointing. By the start of the official season and participation in the Lion Cup Knock-out inter-provincial competition, in addition to their form being poor, they were out of their depth in their encounters with rugby powerhouses such as Transvaal – when they lost 58–3 – Western Province and Northern Transvaal. Things got worse as they struggled to assert the dominance of the previous season. After four matches, Booysen lost his place in the team. Being dropped to club level was good for him because he soon started to regain his old form. Matters on the provincial level, however, did not improve. Their woes continued as the number of defeats climbed. In a state of panic, the provincial selectors engaged in all manner of experiments in team selection. This was aggravated by simmering administrative problems. Ironically, this created new playing opportunities for Booysen. By May 1991 he was back in the provincial team and distinguished himself in a friendly game against the Orange Free State. However, he had to leave the field with a rib injury which complicated his return to representative rugby. When he returned a month later for the Bankfin Currie Cup competition, in the midst of a season of discontent for the province, he once again became a victim of a yo-yo season. After a further five home defeats, he was dropped to the province's second team, the 'Kudus'. With the season on the verge of being lost and the

176

province facing relegation, Booysen returned to the side for the promotion-relegation game against Border. In the background, tensions about non-payment of incentives were also beginning to manifest themselves. Despite the odds, Eastern Transvaal lost its place in the senior league for the next season.

The 1992 season saw the unification of South Africa's opposing and racially-based rugby controlling bodies to give birth to the non-racial South African Rugby Football Union. As the result of the demise of all former ethnic-playing provinces, especially the integration of the Coloured Western Province League into Western Province, the Red Devils were restored to the elite level of South African rugby. As a result of a poor 1992 season and the team's pending relegation, the union witnessed a player exit. The restoration of its status meant that the province had to rebuild its playing resources since only Booysen and two others of the last squad remained.

Booysen made a solid start to the season and in the season-opener against Eastern Free State despite being on the losing side. Reports commented on his 'powerful driving play'. By the start of the Currie Cup competition, he was moved to the Number 8 position to face Northern Transvaal. Unsurprisingly, the team suffered a heavy defeat, 76–0. He, however, suffered a nasty cheekbone injury against Eastern Province and was out of action for around eight weeks. This interfered with his emerging good form. When he returned in May for the match against Natal in the Bankfin competition it was with a group of young and inexperienced players. Player commitment to training and availability for matches was low and there was dissatisfaction with frequent changes in team selection. At that stage they had lost 22 matches on the trot. With Booysen in the team, Easterns scored their first home victory against Border. Once again, reports said that Booysen and his fellow loose-forwards were conspicuous and "they were like falcons on the loose-ball and aggressive on defence".

Booysen took his good form into the Percy Ross Frames Competition and was not intimidated by big-name stars in the ranks of the A-Provinces. He combined try-scoring with aggressive and at times over-robust play which earned him both yellow and red cards and short periods of suspension. Newspapers often referred to Booysen as a fearless and 'fire-blasting flanker'. He also became a serious contender for a place in the team of the Central Unions that was to face the New Zealand All Blacks. Recurring injuries, however, cut across that and in the end shortened his season.

Booysen was back for the new season, six years after making his provincial debut. He made a satisfactory start to the season by not only winning the battle for the loose ball 13–6 against his opponents, but also scored a try. This was followed up by notable performances in the Lion Cup Competition, such as a narrow defeat at the hands of Northern Transvaal, 27–19, and a try against Vaal-Triangle as his team embarked on a mission to rid itself of its 'Cinderella syndrome'. He also played in the historic first friendly between ETVL and Zimbabwe in Harare as well as recording further notable performances against WP and Free State, including scoring a try against the latter. Although he lost his place halfway through the 1993 season with departure of De Vos, the coach, he returned for the Northern Free State game and was part of a memorable 35–17 victory, which he celebrated with a try. He also scored a try against Western Transvaal.

Continued internal problems between the administrators and the coaches, however, undermined the team's overall performance to the extent that they were once again faced with having to play a promotion-relegation match – this time against South Eastern Transvaal. On the day Booysen not only provided the fire for his forward pack, but also emerged as the team's most outstanding player. Unfortunately, he had to leave the field with a broken collarbone and that ended his season. To crown a commendable season, in which he played trials for selection to a South African Development Team destined to tour South America, his club Springs RFC won the club league, Booysen also won the award as Eastern Transvaal Player of the Year.

As the country prepared for its first democratic elections in 1994, Booysen entered his seventh season of first-class rugby. Although he found himself in the starting line-up in a series of friendly games in March, this was the start of a season of mixed fortunes. As a result of some indifferent performances, he was dropped after three matches. Although he regained his place, recurring injuries coupled with below-par performances saw him periodically being dropped to the B-side and the reserve-bench. On those days when he struck form, he contributed by scoring some tries. When the 1994 rugby union season drew to a close, Booysen and other notable union players such as Hercus Mahoney (South Eastern Transvaal), Jaco Webb (Eastern Transvaal) and Joe Herman (Namibia), ventured into rugby league and was selected to represent the South African Rugby League Rhinos against the Queensland Maroons. This immediately created new tensions between the SARL and the rugby union authorities and signalled Booysen's short departure from the latter code.

Booysen returned to rugby union in April 1995 well before the march towards the professionalisation of rugby union after the Rugby World Cup tournament became irreversible. The early season found Booysen playing for Centurion RFC in the Carlton League of the Northern Transvaal (now the Blue Bulls Rugby Union). Considered as one of the toughest of South Africa's domestic leagues, he made his presence felt and did not shy away from physical brawls. Yet by August 1995, in the middle of the domestic rugby union season, he skippered the Rugby League Rhinos to a series win against the British Rugby League Lions, a BARLA amateur team.

With the formal professionalisation of rugby union in South Africa after the Rugby World Cup Tournament, the domestic rugby scene changed irrevocably. By 1998, Booysen returned to his home province, now called the Gauteng Falcons Rugby Union after Eastern Transvaal merged with Vaal Triangle. As a result of his legendary performances in both codes, he was immediately included in their early season squad and was included in the squad scheduled to depart on a tour of Great Britain and Ireland as well as Namibia in preparation for the new Vodacom Competition and the Currie Cup. Playing initially from the reserve bench, he soon found him back in the thick of things and even back to scoring tries. The new professional setup seemingly also had beneficial effects for traditionally second-tier provincial unions with the team succeeding in stringing together four victories in a row. At one stage the Falcons even occupied the third place in the table.

He crowned his return with his 100th game in 1999, 12 seasons after making his representative debut. By 2000 he was awarded the Falcons captaincy for the Vodacom Cup competition and as a result of the free gangway between rugby union and league after professionalisation was also able to continue his league career and to prepare for playing for the Rhinos in the 2000 Rugby League World Cup under the captaincy of Jamie Bloem.

By 2001, after 14 years of commitment and 127 games of top flight rugby union, Booysen finally retires from the sport as one of only a handful of players to have played in the old amateur rugby order, to have managed the transition to professionalism and finally topped it all with a credible rugby league career of 25 international matches. Instead of disappearing, Booysen in his retirement ventured into schools rugby union coaching to put something back into the sport that he loved.

The 1995 Rugby League World Cup is fondly remembered as a tournament of exciting attacking rugby, featuring teams which had not played a major international role before. Coming with the background of the formation of Super League, which had split the sport in Australia and Great Britain, the players provided a tournament which overcame the problems in the management and development of the sport at the time.

The previous World Cup had involved just five countries – Great Britain, Australia, New Zealand, Papua New Guinea and France, and had lasted from 1989 to 1992. It had concluded with an excellent final at Wembley, narrowly won by Australia against Great Britain, but the sport's international leadership recognized the need to broaden the number of participants.

Great Britain split into England and Wales; and the new entrants were Western Samoa, Tonga, Fiji and South Africa. There were three groups: South Africa were in Group 1, along with England, Australia and Fiji. Group 2 featured New Zealand, Tonga and Papua New Guinea and Group 3 had Wales, Western Samoa and France. The top two qualified for the semi-finals from Group 1, along with the other two Group winners. Not surprisingly, England and Australia qualified from Group 1. New Zealand won Group 2 and Wales Group 3. In the final Australia beat England at Wembley.

There was also an Emerging Nations tournament run in parallel with the main competition. South Africa certainly would have been more competitive at that level, but the full tournament needed another team to provide a realistic structure, so they were included in that competition.

South Africa opened their campaign against Fiji, and lost 52–6 at Keighley. Some of the Fijians played in Australia, and were far more experienced than the South African squad, who were missing Jamie Bloem who was suspended from the sport. A World Cup Diary in *Open Rugby* said that South Africa matched Fiji until the second half. Two days later, Australia beat the South Africans 86–6 in front of a 9,191 crowd at Gateshead. Their final match was against England at Headingley. Mark Johnson moved to stand-off to be able to direct the team, and although England won comfortably, 46–0, it was a respectable performance by the South Africans. The World Cup Diary said that as the match progressed, admiration for South Africa's efforts grew, and they "put in a very credible performance". The writer mentioned Boshoff, Booysen and Pierre van Wyk, as well as noting Mark Johnson's role at stand-off. The South Africans' cause was not helped by Pierre Grobbelaar failing a drugs test at the start of the tournament.

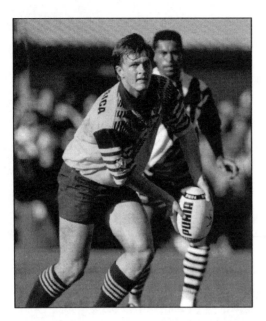

Top left and right: Action from the South Africans first match in the 1995 World Cup against Fiji at Keighley.
Below: The team before the match against England at Headingley. (All photos: David Williams - rlphotos.com)

The South Africa squad for the 1996 Student World Cup. (Photo: David Williams – rlphotos.com)

On parade in Warrington before the 1996 Student World Cup.
(Photo: David Williams – rlphotos.com)

The full South African squad was: Jaco Alberts (S Queensland Crushers – Australia), Barend Alkema, Andrew Ballot (Bay of Plenty – New Zealand), Jaco Booysen (St Helens Devils), Willem Boshoff (Eastern Reds), Francois Cloete (Barea Students), Guy Coombe (Durban Sharks), Tim Fourie (City Scorpions), Pierre Grobbelaar (Vaal Buffaloes), Koot Human (S Queensland Crushers – Australia), Justin Jennings (S Queensland Crushers – Australia), Mark Johnson (Workington Town), Elmar Lubbe (Eastern Reds), Ernest Ludick, Warren McCann, John Mudgeway (Durban Sharks), Eugene Powell (City Scorpions), Nico Serfontein (Hemel Hempstead – UK), Kobus van Deventer (Germiston Warriors), Jaco van Niekerk (Eastern Reds), Pierre van Wyk (Eastern Reds), Jaco Visser, Gideon Watts and Gerald Williams (Durban Sharks).

Of these players, six – Booysen, Cloete, Jennings, Johnson, Powell and van Wyk played in the 2000 World Cup. Four – Alberts, Cloete, Jennings and Visser played in the 1996 Student World Cup.

Despite rugby union allowing professionalism, rugby league was still of interest for some players to develop their careers. One prominent Springbok who also played league was Tiaan Strauss.

Tiaan Strauss

As 'Operation Desert Storm' got underway in the Arabian Gulf in 1990, the star of Tiaan Strauss, born and bred in the arid Kalahari desert region of South Africa shone at its brightest. Like the American campaign sweeping across the Arabian Desert, Strauss – an accomplished rugby union loose-forward for the better part of 10 seasons in South African rugby – collected all manner of honours. He captained a string of representative teams, from the South African Invitational XV, Southern Universities, Southern Unions, South Africa Defence Force XV to Western Province. Following a series of consistent performances, he crowned the 1990 season with South Africa's Rugby Player-of-the-Year award. Starting the season as caretaker captain of Western Province in the Currie Cup and Lion Cup, he skippered his team to fourth position in the former competition and to the final in the latter.

The young University of Stellenbosch law student, who learned his rugby in Upington in the North Western Cape, represented North Western Cape schools in the annual Craven Week tournament in 1983. Strauss was also a field athlete at the SA Championship, excelling in shot put and enjoyed water skiing, tennis and golf. Soon after arriving at Stellenbosch University, he was selected for both the university's and Western Province's under–21 teams. He also played in the Western Province Grand Challenge and Town Challenge competitions.

Strauss made his debut aged 21 for Western Province in the Lion Cup against North Eastern Cape. He made an immediate impression and contributed a try to their 51–0 victory. This, and subsequent performances, saw him keep his place for the Currie Cup series. In his debut against Northern Transvaal, he scored a try in their 31–27 victory and repeated this against Eastern Province. He also played for the Southern Universities against the Northern Universities. By September, after playing seven Currie Cup matches on the trot, WP reached the Currie Cup final. Strauss capped a dream debut season with an outstanding display of forward play in the Currie Cup Final, contributing to Western Province's 22–9 win over Transvaal to take the trophy for the fifth successive time.

Strauss's second season was very different. After a satisfactory start to the 1987 season he was sidelined for two months with a broken bone in his hand. By the time he returned in May, Western Province's only chance of honours was in the Lion Cup. He was included in the South African XV, a shadow Springbok side, for a match against South West Africa (Namibia), but injuries forced him to withdraw prior to the game. By the time that he returned to full fitness, all the major competitions, except the Teljoy Challenge Cup competition, were finished. However, he ended the season with his reputation enhanced.

With the international sports boycott against South Africa taking its toll, Strauss – like many of his peers – made do with domestic competition. He was restricted to playing in local competitions and the ISM Shield between the southern and northern provinces. He also represented Stellenbosch at club and intervarsity level. He also contributed to his team's victory over Northern Transvaal in the Lion Cup Final, but had to accept defeat against the same opposition in the Currie Cup Final.

To mitigate the effect of the sports boycott, the South African Rugby Board worked ceaselessly to entice touring teams to the country. Despite its fellow members disapproving of this practice, the SARB actively promoted the recruitment of rebel tours to play South African teams. These tours provide Strauss and his generation with their first exposure to international rugby.

After starring for the Southern Provinces, Strauss was selected by Western Province to play against the American Grizzlies. However, he missed out through injury. He was selected for a South African multi-racial development team, the Nampak Pioneers, to tour South America. Scheduled to play seven games, this was only the third multi-racial South African rugby team to tour overseas. In his first match against international opposition, Strauss contributed one of the 10 tries in their 100–6 win against Chile. He also scored two tries against the 'Condores', a combined team of Paraguayans and Uruguayans. Strauss was one of the top five players nominated for the South African Rugby Player of the Year award. Although he did not win, this was acknowledgement of a young player eager to stake his claim for international recognition.

In the 1989 season, Strauss played in his 50th game for Western Province. In his 54th game, the quarter-final Lion Cup game against Vaal-Triangle, he took the captaincy after injury to regular captain Carel Du Plessis. Leading from the front, he gave a sterling performance in securing a berth in the Lion Cup Final, including a try in their 55–9 victory. He also skippered his team to the championship, beating Northern Transvaal 21–16.

Strauss staked a serious claim for a place in the national team to face a World XV as part of the SARB's centenary celebrations. He made it to the reserve bench for the President's XV against the tourists. Rugby reporters criticised his omission from the national side and blamed his exclusion on a combination of 'a lack of international experience' and political correctness since some black players gained priority selection for the President's XV. Although Strauss only played in the second half, he distinguished himself. He was vice-captain of the South Africa Students XV team that faced the Defence Force XV in a curtain-raiser for the second test of the Springboks versus the World XV.

Also, he further emphasised his value by energetic and high-quality performances that earned his team a place in the Currie Cup Final and inclusion in the provincial Sevens team for the national tournament. At the end of a busy season, including a 16–16 draw in the Currie Cup final, Strauss went to Italy to play for Nanchetto RFC in the European winter.

1990 was a great season for Tiaan Strauss. He skippered the team to yet another Lion Cup Final. Despite a try by Strauss, they lost to Northern Transvaal. Further honours such as captaining the Southern Universities team, vice-captain of the Craven XV selection team to face Northern Transvaal for a match in honour of the 80th birthday of Dr Craven, inclusion in the Southern Unions XV for their annual game against the north; a nomination as Western Province Sportsman of the Year and another nomination as South Africa's Player-of-the-Year, crowned an extremely busy year. Although Strauss did not win the last mentioned honour, his team finished fourth in the Currie Cup and there was much to be satisfied with as South African began the final transition towards becoming a non-racial democracy.

In 1991, he missed much of the season through injury, but did play in Italy again at the end of the South African season. The 1992 season was a momentous year for South African rugby. Close to 24 months after the release of Nelson Mandela from prison, in March, the politically-divided rugby controlling bodies united to form the South African Rugby Football Union, which also signalled the country's return to international competition. Also, 1992 took the process of political change initiated with the release of Mandela and the unbanning of black political organisations further. Key among these were a national referendum through which white voters were asked to either endorse or reject fundamental changes to the system and by implication, their accepted way of life. On 17 March, three days before the formation of SARFU, Strauss unequivocally declared his position as a supporter of the 'Yes for Change' vote. In April he brought his association with Stellenbosch University to an end by joining Northerns Technical College for the new season. Also, he was reappointed as Western Province's captain.

With South Africa set to return to international test match competition with matches against Australia and New Zealand, a series of trials were held to select South Africa's first unified and non-racial national team. Reward for his consistency over a sustained period came with the captaincy of the Junior Springboks, the country's first truly representative team, against Namibia in Windhoek to formally announce South Africa's official return to international competition. In addition to leading his team to a 79–3 win, Strauss scored a try and won nomination as one of the Parow Senior Sport Stars of the Year. He kept the Junior Springboks captaincy against the touring New Zealand All Blacks. Although his team lost 25–10, Strauss was not disgraced. This was, however, not enough to ensure him selection for the test team. This only came at the end of the season with the selection of the national team to tour the United Kingdom and France. He played six games on tour and impressed sufficiently, especially in defence, to make his test debut against France. In November 1992, he scored South Africa's 400th test try against England at Twickenham.

At provincial level, Strauss played his 100th game for the province. He won the award of the Northerns Technical College Player of the Year as well as the award of South African

Player of the Year. Particularly pleasing was his club winning the Western Province League title and qualifying to represent the province at the annual National Club Championship.

In 1993, he captained the WP team on their pre-season tour to Australia and New Zealand. He made a good start to the new season against Western Australia. Building on this, Strauss was chosen for the first national squad training group under coach Ian Macintosh, but had to withdraw as a result of a kidney problem. Although he was chosen for the final group prior to the test against France, he lost out on the Springbok captaincy. After a reasonable performance in the test, he was given the vice-captaincy for the second test. He also kept his place for the tour to Australia where he had the opportunity to lead the team against an Australian Invitation XV in Adelaide. Overall this was a successful tour for Strauss. At the end of the season he was included in the national team to tour Argentina. Although he was not the vice-captain, he opened the tour against Cordoba as captain. He also led the team to victory against Tucuman and ended the tour as the top try-scorer with five touchdowns.

At provincial level, his individual performances were enough to earn him further honours such as a place among the Western Province Sportsman-of-the-Year and South African Player-of-the-Year nominees. He was third in a French newspaper's Rugby Player-of-the-Year competition. He was also the only South African player to be chosen in the French newspaper *Midi Olympique's* World Rugby XV, and was listed as the season's third best player in the world. Off the field, he was selected as a trustee for the new Trust Fund for Springboks; established to channel some financial benefits for national players through special events and appearances.

As South Africa prepared for its first non-racial democratic elections in April 1994, rugby commentators severely criticised plans to hold trials for the selection of a national team. Most were in favour of continuous assessment, fitness evaluations and training camps for the selected squad. Committed to the task of representing his country at the highest level, Strauss played in the national Sevens tournament which was used as the basis for the selection of the Springbok side to play in the Hong Kong Sevens. Awarded the provincial captaincy for the third successive year, he also led Western Province in the M-Net Ford Night Series Challenge Cup, Lion and Currie Cups. Yet again, the provincial campaign was a frustration for Strauss. Also, he suffered an early season neck injury which saw him miss the first national training camp. When he returned to action in May, he was competing with Francois Pienaar for the Springboks captaincy.

Included in the national team against England, Strauss gave a below par performance, and showed a lack of match fitness. This led him to be omitted for second test. He was, however, included in the touring party to New Zealand. He captained the Springboks for the first test against New Zealand, which the Boks lost 22–14. With Pienaar back as the captain for the second test, Strauss played a solid, if unspectacular match. Much to everyone's surprise, he was dropped to the bench for third test. He fought back to win inclusion in the test squad under new coach Kitch Christie for the series against the Argentineans. He was also included in the team to tour Britain at the end of the season. He was deservedly included in the provisional Springbok group for 1995 World Cup. At provincial level, he led

Western Province to qualification for inclusion in the Super Ten series against the best local, New Zealand and Australian teams.

Entering his 10th season of senior rugby at the age of 30, Strauss was at the pinnacle of his rugby career. With Super Ten rugby and the inaugural Rugby World Cup looming, everything seemed to be ready for one of Western Province's most distinguished players to crown a noteworthy career with the ultimate honour of being crowned Southern Hemisphere and World Champions. Then fate intervened.

First, Strauss was omitted from the Springbok team for the match against Western Samoa followed by his axing from the World Cup squad in May, apparently for the sake of the team and to protect Francois Pienaar, the captain and his foremost opponent. As compensation, he was included in the South African President's XV. When Strauss was omitted from the Springbok side to England and Italy, the writing was on the wall. Against the background of a year of great disappointment, Strauss began to seriously consider various offers from rugby league clubs, including Wigan. This coincided with a threat from SARFU to ban deserters to the 13-man code for a period of three years.

Accepting his fate, and disappointed at being excluded from the opportunity to represent his country in the William Webb Ellis Tournament on home soil, Strauss after 15 tests, joined Cronulla Sharks in Australia for whom he went on to play 14 games, scoring one try, in the 1996 and 1997 Australian rugby league seasons.

After his stint in rugby league, Strauss returned to rugby union and represented New South Wales in Super 12 rugby. By 1999 he qualified through residence to play for Australia and was chosen for the Wallabies. Strauss made his debut for his adopted country against Ireland and went on to play 11 tests for Australia. When Australia played South Africa in August, Strauss became the first player to represent both countries in international rugby. After rugby, as a trained lawyer he joined and at the time of writing continues to work for sports marketing firm Megapro in Cape Town as an executive manager and enjoys the thrills of competitive sport through participation in events such as the Cape Epic Mountain Bike Race.

21. 2000 to 2014: Precious few

The period since the start of the new Millennium has seen a decline in the number of professional South African rugby league players. As professionalism and new structures in the now more commercial sport of rugby union developed, there was even less incentive for players to move from Union to League. If anything, the reverse has been true, with rugby league struggling to hold onto its biggest stars.

For South Africa, the decade opened with an appearance in the 2000 Rugby League World Cup, although disappointingly, all three games were lost. A 66–18 defeat to Tonga was followed by a 16–0 loss to Papua New Guinea, and a 56–6 defeat to France. Jamie Bloem skippered the side, but was sent off against France after 30 minutes. Apart from Bloem, Mark Johnson, Sean Skelton and Canberra's Sean Rutgerson, the rest of the players were based in South Africa.

The full squad was: Leon Barnard (Centurion Lions), Brian Best (Centurion Lions), Jamie Bloem (Halifax Blue Sox), Jaco Booysen (Centurion Lions), Conrad Breytenbach (Pretoria Bulls), Francois Cloete (Pretoria Bulls), Archer Dames (Pretoira Bulls), Quinton de Villiers (Pretoria Bulls), Hercules Erasmus (Centurion Lions), Chris Hurter (Centurion Lions), Justin Jennings (Pretoria Bulls), Mark Johnson (Salford City Reds), Richard Louw (Kempton), Hendrik Mulder (Centurion Lions), Corne Nel (Pretoria Bulls), Ian Noble (Northwest Leopards RU), Tim O'Shea (Johannesburg), Eugene Powell (Johannesburg Scorpions), Sean Rutgerson (Canberra Raiders), Sean Skelton (Marist – Australia), Pierre van Wyk (Centurion Lions), Jaco Webb (Blue Bulls RU).

Sean Rutgerson was an experienced forward who played professional rugby league both in Australia and Great Britain.

Sean Rutgerson

Sean Rutgerson was born on 9 February 1978. After 12 matches for the North Sydney Bears in 1988 and 1999, he joined the Canberra Raiders in 2000. In a four year spell there, he played 56 matches, scoring one try.

Salford rugby league historian Graham Morris reflects on the Salford City Reds career of Sean Rutgerson: "Sean joined the Salford City Reds on a three-year contract commencing from the 2004 season. He was one of a host of new signings by the club in the wake of its return to Super League, having won promotion through winning the previous year's National League Grand Final. The prop forward was one of three southern hemisphere recruits, the former Canberra Raider was joined at The Willows by Manly second row Mark Shipway and former West Tigers full-back Joel Caine who arrived via a brief spell with London Broncos the previous term.

Although Caine was a more than useful acquisition, having set point scoring records at Wests, it was the two forwards – Rutgerson in particular – that quickly established themselves as fans' favourites due to their terrific work-rate and willingness to defend.

A 10-day training camp at Jacksonville in Florida in January was quickly followed by his pre-season home debut in a friendly against Batley Bulldogs on 25 January. A modest 957 crowd was kept waiting whilst the kick-off was delayed 15 minutes, the Batley team coach having taken the wrong exit off the M60 and ended up at the Trafford Centre shopping complex. The unscheduled detour did not deter the National League visitors and they put up a gutsy performance in going down 36–22.

Two further friendly outings followed before Rutgerson saw Super League action in the opening round on 22 February as over 5,000 spectators watched the Reds defeat Widnes Vikings 24–12 at The Willows. Another new experience awaited him one week later when Salford visited London Broncos in the Rugby League Challenge Cup, but his new team suffered an early exit, 24–8.

Salford finished the season in ninth place in the Super League table. Rutgerson scored his first points with a well-taken try in the final fixture at Huddersfield Giants. It was, though, his powerful charges at the defensive line and huge appetite for bringing opponents to a standstill that caught the eye during his first English-based season.

Despite the demands of playing up front, Rutgerson missed only three matches and did likewise in 2005 when he helped the Reds to again finish ninth in Super League. They did, though, fare marginally better in the Challenge Cup; a victory away to Rochdale Hornets being followed-up by another dismissal at the hands of the London Broncos, this time at The Willows. It was against the Broncos, a few weeks later, that Rutgerson registered the first of his two tries of 2005, the other a fortnight later away to Wakefield Trinity Wildcats, although both games ended in an away defeat.

Rutgerson's final season in 2006 was one of Salford's best in its recent history, a fifth placed finish was the highest achieved for 26 years. They also reached the quarter-final stage of the Challenge Cup, losing 44–14 away to eventual runners-up Huddersfield Giants) having eliminated Dewsbury and Wigan on the way, although Rutgerson was unavailable for the former match. This was due to a neck injury sustained on 3 March – the fourth match of the season – after he came off the bench in a 28–10 home victory over Wigan Warriors. The resultant nine-match, two-month absence was his longest spell of inactivity while with the Reds. Following a run-out with Salford's under–21 side in late April he returned to senior action in the 26–12 home win over Wakefield on 5 May.

His inspirational form during 2006 – his death or glory charges generating huge roars of approval from the Popular Stand – was a major factor in Salford qualifying for the club's first Super League play-off series. However, the opening elimination tie away to the Bradford Bulls on 23 September, which resulted in a 52–6 drubbing, was destined to his final appearance for the club. Although the Salford club was believed willing to extend his contract, he elected to return home for family reasons, having created a lot of goodwill and happy memories through his time at The Willows."

In 2009, he became player-coach of the Jacksonville Axemen in the American National Rugby League. It is not known if he is still involved in rugby league.

In 2003, the London Skolars became the first club to make the transition from amateur rugby league to the professional game when they joined National League 2. Based in North

London, some of their recruitment was among the exile communities in London. Three South Africans played for the club in their early seasons in the professional game.

Rubert Jonker was born in January 1979, and played rugby union for the Gauteng Falcons under–21 side. He played his first game of rugby league in 2001 for South Africa against France, and also played against England. He joined the Skolars in 2002, usually playing in the second-row.

He stayed with the club as they joined the professional game, and worked as a teacher near the club's ground. As the team struggled to be competitive, he was one of their more consistent players, and was the team's top try scorer in 2003. This was recognised at the end of the 2004 season when he won the In London award for outstanding achievement in rugby league. He was also chosen for a National League 2 side to play against The New Zealanders at the end of the season. He was also chosen for the National League 2 'Dream Team' in 2004. He missed about half of the 2006 season with a cruciate ligament injury. He only played 3 games in 2007, all off the bench, and then retired due to his knee injury. Overall, he made 64+9 appearances for the Skolars, and scored 23 tries. He then coached the Skolars 'A' team before returning to rugby union as coach of the Haringey Hornets.

In 2004, the Skolars worked with Rugby League South Africa to bring Desi Kadima to the club. The 22 year old had played union for South Africa at schoolboy and under–19 level and had played for the Blue Bulls and North-West Leopards. In rugby league he had played four matches for the full South Africa team, and had played for the Northern Bulls. He scored a try on his debut at Hunslet, but found it difficult to win a regular first team place, and spent some time on loan at National League 3 side St Albans. Overall, he played 7+1 games for the club in 2004, but scored a credible six tries.

Mario du Toit also played for the Skolars from 2003 to 2006, playing a total of 13+7 first team matches, scoring one try. He later coached the 'A' team in partnership with Rubert Jonker. Richard Louw, who had played for South Africa in the 2000 World Cup, and had been playing for St Albans Centurions, joined the Skolars in 2007. Born in June 1979, over two seasons with the club he made 28+18 appearances, scoring three tries, mainly at prop. He then returned to South Africa and joined the Eastern Eagles.

In 2008, Louw was one of the few players with overseas experience in a home-based South Africa squad that toured England, playing and losing four matches. The tour was organised by BARLA, and the South Africans faced Lancashire having arrived in Manchester the day before, and having gone to watch the Grand Final at Old Trafford. They lost 55–12. A couple of days later, the result against Cumbria was more respectable, a 46–36 defeat; but Yorkshire – 66–6 – and then the BARLA Great Britain side – 74–4 – won their matches against the tourists comfortably.

One notable first for the tourists was having a father-son combination in their team. Hennie Rademeyer had played in the 1994 World Sevens, and played in these matches at the age of 47. His son Heinrich also played at half-back in the series, age 23.

South Africa had not played in the qualifying tournament for the 2008 World Cup, but did enter the 2013 tournament. To reduce travelling costs, a three-way tournament was played between South Africa, the USA and Jamaica in October 2011 in New Jersey in the USA. South Africa chose a squad made up of players from their domestic competition, not choosing 11 players who were eligible for the squad and were playing in Europe or the NRL. Despite having considerably a better rugby league pedigree than either the USA or Jamaica, the South Africans were well beaten – 40–4 – by the USA, and then lost 20–6 to Jamaica.

One player who could have played for South Africa, but was not selected, was Christiaan Roets. He has enjoyed a good international career, but for Wales.

Christiaan Roets

Christiaan Roets has played international rugby league regularly since 2009. Despite being born in Pretoria in 1980, his international appearances have been for Wales. He qualifies for the country through residency, and has played rugby league there since 2003. To the end of 2014, he had made 15 senior appearances for Wales, and scored 13 tries, including four in the 2013 Rugby League World Cup. He was also in the Wales team that won the European Cup in 2010. He played all three of Wales's matches, against Scotland, Ireland and France, scoring a try against Ireland. In 2011, he played in all Wales's matches in the Four Nations series, including against New Zealand at Wembley Stadium.

He first played rugby league for Welsh Conference side Swansea Valley Mines in 2003. When the club disbanded in 2006, he joined the Bridgend Blue Bulls, having won a Wales 'A' cap during his time with Swansea. He first played for Wales in 2009, against Serbia, and scored a hat-trick of tries in an 88–8 win. He joined the sport's professional ranks in 2010, when he signed for South Wales Scorpions. Usually playing at centre, he made 40+1 appearances in two seasons, scoring 12 tries. He then switched to North Wales Crusaders, and to the end of 2014 has made 42+4 appearances, with six tries.

He was named in the South Africa squad for the 2013 Rugby League World Cup qualifiers, but the team was chosen from players based in South Africa, and lost to Jamaica and the USA. He has also played rugby union in Wales, for Ystalyfera and Tonmar.

(Photo of Christiaan Roets playing for Wales by Ian Lovell)

A few other South Africans have played in professional rugby league. In 2005, Weldon Saayman played for Workington Town. He had previously played in the Currie Cup and for Bedford in rugby union. In total he made 17 appearances for the Cumbrian side, nine of which were off the bench. He was banned for seven months in 2006 for betting on the outcome of matches. He was injured when he placed the bets, but one involved his own team. He was declared bankrupt in 2007, his last season for the club.

In November 2011, Barrow signed Mike Botes from Furness RUFC. He played in a couple of pre-season friendlies at the start of the 2012 season, but never played in an official match. However, his compatriot Andries Venter, who had played both codes in South Africa, including playing for the national rugby league team did play for Barrow in 2012. He had joined the club from Kendal RUFC, and in 2012 made eight first team appearances, six from the bench.

With it now being so easy to switch codes, some players have become 'rugby' players, changing codes as playing opportunities arise. In Australia, Jarrod Saffy, who was born in Johannesburg in 1984, moved to Australia when he was 15. After playing union, he played league for Wests Tigers in 2006 and 2007, making 8 first grade appearances. He then played for St George Illawarra for three years, making 53 first grade appearances and scored a try. He played in the 2010 Grand Final for the Dragons, becoming the second South African player to do so.

JP du Plessis played rugby league for the Sydney Roosters in 2009 and 2010; Michael Horak played for Perth Reds in their one season in Super League in 1997; Andy Marinos played one first grade game for the Sydney Bulldogs (a brief name change for the Canterbury-Bankstown Bulldogs) before reverting to rugby union and becoming a Welsh international, presumably through residence. And South African Gert Peens, again primarily a rugby union player for Italy, also played for the Italian rugby league team.

At the time of writing, there are very few South African players in top class rugby league. Converts from rugby union are few and far between; and the sport in South Africa, while stronger than it was in the early 2000s, when it almost collapsed, does not have a high profile. It has also not been able to develop a strong base outside the white community.

We plan to examine the full history of South African rugby league in a future book. But it is interesting to speculate about how the sport might have developed had its leadership given full support to Dave Southern's work in developing Mini-League in the townships in the early 1990s. If, instead of trying to find short cuts to lucrative television contacts and links with Super League, the sport had concentrated on working with young players primarily from the African and Coloured racial groups, it could have established a base among those people, and developed the potential for rugby league that Southern showed existed there.

Around 60,000 youngsters played Mini-League. Even accepting that those figures may include players who only had a limited involvement in the sport, if just five per cent of them had stayed with the game as adult players, the sport would have had a base of 3,000 players. It would have been necessary to develop administrative structures to keep these players involved; but surely if that had happened we would not have the sad situation today of South Africa sitting near the bottom of the international table of rugby league nations.

For more than 100 years, South Africans have been involved in rugby league, since Alf Larard, having won Springbok honours and scored their first try, played for Huddersfield; James Megson signed for Leeds and William Mart joined Hull KR in 1910. At certain times, some individual players have made a major contribution to the sport. Tom van Vollenhoven is still involved with St Helens, including being present at the opening of their new stadium, Langtree Park, 44 years after he retired, and presenting the shirts to the players before the 2014 Super League Grand Final. The welcome given to Wilf Rosenberg on his return to Leeds in 2011, to join in the celebrations of their 1961 Championship win also shows the impact that some South African players made. And many other supporters recall the successful players of the 1950s and 1960s. Even some who were not successful, such as Ivor Dorrington or Tommy Gentles, were still fondly remembered as people if not as great rugby league players. In the modern era, London rugby league fans still talk about Mark Johnson and their 1994 team, while Halifax fans recognise Jamie Bloem as someone who always gave 100 per cent to his team's cause.

But not every player was a success. Before 1995, a rugby union player could not give professional rugby league a go and if it didn't work out return to union. Players such as Fred Oliver and Tommy Gentles, who both joined Wigan, one in the 1920s and one in the 1950s, never made it in rugby league and their rugby careers were over. The same applied to the Deysel brothers at Leeds in 1958. Others could play the game, but failed to settle in the north of England which was so very different in many ways to South Africa.

Now, it seems to be unlikely that in the future rugby union players will move to rugby league as they did in the 1920s, 1950s and 1960s. That is why it is so important for rugby league to put down genuine roots in South Africa, and develop players whose primary allegiance is to that code, and are not rugby union players playing to keep fit in their off-season. Internationally, the RLIF should support moves to do that; there is huge potential for the sport in South Africa to build its own identity and become an international force in rugby league.

Notes

[1] AC Parker, *The Springboks 1891-1970* p.22

[2] Op cit p.26

[3] Op cit p. 22 Markotter was a famous South African rugby union coach

[4] Paul Dobson, *Rugby in South Africa* p.52

[5] *Huddersfield Daily Examiner* 27 January 1903

[6] The original club, not the Castleford club that plays in Super League today

[7] The Great Trek was a mass emigration from the British controlled Cape Colony in the 1830s and 1840s by Boers; which resulted in the creation of new republics, including the Orange Free State and the Transvaal. It is a seminal event in Afrikaner history.

[8] Sullivan's recollections and other memories of van Rooyen from *The Illustrated History of Wigan RLFC* by Jack Winstanley p.32

[9] Wigan RLFC 100 Greats p.124

[10] From Twelve locals and a South African p.4

[11] Ibid p.7-8

[12] The Rugby League Challenge Cup – An Illustrated History p.66

[13] Twelve locals and a South African p 12

[14] Quoted in Wigan RLFC 100 Greats by Graham Morris p.123

[15] The Illustrated History of Wigan RLFC by jack Winstanley p. 31

[16] The Challenge Cup – An illustrated history by Les Hoole

[17] The Illustrated History of Wigan RLFC by Jack Winstanley p.32

[18] *An Illustrated History of Wigan RLFC*, p.33

[19] *Paarl Post*, 20 September 1924; p.5

[20] Rugby league players, both professional and amateur were usually allowed to play rugby union while on National Service. Some represented the service they were members of, such as Alex Murphy playing for the RAF, while others were only allowed to play at regimental level. Rugby league did not become a recognised sport in the Armed Forces until 1994.

[21] Bill Fallowfield as quoted in *Rand Daily Mail*, "Shock...rugby amateurs want pro. game", 16 July 1957

[22] *Rand Daily Mail*, "Cape centre for rugby league", 24 January 1957

[23] *Grand Final*, Graham Morris, Vertical Editions, p. 112

[24] *Cape Argus*, "Banished to Common Ground to learn their new game", 12 November 1958

[25] *Cape Argus*, "Consternation over Colin- Rugby Union to 'look into it', 17 October 1961

[26] *Cape Argus*, "Moves to launch rugby league in City: J. Weill here', 23 January 1962

[27] *Cape Argus*, "Moves to launch rugby league in City: J. Weill here', 23 January 1962

[28] *Cape Argus*, "Sponsors of rugby league in S.A. need big names", 19 August 1961

[29] *Cape Argus*, "Rugby league: No game in Bellville", 18 June 1957

[30] *Cape Argus*, "Drastic action is not likely in 'Colin Affair'; 8 November 1961

[31] *Cape Argus*, "Drastic action is not likely in 'Colin Affair'", 8 November 1961

[32] *Sunday Times*, "Pro rugby makes its debut", 18 February 1962

[33] *Cape Argus*, "Lacey group signs four players for W.P. pro rugby", 10 March 1962

[34] *Sunday Times*, "Two groups will run 13-a-side code: No pro rugby merger", 29 April 1962

[35] Match day Programme: The Rugby League of South Africa/Suid Africa, 10 August 1962

[36] Match day Programme: The Rugby League of South Africa/Suid Africa, 21 September 1962

[37] Interview in *Rugby League Journal* No.3 Summer 2003.

[38] *The mighty Bears* p.201

[39] *The Encyclopaedia of Rugby League players* p.209

[40] P 149 – *Trinity – A history of the Wakefield Rugby League Football Club 1872 – 2013*, Mike Rylance, League Publications, 2013

[41] Danie Hartman Craven, 1964. *Rugby in South Africa – 1889 to 1964*. Cape Town, Johnston and Neville; p. 216

[42] The Jewish faith has various strands - from 'Liberal' to 'Orthodox; Orthodox would be seen as a 'stricter' interpretation of the biblical laws.

[43] *Nothing but the Best – Outstanding Leeds Rugby Players 1928-1988*.

[44] Leeds RLFC 100 Greats by Phil Caplan and Peter Smith, Tempus 2001

[45] A Minyan is the word for the 'quorum' of 10 men which is necessary for certain religious functions in Orthodox Judaism.

[46] *Trinity's Wembley Triumphs*, p.58

[47] *The Mighty Bears* p.214

[48] Ibid p.219

[49] Ibid p. 220

[50] Some sources including Allie (2000) based on interviews with Goolam Abed, spells his surname as Neumann and in one instance, namely the paper of Kivedo presented at the Klein Karoo National Arts Festivals, he is also referred to as Peter Newman.

[51] SARU,(2003), *112 Years of Springbok Rugby*; p. 98

[52] *Rochdale Observer*, (2003), "Going back to his roots",
<http://www.rochdaleobserver.co.uk/sport/s/33/33530_going_back_to_his_roots.html>; (27/6/2007)

[53] M. Allie, (2000), *More than a Game*; p. 49

[54] SARU,(2003), *112 Years of Springbok Rugby*; p. 98

[55] Personal Communication, John Downes (Heritage Development Officer: Bradford Bulls Foundation) – Hendrik Snyders; 7/8/2007

[56] Personal Communication, Laurie Grailey (Batley Bull Dogs Club Historian) – Hendrik Snyders; 3/8/2007

[57] D. Appleton, (2003), "*Goolam's long wait finally over*",
<http://www.rochdaleobserver.co.uk/news/s/332/332624_goolams_long_wait_finally_over.html>; (19/4/2008)

[58] D. Appleton, (2001), "*Cricketer who broke down the racial barriers*",
<http://www.rochdaleobserver.co.uk/news/s/29/29664_cricketer_who_broke_down_the_barriers.htm>; (26/7/2007)

[59] Personal Communication, Amy Herisson, Marketing and Membership Coordinator, Sydney Roosters – N. Goos; 27/3/2008

[60] Eastern Suburbs is one of Australia's foundation clubs being part of the small group of clubs that established the code down under. Becoming their player coach within a short time after his conversion to league, therefore speaks volumes of his talent and ability.

[61] Personal Communication, N. Goos – H. Snyders, 28/3/2008; see also V. Qunta, (2007), "*Unsung Heroes of SA Sport*; in *Your Sport*, 2nd Quarter; p. 10.

[62] J. Matyu, (2004), " *'60's rugby star Pikoli dies alone in England*",
<http://www.theherald.co.za/herald/2004/04/16/news/n23_16042004.htm>;(19/04/2008)

[63] p.30 *50 years of bloody Sundays*, Doncaster RLFC 1951 to 2001

[64] p.41 *Leigh RLFC – An Illustrated History*

[65] When the Northern Rugby League split into two Divisions in the 1960s, the Western and Eastern Championships were played to provide extra fixtures, in particular local derbies which could provide a good gate for some of the smaller clubs.

[66] Quoted by Graham Morris in *Wigan RLFC 100 Greats*, p.75

[67] *The Illustrated History of Wigan RLFC*, p.120

[68] Les Hoole, *The Rugby League Challenge Cup – An Illustrated History*, p.134

[69] *Wigan RLFC 1895 to 1986* by Ian Morrison, p.90

[70] *They could catch pigeons* by Ray Hewson p.32

[71] *100 years of rugby* p.121

[72] Danie Craven, *Met die Maties op die rugby veld*; p. 177

[73] Craven; p. 176

[74] A.C. Parker, (1983),*W.P. Rugby Centenary, 1883 - 1983*, Cape Town, WPRFU; p. 70

[75] Danie Craven & Piet Jordaan,1955, *Met die Maties op die rugbyveld*, Cape Town: Nasionale Boekhandel

[76] MCM Van Zyl, 1988, *Noord Transvaal Rugby 50*; Pretoria, NTRVU; p. 193

[77] AC Parker, (1970), *The Springboks, 1891-1970*; London & Johannesburg: Cassell; p. 161

[78] A.C. Parker, (1983),*W.P. Rugby Centenary, 1883 - 1983*, p. 85

[79] Quoted in *The Kiwis – 100 Years of International Rugby League* by John Coffey and Bernie Wood

[80] Craven, *Springbok Annals*; p. 452

[81] *The Star* 24 August 1962

[82] Reg Sweet,1990, *Natal 100: Centenary of the Natal Rugby Union*, Durban: NTRFU; p. 173

[83] Reg Sweet,1990, *Natal 100: Centenary of the Natal Rugby Union*, Durban: NTRFU; p. 183

[84] Frikkie Van Rensburg & Herman Le Roux, 1995, *Vrystaat!: 100 Jaar van Hardloop rugby*, Bloemfontein: OFRFU

[85] *The Star* 22 August 1962

[86] *The Star* 20 August 1962

[87] *The Star* 14 August 1962

[88] *Neil Fox – Rugby League's greatest points scorer* by Robert Gate p.111

[89] ibid

[90] *The Star* 22 August 1962

[91] *The Star* 24 August 1962
[92] The Star 27 August 1962
[93] *The Star* 1 September 1962
[94] ibid.
[95] ibid
[96] *The Star* 3 September 1962
[97] H. Snyders, (2008), *Between the Springbok and Ikhamanga*
[98] A. Williams – Personal Communication
[99] P. Dobson, (1989), *Rugby in South Africa*
[100] P. Dobson, (1989), *Rugby in South Africa*
[101] F. Kemp,(1973), "*Green Vigo, die Superster*"/ ("Green Vigo, the Superstar") in *Rapport Ekstra*
[102] George Gerber, (1973), "*Dis onwaar dat ons Vigo wou keer*" – sê mnr. Loriston"- *Rapport Ekstra*
[103] Rapport Ekstra (1974) "*Green Vigo wil weer vir S.A. speel*", in *Rapport Ekstra*, 20 Januarie
[104] Arnold Whycliff,(1973), "*Give Vigo a Chance*"- The Wigan Observer, Friday, August 17
[105] J. Humphreys (1973), "*Green for go as Vigo ends on-off saga!*", in *Daily Mirror*, July 24; p. 23
[106] F. Kemp,(1973), "*Green Vigo, Die Superster*"/ (Green Vigo , the Super Star") in *Rapport Ekstra*
[107] Colin Clarke in T. Collins & P. Melling (eds.), (2004*), The Glory of their Times*, Vertical Editions
[108] "*The Wigan Wizard*"
[109] "*Saldanha Tiger Roars*"
[110] "*Saldanha Tiger Roars*"
[111] "*The Wigan Wizard*"
[112] George & Marie Gerber, (1978),"*Green Vigo Is Nog Blitsig*" in *Die Burger Ekstra*
[113] "*Good marksman needed by Wigan*",
[114] *Tries and Prayers* p.136
[115] Winstanley p.141
[116] Ibid p.141
[117] *Glory of their Times* p. 111
[118] Green Vigo, Personal Communication, 28 June 2008
[119] Jonty Winch, 1979, *Rhodesia Rugby: A history of the national side, 1898 - 1979*, Salisbury: Zimbabwe Rhodesia Rugby Union; p. 119
[120] SA Rugby Writers Society, 1983, *Toyota Jaarboek 1983 Annual*, Verwoerdburg, SARWS
[121] South African Rugby Football Union, 2003, *112 Years of Springbok Rugby: Tests and heroes*: Cape Town: Highbury Monarch; p. 215
[122] *The Canberra Times*, "South Africa divided on tour", 12 January 1980; p. 33
[123] *The Canberra Times*,, "Zimbabwe rugby decision", 19 May 1980; p. 12
[124] *Gloucestershire Rugby Football Union*, 1980, Match Programme
[125] Edward Griffiths,1997, *Kitch - triumph of a decent man*, Johannesburg: CAB; p. 21
[126] Steve Bale, "Rugby Union: Mordt banned from tour: IRB refuses to accept fitness instructor, 16 September

Appendix 1: Honours: South Africans in British Challenge Cup and Championship Finals

Challenge Cup

Season	Club	Players
1923–24	Wigan	A.J. van Heerden
		G. van Rooyen
1929–30	Widnes	G. van Rooyen
1948–49	Halifax	J.S. Pansegrouw
1958–59	Wigan	W.F. Griffiths
1959–60	Wakefield Trinity	A. Skene
1960–61	St Helens	T. van Vollenhoven
	Wigan	W. F. Griffiths
1961–62	Wakefield Trinity	A. Skene
1962–63	Wakefield Trinity	C.M. Greenwood
		G. Coetzer
1964–65	Wigan	T. Lake
1965–66	St Helens	T. van Vollenhoven
		L. Killeen
		(Lance Todd Trophy winner)
	Wigan	T. Lake
1967–68	Wakefield Trinity	G. Coetzer

Championship Final

Season	Club	Players
1923–24	Batley	H.F. Murray
	Wigan	A.J. van Heerden
		G. van Rooyen
1925–26	Wigan	A.J. van Heerden
		G. van Rooyen
		D. Booysen
1949–50	Huddersfield	K. Morrison
1958–59	St Helens	T. van Vollenhoven
		J. Prinsloo
	Hunslet	R. Colin
1959–60	Wigan	W.F. Griffiths
	Wakefield Trinity	A. Skene
1960–61	Leeds	W. Rosenberg
1961–62	Wakefield Trinity	A. Skene
1964–65	St Helens	T. van Vollenhoven
		L. Killeen
1966–67	Wakefield Trinity	G. Coetzer
	St Helens	T. van Vollenhoven
		L. Killeen
1967–68	Wakefield Trinity	G. Coetzer

Appendix 2: South African international and overseas professional players

(This list does not include players who only played in South Africa. The international appearances may not be complete, and only cover to the qualifying matches for the 2013 RL World Cup.)

First name	Surname	Period	British and Australian clubs	International & representative
Goolam	Abed Hussain	1961-1967	Leeds, Bradford N Batley	
Dawie	Ackerman	1962-63		1962 RLSA versus Great Britain 1963 tour capt
Jaco	Alberts	1995	S Queensland Crushers	1995 WC 2a
Barend	Alkema	1995		1995 v BARLA 1995 WC 3a
Fred	*Anderson*	*1952-1963*	*Australia NRL S. Sydney*	*1963 tour guest*
Johnny	Assor	1992		1992 World 7s
Heinrick	Assor	1993		1993 v N Sydney
Pierre	Assor	1995		1995 v BARLA
Andrew	Ballot	1995	Bay of Plenty (NZ)	1995 WC 3a
David	Barends	1970-1985	Wakefield, York Bradford N, Featherstone R, Batley	Great Britain Other Nationalities
Leon	Barnard	2000		2000 WC 3a 1t 4pt
Harry	Bennett			1962 RLSA versus Great Britain 1963 tour
Brian	Best	2000		2000 WC 3a 1t 4pt
Lesley	Best	1995		1995 v BARLA
Jamie	Bloem	1992-2005	Castleford, Oldham, Doncaster, Widnes Halifax, Huddersfield	2000 WC 3a 3g 6pt SA international 1990s Scotland international
Ken	Boonzaier	1961-62	Leigh	1962 RLSA versus Great Britain
David	Booysen	1924-28	Wigan	
Jaco	Booysens	1995	Dewsbury	1995 WC capt 3a 2000 WC 3a 1995 World 7s SA international 1990s
Willem	Boshoff	1995		1995 WC 3a
Piet (Pieter Hendrik)	Botha	1961-62	Leigh	
Riaan	Botha	2008		2008 tour
Riaan	Botha	2008		2008 tour
Conrad	Breytenbach	2000		2000 WC 1a 1t 4pt
Matt	Brodski	1995		1995 v BARLA
Ted	Brophy	1958-1962	St Helens Blackpool B, Leigh	RLXIII
Athol	Brown	1958-1962	Huddersfield	

Mike	Brown	1962-1967	Halifax, Bradford N Also played in SA	
Carl	Burger	1924-25	Wigan	
Morne	Claassen	2008		2008 tour
Ian W.	Clark	1948 -1955	Huddersfield	
Francois	Cloete	1995 - 2000		1995 WC 2+1a 2000 WC 0+2
Gert (Oupa)	Coetzer	1963-1968	Wakefield Also played in SA	1963 tour
Ronnie	Colin	1957-1959	Hunslet	
Guy	Coombe	1995-96	Dewsbury	1995 WC 3a
K	Coopman	1992		1992 v CIS
Archer	Dames	2000		2000 WC 3a
Noor 'Gubby'	Daniels	1961	Barrow (not first team)	
Wouter	De Jager	2008		2008 tour
Johannes	De Klerk	1961-62	Huddersfield	
Quinton	de Villiers	2000		2000 WC 3a
Jan	de Wall			1963 tour
Gerhardt	de Wet			2013 World Cup qualifiers
Ernie	Deysel	1958-59	Leeds	
Ossie	Deysel	1958-59	Leeds	
Enslin	Dlambulo	1962-67	Bradford N, Keighley	
Ivor	Dorrington	1958-1960	Wakefield T	
Hans	du Plessis			2013 World Cup qualifiers
JP	du Plessis	2009-2010	Sydney Roosters	
Mario	du Toit	2003-2006	London Skolars	SA international
Nick	du Toit	1984-1991	Wigan, Barrow, Chorley, Wakefield T	
Toby	Du Toit	1971–72	Warrington	
Henry	du Toit			2013 World Cup qualifiers
G	Duvenhagge	1992		1992 v CIS
Riaan	Englebrecht			2008 tour 2013 World Cup qualifiers
Hercules	Erasmus	2000		2000 WC 3a
Bart	Erasmus			1963 tour
Lawrence	Evans	1993		1993 v N Sydney
Japie (JJ)	Ferreira	1961-1963	Workington T	
Gene	Forster	1950s	Bradford N (not first team)	
Tony	Foster	1958-59	Whitehaven	
Tim	Fourie	1995-96	Dewsbury	1995 v BARLA 1995 WC 3a
Dirkie	Fourie	2008		2008 tour
Jaco	Fourie	2008		2008 tour
Johan	Fritz			2008 tour 2013 World Cup qualifiers. 1 try
Johnny	Gaydon	1961-1972	St Helens, Widnes	1963 tour
Thomas Alexander	Gentles	1958-1960	Wigan Leeds (not first team)	
Mannetjies (Frederick	Gericke	1963		1962 RLSA versus Great Britain

Wilhelm)				1963 tour
Hugh	Gillespie	1959-60	York	
Colin Marius	Greenwood	1961-1970	Wakefield T, North Sydney, Canterbury	1963 tour
Francois	Greyvensteyn			2008 tour 2013 World Cup qualifiers
Fred (Poensie)	Griffiths	1957-1966	Wigan, N. Sydney, Nowra	1963 tour Australia: Other Nationalities vs NSW Colts
Pierre	Grobbelaar	1994-95	Doncaster 94-95	1995 WC dnp
Jacques	Grobler	2008		2008 tour
Frans	Groenwald	2008		2008 tour
Rudy	Hasse	1962-1964	Bradford N, Wakefield T	
R	Hector	1992		1992 v CIS
Joe	Herman	1995		1995 v BARLA
Jaco	Holtzhauzen	1995		1995 v BARLA
Michael	Horak	1997	Australia (Not NRL first team)	
Koot	Human	1995	S Queensland Crushers (not first team)	1995 WC 1+1a
Chris	Hurter	2000		2000 WC 1+1a
Victor (Ginger)	Jacobs	1960s SA NRL		1963 tour
Conrad	Jacobs	2008		2008 tour
Justin	Jennings	1995-2000	S Queensland Crushers (not first team)	1995 WC 0+1a 2000 WC 1+2a 1996 Student WC
Mark	Johnson	1992-2000	London Crusaders, Workington, Hull, Salford	1995 WC 3a 2000 WC 3a 1992 vs CIS. World 7s
Rubert	Jonker	2001-2007	London Skolars	SA International
P	Joordan	1992		1992 vs CIS
Christo	Joubert			2013 World Cup qualifiers
Desi	Kadima	2004	London Skolars	
Frans	Kellerman	2008		2008 tour
Henry	Kemp	1993		1993 v N Sydney
Len	Killeen	1962-1972	St Helens, Balmain, Penrith	
Dave	Knopf	1950,1954-1956	Wigan (not first team), Halifax, Bradford N	
Deon	Kraemer			2013 WC qualifiers
Eric	Kuppen	1994		1994
Trevor	Lake	1962-1968	Wigan, St George	
Chris	Landsberg	1961-62	Leigh Also played in SA	RL XIII
Percy (Stoffel)	Landsberg	1959-60	St Helens	
Andre	Loader	2008		2008 tour
Arthur (Alf)	Larard	1901-1905	Huddersfield	
Isak	Laubscher	2008		2008 tour
Andre	Loader			2013 World Cup qualifiers. Captain

Nardie	Lombart	1995		SA International
Jan	Lotriet	1958-1960	Wakefield 25 Oct 58	
Hans	Lourens	1962 SA NRL		
Richard	Louw	2000, 2006-2008	St Albans Centurions London Skolars	2008 tour 2000 WC 0+1 Student WC
Robert James	Louw	1985-1987	Wigan	
Christo	Louw			2013 World Cup qualifiers
Elmar	Lubbe	1995		1995 WC 0+1a
Ernest	Ludick	1995		1995 WC 0+2a
Hercus	Mahoney	1995		1995 v BARLA
Andy	Marinos	2000s	Sydney Roosters	
William	Mart	1910	Hull KR	
Warren	McCann	1995		1995 WC dnp
C	McHugh	1992		1992 v CIS
Mervyn (Pin)	McMillan	1957	Hull FC	
James	Megson	1910	Leeds	
Stevie	Meyer			2013World Cup qualifiers
Tom (Thomas)	Moodie	1960-61	Leigh (not first team)	
Ray (Raymond Henry)	Mordt	1985-1987	Wigan	
Ken	Morrison	1948-1955	Huddersfield	
Sivive	Mpondo			2013 World Cup qualifiers
John	Mudgeway	1995		1995 WC 1a
Drikkie	Mulder	2000		2000 WC 0+3
H	Mulder	1992		1992 v CIS
Hendrik	Muller	1993		1993 v N Sydney
Hugh Frederick	Murray	1922-1926	Batley	
Jacob	Ndlovu	2000		2000 WC
Corne	Nel	2000		2000 WC 0+2 1996 Student WC
Dolf	Nel	2008		2008 tour
JP	Nel			2013 World Cup qualifiers
Polla	Nell	1993		1993 v N Sydney
Louis	Neumann	1961-1972	Leeds, Easts, Orange RLFC	
Charlie (Charles Frederick)	Nimb	1962-1964	Hull Also played in SA	1962 RLSA versus Great Britain
Ian	Noble	2000		2000 WC 2a
Tim	O'Shea	2000		2000 WC 1a Student international
Bunny	Oberholzer			1963 tour
Ontie	Odendaal			1963 tour
Fred (WF) Bill	Oliver	1926-1929	Wigan	
Andre	Olwagen			2008 tour 2013 WC qualifiers
Ockert (Ockie)	Oosthuizen	1963		1963 tour
Jack (Jan)	Pansegrouw	1947-1949	Leeds, Halifax	
Roelef	Peacock	1962-63		1963 tour
Hendrik Jacobus Martin	Pelser	1962-63		1962 RLSA versus Great Britan

				1963 tour
Ken	Pelser			1963 tour
Vernon	Petersen	1962-63	Bradford N	
Michael	Peterson	1992		1992 v CIS
Johan	Pieterse			1963 tour
Duncan	Pikoli	1961-1964	Barrow, Liverpool City	
Eugene	Powell	1995-2000		1995 v BARLA 1995 WC 0+2a 2000 WC 3a
Pietrus Johannes (Piet)	Pretorius	1961-1963	Workington T	
Jaco	Pretorious	2008		2008 tour
Rynard	Pretorious	2008		2008 tour
Jacobus Casparus (Jan)	Prinsloo	1958-1962	St Helens, Wakefield T	
Nico	Prinsloo	2008		2008 tour
Rudi	Prinsloo			2013 World Cup qualifiers. 1 try
Heinrich	Rademeyer	2008		2008 tour
Hennie	Rademeyer	2008		1994 World 7s 1995 v BARLA 2008 tour
Ignatius Johannes (Natie)	Rens			1963 tour
Garth	Robertson	1967-68	St Helens	
Christiaan	Roets	2006 to date	S Wales, N. Wales	Wales international
Deon	Roodt	1993		1993 v N Sydney
Glen	Roos	1993		1993 v N Sydney
Wilf	Rosenberg	1959	Leeds, Hull	
Sean	Rutgerson	1998-2006	Salford, North Sydney, Canberra	2000 WC 3a
Mattheus Christian Weldon	Saayman	2005- 2007	Workington T	
John	Sabio	1993		1993 v N Sydney
Jarrod	Saffy	2006-2008	Wests, St George Illawarra	
Gerard	Scholtz	1992		1992 v CIS
Ismail (Salie)	Schroeder	1961	Doncaster	
Nico	Serfontein	1990s	Hemel Hempstead	1995 WC 0+1a
Sean	Skelton	1997-	Marists (N Qld)	2000 WC 1a
Alan Leslie	Skene	1958-1961	Wakefield T, Souths	1963 tour
Gerrie	Slabber			2013 World Cup qualifiers
Marcelle	Slabbert			2013 World Cup qualifiers
Gert	Smit			1962 RLSA versus Great Britain 1963 tour
C	Smythe	1920s	Wigan (not first team)	
Jonathan	Soares			2008 tour 2013World Cup qualifiers
Jacob	Steemag	1992-93		1992 v CIS 1993 v N Sydney
Andre	Stoop	1991-1997	Wigan, London Crusaders, Keighley	
Tiaan	Strauss	1996-1997	Cronulla	

Reoalle	Strijdom	2008		2008 tour
Eddie	Strydom	1995		1995 v BARLA
Christoff	Swanepoel			2013 WC qualifiers
P	Tate	1992		1992 v CIS
Christo	Theunisen	1993		1993 v N Sydney
E	Tran	1992		1992 v CIS
Nick	Turnbull	2003-2005	Sheffield Eagles	
Burger	van der Merve	1993		1993 v N Sydney
Faffa	van der Merwe	1995		1995 v BARLA
Charl	van der Merwe	2008		2008 tour
Pieter	Van der Nest			2013 World Cup qualifiers. 1 goal
Constant	van der Spuy	1924-25	Wigan	
Danie	van der Walt	1960s SA NRL		
Kobus	van Deventer	1995-96	Dewsbury	1995 WC 3a
T	van Dyke	1992		1992 v CIS (capt)
Attie (Adrian Jacobus)	van Heerden	1923-1928	Wigan, Leigh	Other Nationalities
Nicholas	van Heerden	1924-25	Wigan, York	
Andrew	van Loggenberg	2008		2008 tour
Errol	van Niekerk	1969	St Helens	
Jaco	van Nierkerk	1995		1995 v BARLA 1995 WC 0+2
George (Gert Wilhelm – 'Tank')	van Rooyen	1922-1933	Hull KR, Wigan Widnes	
Koos	van Staden	1993		1993 v N Sydney
Tom (Karel Thomas)	van Vollenhoven	1957-1968	St Helens	
Pierre	van Wyk	1995-96	Dewsbury	1995 v BARLA 1995 WC 3a 4g 8pt 2000 WC 2a
Andre	van Wyk	1995		1995 v BARLA
Hennie (Hendrik Jacobus)	van Zyl	1960s		1962 RLSA vs Great Britain
Gerhardhus (Gerry)	van Zyl			1963 tour
Andries	Venter	2011	Barrow	
Johannes	Venter	1997-2000	Canterbury Bulldogs	2000 WC
Willem	Vermaas			1963 tour
Jan	Verwey	1960s SA NRL		1963 tour
Green	Vigo	1973-1984	Wigan, Swinton, Oldham	Other Nationalities
Jaco	Visser	1995		1995 WC 1a
Rian	Voster	1993		1993 v N Sydney
Gideon	Watts	1995		1995 WC 3a 1t 4pt
Jaco	Webb	1995-2000		1995 v BARLA 2000 WC 0+1a
Henry	Wiggins	2008		2008 tour
Gerald	Williams	1995		1995 WC 3a
Mark	Williard	1992		1992 v CIS
Graham	*Wilson*			*1963 tour guest in NZ,*
John Haxton	Winton	1962-1966	Wigan, Oldham	

Appendix 3: National Rugby League and Rugby League South Africa players

(NB These lists are probably not complete.)

National RL players			
Name	**Surname**	**RU clubs, province**	**RL clubs**
J	Barnard		Bloemfontein Aquilas.
K	Bezuidenhout		Johannesburg Celtic
Pieter Hendrik	Botha		Leigh, Boksburg Vikings
Ronnie	Botha		
Piet	Botha		
F	Botha		Bloemfontein Aquilas.
Mike	Brown		Johannesburg Celtic, Halifax
Robbie	Brunton		Johannesburg Celtic
Oupa	Coetzer		Bloemfontein Aquilas, Wakefield T
Ronnie	Colin		Hunslet
Martin (M.C.)	De Beer	Northern Transvaal	Johannesburg Celtic
Ivan	De Jongh		Johannesburg Celtic
Ivan	De Jongh		
Chris	De Nysschen	Natal University RFC , Wasp-Wanderers, Natal, Springbok (no tests)	Johannesburg Celtic Bloemfontein Aquilas.
Peter	Draper	Simmer & Jack	
D.J.	Engelbrecht		
E.J.	Frick		
Piet	Geldenhuys		
A.D.	Geldenhuys		
P	Gerber		Johannesburg Celtic
Chris	Geyer		
Hugh	Gillespie	Boland	York
Bennie	Haycock		
Hannes	Heiberg		
Jannes	Helberg		Bloemfontein Aquilas.
P	Koburg		Bloemfontein Aquilas.
Piet	Kruger (Scrum half)		Johannesburg Celtic
Christoffel	Landsberg		Leigh Bloemfontein Aquilas.
Gert	Laurens		
E	Lax		
Sonny (C)	Liebenberg	E Transvaal	Johannesburg Celtic
T	Lienbenberg		Bloemfontein Aquilas.
Hans	Lourens		
Gert	Louw		
Johan	Mitchell	N Transvaal	Pretoria Koedoes
Tom	Moodie		Leigh
C	Otto		
Joe	Peacock		
Ken	Pelser	Johannesburg Municipal	Johannesburg Celtic
Sarel	Pelser	Boksburg	
Rudolph	Pothas		Bloemfontein Aquilas.
H	Raach		Bloemfontein Aquilas.
Bennie	Raath		
R	Richter		Johannesburg Celtic
Alfred	Smith		Johannesburg Celtic
Alfred	Smith		

K	Snyman		Bloemfontein Aquilas
J.	Stone		Bloemfontein Aquilas.
Jack	Stoney		
Theo	Swart		
Theo ('Blackie')	Swart		
Dawid (D J)	Van der Merwe	Harlequins, Silverton, Northern Transvaal	Pretoria Koedoes
Daantjie	Van der Walt (Also RLSA)		
J.L.	Van Niekerk		
Naas	Van Rooyen		
	Van Schaik		
Johan	Van Zyl		
Tony	Van Zylichgem	N Transvaal	Pretoria Koedoes
Gert	Venter		
J	Venter		
Corrie	Vermaar	N Transvaal	Pretoria Koedoes
G	Vester		Johannesburg Celtic
A	Vlok		Bloemfontein Aquilas
Jan	Weideman		
A	Wright		Johannesburg Celtic

Rugby League South Africa (RLSA) Weil Cup Competition			
Name	**Surname**	**RU clubs & province**	**RL clubs**
Dawie (D.S.P.)	Ackerman	Diggers/ Transvaal Springbok	Southern Suburbs
John (J.J.)	Baartman		Southern Suburbs
Harry	Bennett	Eastern Transvaal, Springs	Eastern Transvaal
Christiaan Esias (Chris)	Bezuidenhout	Springbok	Pretoria
Ken	Boonzaier	Eastern Transvaal	Leigh, Vaal
Piet (P.G.)	Booysen		Southern Suburbs
T	Botha		Eastern Transvaal
B	Boyson		Eastern Transvaal
Coetzee	Burger	Pretoria, N Transvaal, E Province	Pretoria
Johnnie	Buys	Transvaal	Southern Suburbs
Pieter	Coetzee	Pirates, Municipals	Southern Suburbs
J	Coetzee		Southern Suburbs
Ronnie	Colin	Gardens	Hunslet, Johannesburg City
Flip	de Lange		Pretoria
B	de Villiers		Johannesburg City
Dirk	de Vos	Simmer & Jack	
Jan	de Waal	Vereniging, ISCOR	Vaal
Andrew	du Plessis		Southern Suburbs, Pretoria
Bart	Erasmus		Southern Suburbs
Gene	Forster	Bradford Northern	Manager / Director
Joe	Foxcroft	Transvaal	Johannesburg City
Schalk	Geel	Transvaal	Southern Suburbs
Mannetjies	Gericke	Diggers, Transvaal, Springbok	Southern Suburbs
	Herholdt		Vaal
Frans	Holtzhausen		Pretoria
Victor (Ginger) (V.H.)	Jacobs	Union / Transvaal	Southern Suburbs

Martheus	Jaonneck		Johannesburg City
Willem	Jonker	Iscor	
P	Jordaan		Johannesburg City
Koos	Krugel	Vereniging	Vaal
Albie	Kruger		Pretoria Koedoes
Ralph	Kruger	Simmer & Jack	Johannesburg City
D	Lingaard		Eastern Transvaal
Lommies (Ryan B)	Lombard	N Transvaal	Pretoria
Giel	Lubbe	Transvaal ISCOR	Vaal
Basil	Lucas	E Transvaal, Unicor, Springs	
D	Luggard		
Dirk	Luus (initially as amateur)		Eastern Transvaal
Mike	Murphy		Eastern Transvaal
Fanie	Naude	Vereniging	Eastern Transvaal
Charlie	Nimb	Western Province, Springbok	Johannesburg City, Hull FC
P	O' Kelly		Vaal
T	O' Kelly		Vaal
Shorty	Oberholtster	Diggers	
Phillip (P.C.)	Oberholzer	Diggers, Pirates, Rand Leases	Southern Suburbs
M C (Ontie)	Odendaal	Oostelikes	Pretoria
P	Oliver		Johannesburg City
Ok	Oosthuizen	Simmer & Jack, Transvaal	Johannesburg City
Tjaart	Oosthuizen	Simmer & Jack	Johannesburg City
Piet	Opperman	Western Areas	
Roelof	Peacock		Pretoria
Martin	Pelser	Rand Leases RFC. Transvaal, Springbok	Johannesburg City
F	Pelser		Johannesburg City
O	Philpott		Johannesburg City
Johan	Pieterse	Transvaal	Johannesburg City
Harry	Potgieter	Vereniging	Vaal, Eastern Transvaal
Henry	Potgiter		Vaal
Jan 'Das'	Prinsloo	Pretoria, Northern Transvaal	Pretoria
Natie (I.J.)	Rens	Transvaal, Springbok	Southern Suburbs (captain)
Boet (J.G.)	Rheeders	Union	Southern Suburbs
W.S. (Roelie)	Roelofse	Diggers	Southern Suburbs
Tommy	Slabbert		Pretoria
Gert	Smit	Boland, N Transvaal, Eastern Transvaal, Springbok	Vaal, East Rand
S	Steenkamp		Eastern Transvaal
Gideon	Stols	Vereniging	Vaal
Denis	Sutherland	Unicor	Eastern Transvaal
A J (Ampie)	Theunissen	Oostelikes	Pretoria
Ben	Usher		Johannesburg City
P	Van der Walt		Eastern Transvaal
Christo	Van Wyk	Diggers	Johannesburg City
Hennie (H.J.)	Van Zyl	Transvaal, Springbok	Southern Suburbs
Witbank	Van Zyl	Diggers	Southern Suburbs
Willem	Vermaas	N Transvaal	Pretoria
Corrie	Vermaak	Pretoria	Pretoria
Jan (J.J.)	Verwey		Southern Suburbs
Hennie	Visser		Eastern Transvaal
Brian	Wise	Diggers	Eastern Transvaal
Mike	Wise		East Rand
Pieter (P.J.)	Woest	Diggers	Southern Suburbs

Sources and bibliography

Sources used for particular players

Jaco Booysen:
Beeld Newspaper (Various issues).
Duane Heath (ed.), *SA Rugby Annual 2014*, Cape Town: SARU

Ted Brophy:
Jonty Winch, 1979, *Rhodesia Rugby: A history of the national side, 1898 - 1979*, Salisbury: Zimbabwe Rhodesia Rugby Union
The Northern Rhodesia Journal, Volume III, Number 2, 1956

Mike Brown
Germiston-Simmer RFC History: Available from
http://www.pitchero.com/clubs/germistonrugbyclub/a/history-8846.html
J.T. Ferreira; J.P. Blignaut; P.J. Landman & J.F. Du Toit, 1989, *Transvaal Rugby Football Union: 100 years*, Johannesburg: TRFU
Sunday Times various editions.

Ivor Dorrington:
J.A. Donaldson, 1949, *The South African Sporting Encyclopaedia and Who's Who*, Johannesburg: Donaldson's Publications
A.C. Parker, 1983, *W.P. Rugby Centenary, 1883 - 1983*; Cape Town, WPRFU

Jape Ferreira and Piet Pretorius
Transvaal RFU, *Transvaal Rugby Football Union: 100 Years*: Johannesburg, TRFU

Hugh Gillespie:
A.C. Parker, 1983, *W.P. Rugby Centenary, 1883 - 1983*; Cape Town, WPRF
Paul Theron, 1989, *Boland Rugby: Die eerste halfeeu*, Wellington, BRU
SA Rugby Football Board - Rugby Album of Press Cuttings

Rudi Hasse:
Danie Hartman Craven, 1964, *Springbok Annale / Annals: Internasionale Toere na en van Suid Africa / International Tours to and from South Africa, 1981 - 1964*, Johannesburg, Mimosa Publishers
A.C. Parker, 1983, *W.P. Rugby Centenary, 1883 - 1983*; Cape Town, WPRF

James Megson:
Hans van Zyl & Piet van der Schyff, 1996, *Mielieboersage: Wes-Transvaal Rugby 75 (1920 - 1995)*, Potchefstroom: Northwest Rugby Union

Fred Oliver:
J.T. Ferreira; J.P. Blignaut; P.J. Landman & J.F. Du Toit, 1989, *Transvaal Rugby Football Union: 100 years*, Johannesburg: TRFU
Diggers RFC, *Diggers Rugbyvoetbal Klub, 1893 - 1983*: Johannesburg, DRFC
Danie Hartman Craven, 1964, *Springbok Annale / Annals: Internasionale Toere na en van Suid Africa / International Tours to and from South Africa, 1981 - 1964*, Johannesburg, Mimosa Publishers

Jack Pansegrouw:
J.T. Ferreira; J.P. Blignaut; P.J. Landman & J.F. Du Toit, 1989, *Transvaal Rugby Football Union: 100 years*, Johannesburg: TRFU
Diggers RFC, *Diggers Rugbyvoetbal Klub, 1893 - 1983*: Johannesburg, DRFC

Martin and Ken Pelser:
Transvaal RFU, *Transvaal Rugby Football Union: 100 Years*: Johannesburg, TRFU

Natie Rens:
J.T. Ferreira; J.P. Blignaut; P.J. Landman & J.F. Du Toit, 1989, *Transvaal Rugby Football Union: 100 years*, Johannesburg: TRFU
Diggers RFC, *Diggers Rugbyvoetbal Klub, 1893 - 1983*: Johannesburg, DRFC
Danie Hartman Craven, 1964, *Springbok Annale / Annals: Internasionale Toere na en van Suid Africa / International Tours to and from South Africa, 1981 - 1964*, Johannesburg, Mimosa Publishers

Andre Stoop:
South African Rugby Annual (various editions)
http://www.espscrum.com

Tom van Vollenhoven:
Alex Service, 1993, *The flying Springbok: The rugby career of Tom van Vollenhoven, 1955 - 1968*, A. Service
Danie Craven,1964, *Springbok Annale / Annals: Internasionale Toere na en van Suid Afrika / International Tours to and from South Africa*, Johannesburg, Mimosa Publishers
M.C. Van Zyl (ed.), 1988, *Noord Transvaal Rugby 50*, Pretoria, NTRU
Jonty Winch, 1979, *Rhodesia Rugby: A history of the national side, 1898 - 1979*, Salisbury, The Zimbabwe Rhodesia Rugby Union

Hennie van Zyl:
Diggers RFC, *Diggers Rugbyvoetbal Klub, 1893 - 1983*: Johannesburg, DRFC
Transvaal RFU, *Transvaal Rugby Football Union: 100 Years*: Johannesburg, TRFU

Green Vigo:
Booley, A; (1998), *Forgotten Heroes: History of Black Rugby 1882 - 1992*, Cape Town, Manie Booley Publications
Dobson, P; (1989), *Rugby in South Africa: A history, 1861 - 1988*, Cape Town, The South African Rugby Board
The Central Park Years (2001)
Web Page: Vince Karalius at *http:en.wikipedia.org/wiki/Vince_Karalius*
Web Page: Virtual Rugby League Hall of Fame: Vince Karalius at http:// www.rlhalloffame.org.uk/Karalius.htm
Web Page: http://www.wiganwarriors.com/SquadMember.asp?teamid=5&id=243
Green Gregory Vigo, R v. [1998] EWCA Crim 2354 (16 July, 1998,)
Web Page: http:// www.bailii.org/ew/cases/EWCA/Crim/1998/2354.html
Web Page: *http://wigan.rlfans.com/fusion_pages/index.php?pagr_id=393*
Web Page: *http:www.rugbyleague heritage project.com*
Oral Testimony / Personal Communication:
Green Vigo to Frank Daniels, 1 February 2007
Green Vigo to Hendrik Snyders, 1 February 2007

John Winton
Telephone interview: John Winton, Tuesday, 28 October 2014
Jonty Winch, 1979, *Rhodesia Rugby: A history of the national side, 1898 - 1979*, Salisbury: Zimbabwe Rhodesia Rugby Union
Danie Craven, *Springbok Annale / Annals, 1891 - 1964*; Cape Town: SA Rugby Football Board

Bibliography

Books

100 years of rugby – The history of Wakefield Trinity 1873 to 1973 by J.C. Lindley, The Wakefield Trinity Centenary Committee, 1973

A lad from Donkey Common by Austin Rhodes, London League Publications Ltd, 2012

A 'Ton' full of Memories by Brian F. Cartwright, self-published 1986

Ad & Wal by Peter Hain, Biteback Publishing, 2014

Bradford Northern – The History 1863 – 1989 by Nigel Williams, 1989

Chocolate, Blue and Gold – 50 years of Whitehaven RLFC by Harry Edgar, Edgar Publishing / Open Rugby Nostalgia, 1998

Doc – The life of Danie Craven by Paul Dobson, Human & Rousseau, 1994

Eddie Waring Rugby League Annual – various editions

For the love of Rugby by Rob Louw with John Cameron-Dow, Hans Strydom Publishers, 1987

Gillette Rugby League Yearbook edited by Tim Butcher, various editions, League Publications Ltd

Grand Final by Graham Morris, Vertical Editions, 2007

History of Rugby League edited by Irving Saxton, various editions

Keeping the Dream Alive – Barrow RFC complete who's who by Dave Huitson, Keith Nutter & Steve Andrews

Leigh RLFC – An Illustrated History by Michel Latham and Mike Hulme, Mike RL Publications, 1990

Leigh Rugby League Club – A comprehensive record 1895 – 1994 by Michael Latham, Mike RL Publications, 1994

Rothman's Rugby League Yearbook Raymond Fletcher and David Howes, various editions

Rugby in South Africa – A history 1861 – 1988 by Paul Dobson, The South African Rugby Board, 1989

Rugby League Review No.2 edited by Peter Lush & Dave Farrar, London League Publications Ltd 2008

Rugby League test matches in Australia by Alan Whiticker and Ian Collis, ABC Books, 1994

Teams & scorers by Irving Saxton Rugby League Record Keepers club

The complete book of Springbok Rugby Records by Kobus Smit, Don Nelson, 2007

The Encyclopaedia of Rugby League Players by Alan Whiticker and Glen Hudson, Gary Allen Pty, 2007

The Fartown Rugby League Yearbook – various editions

The Illustrated History of Wigan RLFC by Jack Winstanley, Smiths Books (Wigan), 1987

The March of the Saints by Alex Service, self-published 1988

The Mighty Bears – A social history of North Sydney Rugby League by Andrew Moore, Pan Macmillan Australia Pt, 1996

The Phoenix Book of International Rugby Records by John Griffiths, J.M. Dent & Sons, 1987

The Rugby League Challenge Cup by Les Hoole, Breedon Books, 1998

They played for Wigan by Michael Latham and Robert Gate, Mike RL Publications 1992

Trinity – A history of the Wakefield Rugby League Football Club 1872 – 2013 by Mike Rylance, League Publications Ltd 2013

Workington Town RLFC 1945 – 1995 by Joe Holliday, Richard Matthew Publications 1996

Magazines, journals and newspapers

Huddersfield Daily Examiner – various issues

Johannesburg Star – various issues

League Weekly – various issues

Open Rugby – various issues

Our Game issue 14, edited by Peter Lush & Dave Farrar, London League Publications Ltd 2006

Rugby League Express – various issues

Rugby League Journal – various issues

Rugby League Review – various issues

Rugby League World – various issues

Rugby Leaguer – various issues

Other books from London League Publications Ltd:

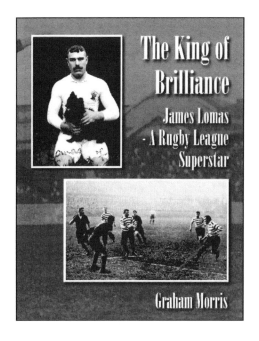

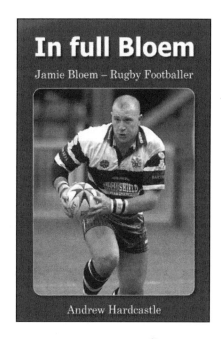

In full Bloem: The explosive biography of South African rugby league star Jamie Bloem, current referee and former Halifax, Widnes, Doncaster and Huddersfield player. He also played regularly for South Africa, and was capped by Scotland.
Published in February 2013 @ £14.95 (hardback), just £8.95 post free in the UK direct from London League Publications Ltd.

The King of Brilliance: Great book about one of the sport's genuine legends. James Lomas played for Bramley, Salford, Oldham and York, and won representative honours for Lancashire, Cumberland, England and Great Britain. He captained the first Lions team to tour Australia and New Zealand in 1910. This is the first biography of him.
Published in October 2011 at £16.95 (hardback). Special offer: £9.95 post free in the UK available direct from London League Publications Ltd.

All our books can be ordered from any bookshop @ full price. To order direct from London League Publications Ltd visit our website: www.llpshop.co.uk or write to LLP, PO Box 65784, London NW2 9NS (cheques payable to London League Publications Ltd).

"Come on Northern"

The fall and rise of
Bradford Northern RLFC 1954 to 1965

Trevor Delaney

The collapse of Bradford Northern RLFC in December 1963 sent shock waves throughout rugby league in Great Britain. Northern were the first team to appear in three successive Wembley Cup finals, from 1947 to 1949, and were top of the league at the start of the 1954–55 season.

However, by December 1963, this once proud club had sunk to the bottom of the league table and withdrew from the competition in mid-season. It was the first time since the 1920s that a team had pulled out of the league without completing their fixtures. Their membership of the Rugby Football League was terminated and that season's record was expunged.

No club in the game's history had fallen from the heights quite like the old Northern. Their subsequent re-entry to the league was a great achievement for two men of vision – former Odsal greats, Trevor Foster and Joe Phillips.

The acclaimed rugby league historian, Trevor Delaney, recalls this period in the club's turbulent history. "*Come on Northern*" is an essential read for everyone interested in rugby league. Available for just £13.00 post free in the UK direct from London League Publications Ltd. Credit card orders via www.llpshop.co.uk; payment by cheque to PO Box 65784, London NW2 9NS. Available in bookshops at £13.95.